Blueprint for a Christian World

An Analysis of the Wesleyan Way

By
Mary Alice Tenney

First Fruits Press
Wilmore, Kentucky
c2016

Blueprint for a Christian world: an analysis of the Wesleyan way.
By Mary Alice Tenney.

First Fruits Press, ©2016
Previously published by Light and Life Press, ©1953.

ISBN: 9781621715986 (print), 9781621715993 (digital), 9781621716006 (kindle)

Digital version at http://place.asburyseminary.edu/freemethodistbooks/23/

First Fruits Press is a digital imprint of the Asbury Theological Seminary, B.L. Fisher Library. Asbury Theological Seminary is the legal owner of the material previously published by the Pentecostal Publishing Co. and reserves the right to release new editions of this material as well as new material produced by Asbury Theological Seminary. Its publications are available for noncommercial and educational uses, such as research, teaching and private study. First Fruits Press has licensed the digital version of this work under the Creative Commons Attribution Noncommercial 3.0 United States License. To view a copy of this license, visit http://creativecommons.org/licenses/by-nc/3.0/us/.

For all other uses, contact:

First Fruits Press
B.L. Fisher Library
Asbury Theological Seminary
204 N. Lexington Ave.
Wilmore, KY 40390
http://place.asburyseminary.edu/firstfruits

Tenney, Mary Alice, 1889-1971.
   Blueprint for a Christian world: an analysis of the Wesleyan way / Mary Alice Tenney. Wilmore, Kentucky : First Fruits Press, ©2016.
        292 pages ; 21 cm.
        Includes bibliographical references.
        What is Christianity? -- The issues at stake -- Some other ways -- Still other ways -- The seeking -- The finding -- "An highway shall be there and a way" -- The disciplines of the way -- The Christian use of time -- "Time in masquerade" -- "The world is too much with us" -- Mammon and the way -- Stewardship and the way -- Those who walked the way -- The Wesleyan way in perspective.
        Reprint. Previously published: Winona Lake, Indiana : Light and Life Press, ©1953.
        ISBN - 13: 9781621715986 (pbk.)
        1. Methodism. I. Title.
BX8331 .T42 2016   287

Cover design by Jon Ramsay

asburyseminary.edu
800.2ASBURY
204 North Lexington Avenue
Wilmore, Kentucky 40390

First Fruits Press
The Academic Open Press of Asbury Theological Seminary
204 N. Lexington Ave., Wilmore, KY 40390
859-858-2236
first.fruits@asburyseminary.edu
asbury.to/firstfruits

Blueprint for a Christian World

An Analysis of The Wesleyan Way

BLUEPRINT
for a
CHRISTIAN WORLD
An Analysis of The Wesleyan Way

MARY ALICE TENNEY

LIGHT AND LIFE PRESS
WINONA LAKE, INDIANA
1953

Copyright, 1953
by
Light and Life Press

*To Minta
Who Lives
The Wesleyan Way*

Preface

The writer owes a great debt of gratitude to a host of friends who have given assistance and encouragement from the time research was begun in 1938 preparatory to a doctoral dissertation on the subject of *Early Methodist Autobiography*. The counsel of Professor Helen C. White, University of Wisconsin, at that time proved invaluable. Much appreciated aid in continuing research has been frequently given by Dr. Neal F. Doubleday, Millikin University, and Professor Arthur W. Secord, University of Illinois.

To Florence and Ernest Vinson, who suggested and sponsored study in England, and to all those former students of Greenville College who gave so generously to the travel fund, heartfelt thanks are given. To English friends, also, goes an expression of deep gratitude: to the staff of Epworth Press associated with the Methodist Book Room, especially to Dr. Leslie Church, Robert Young, and Margaret Simpson; to the gracious friends at *Littlegarth,* especially to Doris Morgan; and to Dr. W. E. Sangster for his wise and stimulating suggestions.

The writer wishes to express appreciation for the leave of absence granted by President Long and the Trustees of Greenville College, and for the kindly interest shown by members of the Greenville College staff, particularly for the assistance from the librarians, Ruby Dare and Dorothy King. She gratefully acknowledges her debt to Dr. George Turner, Asbury Seminary, for reading the manuscript, and to Nadine Roller for preparing the script, and to various advisors at the Light and Life Press, in particular Mr. B. H. Gaddis, and Edna Evans. To Minta Secord thanks are due for the plans for the format of the book.

Acknowledgment is gratefully given to the following persons who have permitted use of copyright quotations:

To Abingdon-Cokesbury Press quotations from *The Way*, by E. Stanley Jones, and *American Churches: An Interpretation*, by W. W. Sweet;

To Mrs. Marjorie Meador for quotations from *English Society in the Eighteenth Century*, by J. B. Botsford;

To Epworth Press for brief quotations from various publications for which they hold the copyright.

MARY ALICE TENNEY

Contents

Chapter		Page
	Foreword	11
I.	What Is Christianity?	13
II.	The Issues at Stake	25
III.	Some Other Ways	41
IV.	Still Other Ways	53
V.	The Seeking	65
VI.	The Finding	81
VII.	"An Highway Shall Be There and a Way"	101
VIII.	The Disciplines of the Way	119
IX.	The Christian Use of Time	139
X.	"Time in Masquerade"	155
XI.	"The World Is Too Much With Us"	187
XII.	Mammon and the Way	203
XIII.	Stewardship and the Way	217
XIV.	Those Who Walked the Way	239
XV.	The Wesleyan Way in Perspective	263
	Conclusion	279
	Appendix	285
	Index	289

Foreword

"The early Methodists had something." This was my first impression when, about ten years ago, I read their unique religious confessions. It has been the impression of most readers, from the time when Coleridge read and reread Southey's history of Methodism to our own day when the psychological analysts have explored the autobiographies of early Methodists for evidence on the character of religious experience.

Today, after further examination of the records here and in England, I am convinced beyond the shadow of a doubt that they had touched Reality as no group of Christian believers have been able to do in our time. Furthermore, they succeeded in disseminating their good news to an extent that approaches the accomplishment of the early church.

Men still find God, solitary men, and men en masse, but no mass movement today even approximates the power of early Methodism in convincing the world of the all-sufficiency of Christianity to meet human need. The early Methodist was able to impregnate with his conception of Christianity almost every religious body of the nineteenth century, and, thereby, to change the very face of England, morally, socially, economically, and even politically.

What was the secret of the power of Methodism? Many books have been written to answer this question. The convergence of age forces, says one; the genius of Wesley, says another; the powerful organization which he built, say some; the excellence of Methodist doctrine, say others. But do these answers taken all together furnish sufficient explanation? Would these reasons be sufficient to account for the rapid spread of early Christianity? Many historians have seen a similarity between early Christianity and Methodism in their amazing power of infiltration.

Students of early Christianity have long been impressed with its distinctive way of life and have emphasized the fact that very soon after Christ's departure his followers became known as the people of "the Way," because of their unique conduct pattern. But no one has given much attention to the way of life adopted by early Methodists as a consequence of their discovery of God. If it is true that one secret of the power of the early church is found in the character of its adherents, and, if their character was shaped by the disciplines of "the Way" (undeniable facts), then surely the power of early Methodism is to be accounted for to some degree in their distinctive way of life.

Early in my study I found that Wesley's solution for the eighteenth century religious dilemma was expressed almost entirely in terms of Christian character. His answer to the skepticism created by deism was twofold, the internal evidence within the converted soul and the external witness of a way of life that was lived on the level of miracle. The religious experience which accompanied the character pattern has received sufficient study in recent years, but the unique way of life adopted in consequence by early Methodists calls forth ridicule or simply tolerant curiosity. The Wesleyan way has become a museum piece, a quaint antique of bygone days, interesting to the historian, but valueless for assistance in the solution of modern problems.

This is not a proper approach to any movement, religious or otherwise. We must look always beneath practices for the motivating principles, and if the principles prove to be sound, the practices should be analyzed for values they may possess for our time. A movement which sought as honestly as did Methodism to rediscover the principles of early Christianity and which feared nothing but being untrue to the lofty, heroic ideals set up by Christ and Paul surely could not have been entirely mistaken in either its principles or its practices. This belief has led to the study which follows.

I

What Is Christianity?

The Church of St. Mary the Virgin for seven centuries has been the center of the religious life of Oxford University. Its glorious spire soaring above the pile of towers and turrets has been a symbol of the historic relationship which has continued to exist through the years between the University and the Church, as also between the National Church and the State.

Even today this relationship is still recognized in the use of the ancient Bidding Prayer, which opens the University service with the petition "that there may never be wanting a succession of persons duly qualified for the service of God in church and state." The responsibility of the University for providing moral and spiritual leadership for the nation has been profoundly sensed from time to time through the passing centuries, prompting some mighty sermons, and issuing in some cataclysmic events.

Here John Wycliffe denounced the clerical abuses of the fourteenth century church. Here in 1554 Cranmer, Ridley and Latimer were brought for trial. Near the throne now occupied by the Vice Chancellor stands a scarred pillar marking the place where Cranmer received his sentence to martyrdom. From the ancient pulpit Pusey in the nineteenth century gave his scholarly discourses and Newman cast the spell of his irresistible personality over the listening throngs as he spoke for the changing phases of the Oxford Movement.

On the morning of August 24, 1744, just a century before the Oxford Movement, a great crowd, conscious of impending drama, had gathered for the St. Bartholomew Day sermon. As is the practice at regular intervals, a priest holding the M.A. degree was to take his required turn in the pulpit, a duty which fell to every ordained Fellow once in three years, and which had been fulfilled by this morning's preacher six times already.

An audience, agog with curiosity, composed of townspeople, undergraduates, Fellows, Professors and Heads of houses, packed the nave. The magnet which had drawn them there was the black-haired, black-robed little man who followed the Vice Chancellor down the aisle at the head of the scarlet-robed procession of doctors of divinity. With varying degrees of approbation they watched him ascend the pulpit opposite the throne of the Vice Chancellor, and, at the conclusion of the brief preliminary exercises, stand and announce with pleasing emphasis his text, "And they were all filled with the Holy Ghost."

In the judgment of a young undergraduate by the name of Kennicott, afterward an eminent scholar and a Canon of Christ Church, who left on record a description of the service, the "peculiar composure of the speaker's countenance . . . showed him to be an uncommon man."[1] His scholarliness and engaging address stamped him as "a man of great parts." His discourse was pronounced by all to be "uncommonly pleasing in style"; yet vehement disapproval was expressed because of his daring assertion that Oxford, neither in its students, nor its teachers, nor its citizens, was Christian, and that England could not properly be called a Christian nation.

In flaming tones of authority he charged the University with failure to prepare men for "the service of God in church and state." Once more the words of the Bidding Prayer were literally interpreted and a new voice joined the chorus of Oxonians who had reasserted the faith of the living church. The shock felt by the undergraduate ran through the whole audience. The Dean of Christ Church, for example, while conceding that the speaker would always be regarded as a "man of sound sense,"[2] yet contradictorily applied to him the most invidious of epithets used in the eighteenth century: "enthusiastic"—in modern terminology, "fanatical."

This was John Wesley's last appearance as University

preacher at Oxford. After the sermon, his brother, Charles, tells us the little group of Methodist disciples made their way through the indignant mob, recognized by none of their former friends. Shortly afterward the Vice Chancellor requested a copy of the sermon and submitted it to all the professors of theology, who had power to suspend a refractory Fellow from preaching within the University precincts unless he withdrew his statements. The penalty, however, was not suspension but, rather, "a mortifying neglect." Thereafter, whenever Wesley's turn came round, he was simply ignored and another Fellow was quietly paid to fill his place. The fact was that his sermon could not possibly have been proved heretical, for it was a literal interpretation of the subject under discussion, "Scriptural Christianity," and his application of the principles derived was without question justified by circumstances.

John Wesley had anticipated this outcome. At his turn three years before he had spoken fearlessly to a congregation "so numerous" as he had "seldom seen at Oxford,"[3] drawn there by nation-wide rumors concerning his work. His sermon on "The Almost Christian" had given great offense by its arraignment of his audience as only "half-Christian." During the three years since, his travels up and down England had made him increasingly conscious of a universal ignorance of the real nature of Christianity; and the phenomenal response of the masses to his message had convinced him that he had rediscovered a lost meaning. He had to proclaim it, whatever the consequence.

And so into the sermon on Bartholomew's Day he poured all the gathered emotion of the past three years and the moral indignation of one who sees an institution which he loves lost to its original purpose. John Wesley was deeply devoted to his Alma Mater. In an unpreached sermon, which he had been dissuaded from giving by Lady Huntingdon, he speaks of "a full, settled conviction" that he owed a "labour of love" to his "tender parent" from whom he had received advantages that he would treasure with gratitude to his dying day.[4]

But he was well aware of the settled opposition at Oxford toward the developments which had attended his efforts to bring England to a true understanding of Christianity. No one, indeed, unless he had had intimate acquaintance with the first phases of Methodism could have sympathized with his resort to field-preaching, nor have understood the hysteria which accompanied his appeals for moral decision to the emotional lower classes, nor approved his segregation of them into societies for the nurture of their newly found religious life. Most dubious of all his irregularities had been his teaching that God may be known as living reality by every man, whatever his social status. The eighteenth century had no liking for either supernaturalism, free emotional expression or social leveling.

Wesley, facing the intellectual leaders of England and boldly applying the principles of scriptural Christianity to their thought and conduct, was animated by the same quality of courage as had prompted Cranmer. Yet he was not conscious of his role as a hero. He proceeded calmly back to London, preaching on the way in the evening at High Wycombe, and recording in his diary his satisfaction that now, because of the Vice Chancellor's demand for his sermon, it would be read "by every man of eminence in the University."[5] The message for which Wesley was willing even to die would now get a wider hearing among the intellectuals. What was this message? What was his interpretation of "Scriptural Christianity," the topic of his ill-fated sermon?

Kennicott, the brilliant young undergraduate from whom we have been quoting, caught unmistakably Wesley's meaning: The Holy Spirit was given to all men, not only to the apostles, but also to those "persons who had no business to perform besides the reformation of their own lives"; and if the Holy Spirit "was necessary for men as private persons at first, it must be so in all ages."[6] Christianity, according to Wesley, never had meant primarily intellectual assent to doctrine. It had always meant a new life, characterized by new purposes, new principles, new dispositions and new practices, and these were incumbent upon all who call themselves Christian.

The opening section of his sermon had described the influence of early Christianity upon the life of an individual who had entered upon the new way of life after sincere penitence and a discovery of the great love of God. Faith had brought an insight into eternal values, and with this came peace and joy and power over sin. Humility, gentleness, meekness, temperance, and love of truth grew where once had flourished pride, passion, lust, vanity, dishonesty, covetousness and false ambition. A dominant disposition gave birth to all these virtues. It was love—love to God, expressed in complete obedience to His will, and love for men, expressed in tireless service to all in need.

"It may be easily believed," said Wesley, "he who had this love in his heart would work no evil to his neighbour. It was impossible for him, knowingly and designedly, to do harm to any man. He was at the greatest distance from cruelty and wrong, from any unjust or unkind action . . . He put away all lying, falsehood, and fraud . . . He spoke evil of no man . . . But it did not satisfy him, barely to abstain from doing evil . . . he fed the hungry, clothed the naked, helped the fatherless or stranger, visited and assisted them that were sick or in prison. He gave all his goods to feed the poor. . . ."[7]

In his second division Wesley described the society which logically resulted from the adoption of the Christian way of life. These new lovers of mankind could not rest until they had saved the world from its misery. They found a way of speaking to every man's condition and steadily extended the outreach of Christianity. Yet, since positive opposition to evil, a necessary concomitant of Christianity, always offends the devotees of false religion—the lovers of pleasure, worldly honor or riches—persecution in all its forms arose; more and more were enraged at these who "turned the world upside down." Nevertheless, Christianity continued to spread.[8]

Such a state of affairs, Wesley believed, will not go on forever. In the third division he declared that "the time will come when Christianity will prevail over all, and cover the earth." He invited his audience to "stand a little" and survey "this strange sight, a *Christian world.*" [9] War is no more; civil discord, oppression, injustice, poverty are gone. Just as in the conversion of the individual, good tempers had replaced the bad, so now peace, equality, honesty, justice and human love and kindness prevail among all men. This Christian order, declared Wesley, is the end *assured* by Christianity, when it is accepted, not merely as belief, but as a way of life.

This logical development of the meaning and end of scriptural Christianity seems to have been acceptable to Wesley's audience. Had the sermon ended here there would probably have been no unpleasant consequences. It was his uncompromising application of the criteria which he had set up that provoked the opinion voiced by Kennicott, "He expressed himself like a very good scholar, but a rigid zealot." [10]

At the close of this exposition of the text Wesley had turned upon his audience and asked, "Where does this Christianity now exist? Where, I pray, do the Christians live? Which is the country, the inhabitants whereof are all thus filled with the Holy Ghost? . . . With what propriety can we term *any* a Christian country, which does not answer this description? Why then, let us confess that we have never seen a Christian country upon earth?" [11]

It is probable that any eighteenth century audience, and, for that matter, any twentieth century audience, would agree with Wesley's judgment that no really Christian country has ever existed. But Wesley could not allow the matter to rest there, as can no serious Christian today. "Why," we must ask, "after all these centuries, is the world still so unchristian?" This, for Wesley, was not an academic question to be settled by the theologians. The failure to achieve a Christian world was chargeable, he believed, to those who professed to be Christian. The responsibility for the existing state of Christendom rested upon

WHAT IS CHRISTIANITY? 19

every member of the audience that morning at St. Mary's, and he proceeded to make plain some of those responsibilities.

Begging them to accept great plainness of speech and to listen open-mindedly, he addressed himself first to his superiors, the Magistrates, Heads and Governours of the University, and asked them whether their lives and their dispositions toward those whom they taught exhibited Christian love and dignity; whether their teaching had "an actual tendency to the love of God, and of all mankind; whether their first desire for their students was that they might adorn the Gospel of Christ." He hastened to add that he was *not* speaking of the training of prospective clergymen, but the instruction of all "as if they were intended to be Christians."[12] In other words, if Oxford were a Christian institution, should not its primary function be the making of Christians, and should not its heads exemplify the Christian way of life? A fair question, if Christianity is what Wesley had described it to be, and particularly at a time when Oxford was professedly the instrument of the Church.

He next turned his attention to their vocational diligence and asked, "Do you put forth all your strength in the vast work you have undertaken? Do you labour herein with all your might? . . . using every talent which God hath lent you, and that to the uttermost of your power?"[13] This was not an impertinent question in view of the existing state of learning at the universities.[14]

Godley from his examination of available data concludes that "those in authority were for the most part gluttons or loose livers."[15] Even the bishop of Oxford in 1733 was labeled by students "the mitred Hog." Endowments were misused, obligations neglected, statutes violated.[16] Their neglect of their instructional duties, in and of itself, was serious enough to warrant Wesley's question about their industry. Teaching was regarded as "an interlude" rather than the main vocation; examinations were a farce, sometimes even they were the objects of bribery;[17] and the positions of both professors and tutors were often simply rewards for political support.

Professors in general had ceased to lecture. Godley finds that as late as 1800 not more than one in three of the Oxford professors was lecturing and concludes that this estimate "would perhaps be too optimistic in reference to the Oxford of a century earlier."[18] Apparently a seminar was given upon the request of a sufficient number of serious minded students, but in so apathetic an intellectual atmosphere few students would desire it.[19] As a natural consequence, the vast storehouse of the Bodleian library was hardly used.[20]

In the absence of lectureships, the chief responsibility for instruction devolved upon the Fellows. Yet they were the objects of criticism and ridicule by almost everyone who has left any reference to university life. Wesley knew through long association with them how they prostituted their calling, for he had been called back to Lincoln College in 1729 to aid in reforms among them. Lincoln, however, was an exception in its effort toward betterment.[21]

The real condition at most colleges was accurately described by Nicholas Amherst of St. John's when he wrote: "When any person is chosen fellow of a College, he . . . is settled for life in ease and plenty. He wastes the rest of his days in luxury and idleness; he enjoys himself and is dead to the world; for a Senior fellow of a College lives and moulders away in a supine and regular course of eating, drinking, sleeping, and cheating the juniors."[22]

One of Wesley's duties at Lincoln had been to raise the standards for the disputation, an instructional method much used at the time. The same Amherst complained that the final disputation for the degree was "no more than a formal repetition of a set of syllogisms upon some ridiculous question in logick, which they get by rote, or perhaps only read out of their caps, which lie before them with their notes in them. These commodious sets of syllogisms are called 'Strings,' and descend from undergraduate to undergraduate in a regular succession."[23]

These were the conditions which provoked Wesley's pointed questions to tutors and students. Fitchett says that "Oxford, when Wesley trod its streets, was, for the average student, an education in the bad art of subscribing to articles he ridiculed, swearing to keep laws he ignored, and pretending to attend lectures which had no existence. The professors drew salaries for lectures which were never delivered, and took oaths to obey laws which they never so much as read."[24] The members of this institution, from the Heads down to the youngest student, were participating in a living lie; and one man whose moral conscience had been awakened could not be still.

He accused the Fellows of "pride and haughtiness of spirit, impatience and peevishness"[25] in their relationships with students. He prayed that they might be forgiven the reproach brought upon them by their "sloth and indolence, gluttony and sensuality, and even a proverbial uselessness."[26] Those Fellows, in particular, who prepared young men for the ministry he denounced unsparingly.

The undergraduates he branded as "a generation of triflers, triflers with God, with one another,"[27] and with their own souls, accusing them of Sabbath desecration and profanity, matters forbidden by the statutes, and of drunkenness and uncleanness. The accusation most objected to was his use of the term "perjury" to describe their careless subscription to statutes which they made no pretense even of reading. Oaths meant little in English society at this time, and this was not the last instance of Wesley's lively censure of tacit falsehood.

He was probably wrong in placing upon students the responsibility for an evil bred by a vicious system. The rules for conduct, like the academic rules, were "survivals" retained by a conservative faculty but meaningless even to conservatism.[28] Students were perforce perjurers because their elders had lost the principles which had called forth the rules. This loss of primary truths permeated the entire social fabric of England, and while Wesley should have seen the injustice of indicting the younger generation for faults forced upon them, he was doing here what he did on so many occasions: presenting facts that exposed the terrible chasm between the profession of Christian morality and its actual practice. He was convinced that England no longer knew Christianity. The whole nation lay under that paralyzing spiritual apathy which results from clinging to forms, customs and laws divorced from their original, life-giving sources.

In a period so sunk in moral insensibility the maintenance of the *status quo* is always the first consideration. A movement which questions in any way the existing order is feared. Wesley's last three sermons at Oxford probed deeply into the state of eighteenth century religion. The officials at Oxford would not tolerate it; neither would the leaders of the church. The storm of opposition evoked was terrific.

During the six years preceding Wesley's last appearance in the pulpit at St. Mary's at least 175 publications were issued in the attack upon Methodism.[29] They contained in essence the objections which were to be raised for years against the movement. An examination of these reveals the three major areas where Wesley had come into conflict with his age in his interpretation of the Christian Way. He had pitted himself against its humanistic theology; he had denounced its moral compromise; he had exposed its social injustice.

These obstacles to the establishment of a Christian order he met with three great declarations: First, Christianity is "the life of God in the soul of man" and can never be known or practiced by mere human effort; secondly, Christianity is superlative in its standard of moral perfection; thirdly, Christianity demands a love of mankind which extends to all alike and ministers to every human need. What was there in these declarations to evoke such violent hostility?

1. "Dr. Kennicott and Mr. Wesley's Last Sermon," *The Wesleyan-Methodist Magazine*, LXXXIX, Part I (January, 1866), 47.
2. *Ibid.*, p. 48.
3. *The Journal of the Rev. John Wesley, A.M.*, ed. Curnock (London: Robert Culley, 1909), II, 478.
4. John Wesley, "True Christianity Defended," *Works* (3rd ed.; London: John Mason, 1829), VII, 452.
5. *Journal*, III, 148.
6. *The Wesleyan-Methodist Magazine*, op. cit., p. 47.
7. *Wesley's Standard Sermons*, ed. Sugden (London: Epworth Press, 1921) I, 96-7.
8. *Ibid.*, p. 100.
9. *Loc. cit.*
10. *The Wesleyan-Methodist Magazine*, op. cit., p. 47.
11. *Sermons*, I, 102.
12. *Ibid.*, p. 107.
13. *Loc. cit.*
14. See G. M. Trevelyan, *British History in the Nineteenth Century and After* (London: Longmans, 1937), pp. 26-8.
15. A. D. Godley, *Oxford in the Eighteenth Century* (London: Methuen & Co., 1908), p. 196.
16. J. W. Bready, *England: Before and After Wesley* (London: Hodder & Stoughton, 1939), p. 55.
17. Godley, *op cit.*, p. 178.
18. *Ibid.*, p. 43.
19. *Ibid.*, p. 46.
20. *Ibid.*, p. 50.
21. J. S. Simon, *John Wesley and the Religious Societies* (London: Epworth Press, 1921), p. 89. Wesley was recalled by the Rector in 1729 and remained until he went to Georgia in 1735. He was commended by the Vice-Chancellor for his energetic work as tutor, Greek Lecturer, and Moderator of the Classes. Simon says that Lincoln had its "golden age" from 1730 to 1740, but Godley terms the period from 1714 to 1760 the "dark age" for most colleges.
22. *Sermons*, I, 107, note.
23. Godley, *op. cit.*, p. 176.
24. W. H. Fitchett, *Wesley and His Century* (London: Smith, Elder & Co., 1906), p. 46.
25. *Sermons*, I, 108.
26. *Loc. cit.*
27. *Ibid.*, p. 110. It is interesting to find that Kennicott approved of this label.
28. Godley, *op. cit.*, p. 186.
29. See Richard Green, *Anti-Methodist Publications issued during the Eighteenth Century* (London: C. H. Kelly, 1902)

II

The Issues at Stake

What, first of all, was objectionable in Wesley's declaration that God may be known as reality? Simply this: that his preaching of evangelical faith had exposed the fact that the age had drifted into a virtual abandonment of supernaturalism. The doctrine of the Holy Spirit had been so discounted that those who accepted its full implications were suspected of fanaticism.

This was the attitude of his University audience, as implied by Wesley in the sermon just reviewed. He asked them: "Who of you is in any degree acquainted with the work of his Spirit, his supernatural work in the souls of men? Can you bear, unless now and then in a church, any talk of the Holy Ghost? Would you not take it for granted, if one began such a conversation, that it was either hypocrisy or enthusiasm?"[1]

The deepest evil of the age to Wesley's mind was its loss of faith. It had pushed God out to the rim of the universe and forgotten Him. The great masses never thought of Him, and those who professed interest knew Him only through speculation or a lukewarm performance of prescribed duties. "Practical atheism," that is, the *practice* of unbelief, was so general, Wesley said, that the average man was not "content with being utterly ignorant of spiritual things," but denied "the very existence of them."[2]

He was certain, however, of a remedy for this. The Son of God, he said, *"begins* his work in man by enabling us to believe in him. He opens and enlightens the eyes of our understanding ... takes away the veil which the 'god of this world' has spread over our hearts. And we then see, not by a chain of *reasoning,* but by a kind of *intuition,* by a direct view, that God has forgiven us our sins."³ Only then does atheism disappear.

He believed that God has given men spiritual senses for apprehending the supernatural. To the practical atheist this, of course, was pure foolishness. "How," asked the average man, "can these things be? How can any man know that he is alive to God?" Wesley replied, "Even as you know that your body is now alive. Faith is the life of the soul . . . . that divine consciousness, the *witness* of God, which is more and greater than ten thousand witnesses!"⁴

It was this direct view of God, this intuition of the reality of the supernatural, that Wesley's age would not tolerate. Although the theory of divine immanence was still an accepted doctrine among his clerical opponents, as a principle actuating daily conduct it was considered dangerous, for it might lead into the exaggerated claims to divine guidance made by the "enthusiasts" of the seventeenth century Civil War period. It was argued that if a man were allowed to claim illumination by the Spirit at one point, there would be no end to claims he might extravagantly make on every imaginable detail of life.

Wesley was well aware of this danger. He had been reared by parents whose withdrawal from Dissent had been motivated in part by their dislike for these extravagant claims and the great national discords resulting from them. He admitted that "many have mistaken the voice of their own imagination for this witness of the Spirit of God, while they were doing the work of the devil! These are truly and properly enthusiasts . . . Who then," he grants, "can be surprised, if many reasonable men, seeing the dreadful effects of this delusion, and labouring to keep at the utmost distance from it, should sometimes lean toward another extreme? . . . "⁵

He understood perfectly why some questioned whether the witness of the Spirit could be "the privilege of *ordinary* Christians and not, rather, one of those *extraordinary* gifts which they suppose belonged only to the apostolic age? But," he argued, "is there any necessity laid upon us of running into one extreme or the other? May we not steer a middle course—keep a sufficient distance from that spirit of error and enthusiasm, without denying the gift of God, and giving up the great privilege of his children?"⁶

While regretting the excesses to which the doctrine of the Holy Spirit had led in the last century, he saw the necessity of recovering it in its full meaning for his own day. He was in fact convinced that the age denial of the vision of God to the ordinary man had become a denial of Christianity itself. "Is not almost the very notion of this religion lost? . . ." he asked. "Nay, is it not utterly despised? Is it not wholly set at nought, and trodden under foot? Were anyone to witness these things before God, would he not be accounted a madman, and enthusiast?"⁷

This description does not exaggerate the dominance of secularism. The anti-Methodist pamphlets and sermons afford abundant explanation for Wesley's consciousness of bitter hostility. Most of them apply the term "enthusiast" to him and accuse him of preaching such things as "unaccountable sensations, violent emotions," and "filling the heads of the unwary and ignorant with wild, perplexive notions," boasting of "immediate inspirations," and even of laying "claim to miracles."⁸

An article in the *Scots Magazine* advised the Methodists to "go over to their proper companies, their favorites, the Dissenters, and utter their extemporary effusions in a conventicle; but not be suffered in our churches hypocritically to use our forms, which they despise. Let them carry their spirit of delusion among their brethren, the Quakers. . ."⁹

Even those pamphleteers who attempted to avoid rancor and deal constructively with Wesley's theory of faith betray an amazing ignorance of religious experience. Their approaches were of two sorts. The first was an analysis of faith in terms of the Anglican doctrine of baptism. Regeneration, which to Wesley meant transformation of life and acquaintance with divine reality, was interpreted by them as nothing but entrance into the covenant of baptism. Dr. Daniel Waterland, one of the chaplains to George II, argued the impropriety of speaking of the New Birth apart from baptism, insisting that it gave the common people wrong ideas, taught them to disregard their baptismal vows, to look for inward feelings instead of carefully examining their past life, and to attribute everything to the Holy Spirit.[10]

Another opponent went so far in his humanism as to insist that the "Proper Religion is a Religion of the Mind, a Religion of Virtue and Charity."[11] In a discussion of the subject of "walking by faith rather than by sight," one writer concluded that no one can have any assurance of what his state is, for if he could, he would be walking by sight and not by faith.[12] The total absence of spiritual perception and, worse than that, the deadly hostility to those possessing it is all too evident in these pamphlets.

William Law, author of the greatest devotional classics of the eighteenth century, and recognized now as exerting major influence upon Wesley's central message,[13] perceived the dilemma produced by humanism and commented satirically upon the "learned pains" which some people were taking "to root up the Belief of our having a Life and Birth from Jesus Christ. . . . They run from *Book* to *Book,* from *Language* to *Language,* they call upon every *Disputant,* consult all *Criticks,* search all *Lexicons,* to shew us, that according to Scripture, and Antiquity, and the Rules of true Criticism, Regeneration *need signify* no more than what is meant by the federal Rite of Baptism."[14]

Law decries this as a misuse of learning, saying that, "we need not look at Rome, or Geneva, or the ancient Rabbis of the Jewish Sanhedrin, to see what miserable work Learning can make with the Holy Scriptures. For it must be said, that the true Messiah is not *rightly owned,* the Christian religion is not *truly known,* nor its Benefits rightly *sought,* till the Soul is all Love, and Faith, and Hunger, and Thirst, after this new *Life, Birth,* and real Formation of Jesus Christ in it, till without

Fear of *Enthusiasm* it seeks, and expects all its Redemption from it." [15]

The second method for disposing of Wesley's theory of faith came from controversialists who were truly concerned for the moral state of England, but who took the New Birth to be a figurative term for practical righteousness, and the Witness one's consciousness of performing good works. This definition of faith in terms of duties, obedience and submission to one's station in life was the line of argument taken by Dr. Gibson, Bishop of London, in his Pastoral Letter to his diocese in 1739.[16] Bishop Gibson, undoubtedly the most able of the early opponents to Methodism was a good man, the sponsor of the leading reform movements of the time. He professed open-mindedness toward the new movement and proposed to chart a middle course between the prevailing secularism and the dangers of enthusiasm; yet he devoted two-thirds of his address to warnings against Methodism.

Apparently incapable of distinguishing between the valid and the specious in religious experience, he discouraged all aspiration for the assurance of God's presence and guidance and recommended instead dutiful attention to public and private devotion, willing acquiescence to one's station in life, and fulfillment of one's moral obligations.

He promised his readers that if they would attend to these rules in earnest, they would grow "more and more into a Love of their Duty, and by consequence into a Love of God." Nor would they need "any other Evidence, besides those good Dispositions they find in their Hearts ... they will be accepted and rewarded of God, according to the Degree and Measure of Goodness to which they have arrived in this Life." [17]

What is Christianity, according to Bishop Gibson? His exposition reveals clearly the humanism latent in the best religious thought of the day. Christianity is a supplement to that natural religion which is the common possession of all men. Christianity came to give "a true notion of natural Religion, and a just

Sense of ... obligation to the Performance of moral Duties." [18] It is distinguished from other religions only in its "higher Hopes" and its "greater Degrees of Purity and Perfection." [19]

Bishop Gibson, for all his moral intensity, had little insight into the reality of a spiritual world or the inwardness of the Christian religion. One of Wesley's advocates, recognizing the blindness of Churchmen to the real issues involved in the controversy, declared that the denial of conscious supernatural assistance in the life of every real Christian amounted to the "denial of the real meaning of Grace as treated in the tenth Article of the Church." The word Grace had actually "lost its meaning." [20] To the reticence or confusion of the clergy on this subject he attributed the spread of Deism,[21] a judgment that is undoubtedly true.

We may say, then, that the first issue between Wesley and his age arose from his insistence that the exclusion of the miraculous from the popular religion of the time branded it as non-Christian. He had a profound conviction that the life of the Christian can be lived only "on a supernatural level"; that Christ's "ideal is so vast" that it can be achieved only through miracle.[22] Wesley in his own search for the Way had come to that moment described by C. S. Lewis when "one reaches a sort of Rubicon." "One goes across; or not," says Lewis. "But if one does, there is no manner of security against miracles." [23]

Because of his belief that nominal Christians of his day were not living on this supernatural level Wesley found himself in conflict also with their scale of ethical values, for a man who lives in relation to the world perceived by faith cannot derive his values from the world perceived only by the physical senses.

The pamphleteers who declared that miracle was not necessary to the Age of Enlightenment argued also that the high standard of conduct demanded by Christ had been necessary only to the founding of Christianity. This sort of sophistry is found frequently in the eighteenth century sermon. In fact, the pattern for it was set in the previous century by such prominent

Churchmen as Archbishop Tillotson, who went to great lengths to show that nothing in the Christian religion is "unsuitable to our reason or prejudicial to our interest." He explained away all the rigorous requirements that had brought persecution upon the early Church, affirming that they "related to the conditions of the Church before the kingdoms of the world adopted the official profession of Christianity, and were therefore no longer relevant to contemporary circumstances." [34]

Watson in his study of a typical clergyman of the eighteenth century says that pulpit teaching had tended "to degrade the Divine benevolence into mere good nature and to minimise the achievement required by God of His creatures . . . Let them be kind, and honest, let them be sober on market days, and then they will probably reap a good harvest." [35] Sykes, after examining many sources, concludes that "every means had been adopted to temper the demands of Christianity to the infirmities of unregenerate human nature, and to promise the consolations of religion to the weakest of its professors." [36]

Moral decadence on a national scale inevitably attended such adulteration of the Christian message. Even some of Wesley's critics recognized this fact. Blackstone, who attacked severely Wesley's last sermon at Oxford, later in life declared, after visiting many London churches, that he had not heard "a single discourse which had more Christianity in it than the writings of Cicero." [37] Lord Bolingbroke, a deist, is reported to have said to a group of clergymen, "Let me seriously tell you that the greatest miracle in the world is the subsistence of Christianity and its continued preservation as a religion, when the preaching of it is committed to the care of such unchristian men as you." [38]

All who have studied the century, whether in its economic, social or religious aspects, agree that the peak of social and moral disorder was reached about the time of Wesley's conversion in 1738. Mrs. George, for instance, concludes after voluminous collecting of data on social and economic conditions that the horrors of the period between 1720 and 1750 cannot be exaggerated. Economic conditions were comparatively good, she says; yet the waste of life was appalling, because of social and moral ruin."[29]

The reason traditionally given for this moral decline is the continuing reaction against Puritanism. But the cause lay far deeper in a lack of moral leadership. No one in the State Church had come forward to deal positively with spiritual apathy and practical atheism. The pulpit offered little instruction that was distinctively Christian, and pastoral work was almost unknown. Portus, reviewing the conditions that called forth the organization of the few struggling religious societies, says that "there is little reason to doubt" that the evils of the day arose primarily from "the moral and spiritual unpreparedness of the nation at large."[30] A vicious circle had been set up in which spiritual ignorance brought about low morals, which in turn produced ever increasing unbelief.

Wesley, first enlightened concerning this state of affairs through his association with the religious societies, looked upon the current preaching as simply an accommodation to the spirit of the times, far removed from the Christian message. He accused the popular preacher of prostituting his calling. "How few," he complained, "are there that, either in writing or preaching, declare the genuine gospel of Christ, in the simplicity and purity wherewith it is set forth in the venerable records of our own Church! And how are we inclosed on every side with those who, neither knowing the doctrines of our Church, nor the Scriptures, nor the power of God, have found out to themselves inventions wherewith they constantly corrupt others also!"[31]

The direct result of a compromising clergy was an unregenerate laity. William Law, answering one of the pamphleteers who had accused the Methodists of being "righteous overmuch," described two-thirds of those reputed to be religious as "conniving at favourite Sins," enslaved to "Ease, Softness and sensible Pleasures," insensible of "their corrupt, unreformed, unregenerate State" and "satisfied with poor Beginnings, Names and Appearances of Virtue. . . ." [82]

The indirect result of compromise within the Church was the "practical atheism" of the masses and the consequent flood of national vice. As a matter of fact, the majority of men were living so far below the standards recognized even by the great pagan teachers, such as Confucius and Plato, that the church member who approximated these standards congratulated himself upon being Christian. Few clergymen had sufficient perception themselves to recognize the non-Christian source of current ethics.

As early as 1733 Wesley told an Oxford audience that "he who now preaches the essential duties of Christianity runs the hazard of being esteemed, by a great part of his hearers, 'a setter forth of new doctrines.' Most men have so *lived away* the substance of that religion, the profession whereof they still retain, that no sooner are any of those truths proposed which differentiate the Spirit of Christ from the spirit of the world, than they cry out, 'Thou bringest strange things to our ears; we would know what these things mean'; though he is only preaching to them 'Jesus and the resurrection,' with the necessary consequence of it—If Christ be risen, ye ought then to die unto the world, and to live wholly unto God." [83]

This does not mean that earnest Churchmen dedicated to their calling were not alarmed over the spread of paganism. Bishop Butler, when he published his *Analogy of Religion, Natural and Revealed* in 1736, said: "It is come, I know not how, to be taken for granted by many persons that Christianity is not so much as a subject of inquiry, but that it is, now at length, discovered to be fictitious. And accordingly they treat it as if in the present age this were an agreed point among all people of discernment, and nothing remained but to set it up as a principal subject of mirth and ridicule. . . ." [84]

Many men shared with Wesley a deep anxiety for the future of the Christian faith, but their solution for the dilemma was either a renewal of the speculative approach by a fresh defense of Christian doctrine or a repetition of the ethical emphasis by entreaties to more regular church attendance and a life of virtue. Wesley, without undervaluing either the intellectualistic or ethical approaches, recognized the impotence of humanism and recommended a return to the Originator of Christianity for divine reillumination and recovery of a lost way of life.

The moral severity of Wesley's teaching provoked great opposition; in fact, Wesley sometimes thought of it as the primary cause for the persecution which he met. Many, he said, complained that the Methodists "make the way to heaven too narrow." It had been "the original objection (as it was almost the only one for some time)," and he considered it still in 1745 "secretly at the bottom of a thousand more, which appear in various forms." [35]

The pamphlets written by Dr. Trapp, a High Church leader, whose ambitions turned, like those of many High Churchmen, toward political and literary leadership,[36] are representative of the counter defense of moral compromise. He charged the Methodists with the "Folly, Sin and Danger of Being Righteous Overmuch," and argued that "all Christians must indulge in some vanities." [37] He interpreted Christ's commands on these matters as only "proverbial and hyperbolical," and not to be taken in their "first, literal and most rigorous Signification." [38] He believed that the official adoption of Christianity in the fourth century had brought to an end, not only the dispensation of immediate inspiration, but also the necessity for the distinctively Christian disciplines. The Age of Enlightenment needed only to look to its own high state of culture for salvation.[39]

Law, who came to Wesley's help in answering the early attacks upon Methodism, declared that such "commentators had construed away the text" of the Gospel. Philosophy "had corrupted the meaning"; preaching had "softened its unpleasant truth, and reconciled the spirit of Christ and the spirit of the world." He reaffirmed Wesley's insistence that "the same Spirit which first planted the Gospel, is now required to recover and restore it amongst us." [40]

The third cleavage between Wesley and the eighteenth century Church arose from his literal rendering of Christ's message to the lower classes. The first published attack upon him came during his Oxford days in an article in *Fogg's Journal* entitled "The Oxford Methodists." All three points of divergence which we have enumerated appear here: the charge of "enthusiasm," the objection to Methodist piety, and a protest against their work among the needy, such as visiting and relieving the prisoners and the sick, instructing poor children, and denying themselves diversions in order thereby to have funds for this work.[41]

Wesley's father, who encouraged the endeavors of the Holy Club, stated that their chief offense was their ministry to the prisoners. John Gambold, who was a member of the Club, and whose testimony is reliable, wrote that "nothing was so much disliked as their charitable work." [42] He complained that any sort of religious fervor would be tolerated, but if one became "a friend of publicans and sinners," willing to sit "down upon the level with them" he would be treated with abhorrence.[43]

Wesley wrote to Bishop Secker that even before he "preached or knew salvation by faith" he was excluded from several pulpits for proclaiming that the love of God and mankind was "the substance of religion." [44] The very core of early Methodism was its logical application of this truth to actual human need, and from the beginning Wesley was made aware of violent hostility to his welfare work.

An undertone of caution and fear runs through the whole pamphlet war. Cannot one have too much charity? To be sure, one should have benevolence, but not to the extent of unsettling the social order. And does not this Methodist plea for the restoration of primitive Christianity lead in this direction?

One is not surprised to find this point of view accompanying the moral complacency of Dr. Trapp. He grants that "we cannot love God *excessively,* or too much, nor our Neighbours neither, with regard to the *inward Temper* and Disposition of our Souls . . . But," he warns, "with regard to *outward Actions* we may be drawn into many Errors, and *unjustifiable Practises,* for want of *truly distinguishing the Circumstances of Persons,* and Things, by a *mistaken Notion* of Charity, and *Love* to our *Neighbours.* . . . " He asserts, though quite mistakenly, that some of the Methodists are for having all things in common and predicts that "if due care be not taken, . . . the Consequence . . . must be the Dissolution of *Government,* and *human Society."* "

The example set by the early church is disposed of perfunctorily by the smug observation: "The difference between our Case *now,* when whole Nations and Kingdoms are Christian, and That of Christians in the *Days of the Apostles,* is so evident; that I will not affront the Reader's Judgment by saying any more of it." " The complacency with which this worldly-minded Churchman could view social and economic injustice is appalling; but it is a product of the humanistic optimism of the Age of Enlightenment. To suggest a reversion to first century ideals was to "affront the Reader's Judgment" concerning the superlative values of the eighteenth century.

Most of the pamphlets emphasize the acceptance by the individual of his social status as a constituent element of religion. *The Whole Duty of Man,* with its defense of the master-servant caste system, was the most highly recommended devotional classic of the time." We have seen how Bishop Gibson made "a willing acquiescence in one's station in life" essential to practical righteousness. He declared also that the Scriptures "deal much with the Duty of Diligence in our Stations" and indicate that a great part of "the Christian life consists in a regular and conscientious Discharge of those Duties." "

This routine of daily tasks was greatly interrupted, the critics said, by Methodist "enthusiastic ardour," which could not be practiced "without breaking in upon the common duties of life." More than that, "the same exalted strains and notions" tended to "weaken the natural and civil relations among men, by leading the inferiors, into whose heads those notions are infused, to disesteem of their superiors; while they consider them in a much lower dispensation than themselves. . . ." [50] Wesley's reply to this subtle thrust at the democratizing influence of the Gospel was: "I have mentioned before what those exalted notions are: These do not tend to weaken either the natural and civil relations among men; or to lead inferiors to a disesteem of their superiors, even where those superiors are neither good nor sober men." [51]

Frequently even fear of riot was expressed, and in the course of the Revival this fear was effectively appealed to and often fanned into a flame. The earliest pamphleteers made the most of the argument; for example, Bowman, in *The Imposture of Methodism Displayed* predicted that "Mutinies, Riots, Robberies, and Disorders of every Kind, are the natural Consequences of a *Levelling* Scheme, and a Community of Goods." [52] The ugly arrogance of a fixed cultural system which completely ignored the pagan state of the masses appears in his assertion that the movement, if right, would not take place among "the illiterate, unthinking Mob," but would be promoted with "those happy Aids and Assistances, which the Arts, Education and Literature are alone capable of giving it." [53]

But it was to this "illiterate, unthinking Mob" that Wesley felt particularly called. He saw that the preaching of the Gospel to the poor was one of the features of early Christianity most neglected by the eighteenth century, and he was willing to accept all the consequences that must follow upon so revolutionary a departure. The remoteness of the Church from the masses, its utter indifference to their needs, and its abject subservience to the aristocracy are all woefully revealed by Wesley's statement in his *Short History of Methodism* that one of the common complaints from the very beginning of the Revival was that "the people crowd so that they block up the church and leave no room for the best of the parish." [54]

The Church in Wesley's youth had become the preserve of the cultured. It had become so impregnated with humanism that it could no longer distinguish between the specious and the genuine in religious experience. It had banished the miraculous, the distinguishing feature of Christianity. In consequence, it had lost the principles and the pattern that made Christianity in its beginnings a world-conquering force, sweeping into its fold both rich and poor. Wesley's call for a return to "Scriptural Christianity" threw him into conflict with the humanism of popular religion, with its compromise with evil and with its extenuation of an unchristian social and economic system.

At the time of the St. Bartholomew Day's sermon Wesley was forty-one. In the previous year he had written one of his most able defenses of his views, *The Appeal to Men of Reason and Religion*. Even three years before in an unpreached sermon on "True Christianity Defended" he had already defined his position. We may say therefore that before he was forty he had achieved a view of the Christian way that was antithetical to that prevalently held in the Church of England.

Where had he found this view? Had he formulated it from current conceptions of Christianity? Had he found it through speculative thought, by critical and historical research, or, as George Fox had found it a century before, by personal religious experience? These are some of the questions that must be answered before one can understand the way of life adopted by Wesley and his followers.

---

1. *Sermons*, op. cit., p. 110.
2. *Ibid.*, p. 74.
3. *Works*, VI, 274.
4. *Sermons*, I, 74.
5. *Ibid.*, pp. 202-3.
6. *Loc. cit.*
7. *Works*, VII, 462.
8. Luke Tyerman, *The Life and Times of John Wesley* (London: Hodder & Stoughton, 1871), I, 240.
9. *Ibid.*, p. 239. Hogarth's famous picture, "Credulity, Superstition and Fanaticism," 1762, is a satire upon Methodism.
10. Daniel Waterland, "Regeneration Stated and Explained according to Scripture and Antiquity," (London: W. Innys & R. Manby, 1740), p. 9. He declares

that "As there can be no second Baptism, so there can be no second New Birth."
11. Anonymous, "A Short Preservative against the Doctrines reviv'd by Mr. Whitefield and his Adherents" (London: H. Whitridge, 1739), pp. 24, 25.
12. James Bate, "Methodism Displayed," (London: John Carter, 1739), p. 5.
13. See R. Newton Flew, *The Idea of Perfection in Christian Theology* (Oxford: University Press, 1934), p. 314.
Also Eric Baker, *A Herald of the Evangelical Revival* (London: Epworth Press, 1948), pp. 65 et seq., 174 et seq.
14. William Law, "An Earnest and Serious Answer to Dr. Trapp's Discourse . . ." (London: Innys & J. Richardson, 1940), p. 39.
15. *Ibid.*, p. 40.
16. Edmund Gibson, "The Bishop of London's Pastoral Letter to the People of his Diocese" (By way of Caution, Against Lukewarmness on one hand, and Enthusiasm on the other) (London: S. Budkley, 1739).
17. *Ibid.*, p. 18.
18. *Ibid.*, p. 42.
19. *Ibid.*, p. 43.
20. Robert Seagrave, "An Answer to Rev. Dr. Trapp's Four Sermons against Whitefield, Showing the Sin and Folly of being Angry Overmuch," (London: Oswald, 1739), p. 17.
21. *Ibid.*, p. 18.
22. Flew, *op. cit.*, p. 16.
23. C. S. Lewis, *Miracles* (New York: Macmillan, 1947), p. 114.
24. Norman Sykes, *Church and State in England in the Eighteenth Century* (Cambridge: University Press, 1934), p. 259.
25. E. W. Watson, "An Eighteenth Century Clergyman," *Church Quarterly Review*, CV, No. 210, as quoted in Sykes, *op. cit.*, p. 262.
26. Sykes, *op. cit.*, p. 262.
27. Abbey and Overton, *The English Church in the Eighteenth Century* (London: Longmans, Green, and Co., 1878), p. 37. This was a hasty generalization based on insufficient evidence, but Abbey and Overton state that sermons were as a rule controversial, and appealed mainly to prudential motives.
28. A. D. Belden, *George Whitefield—The Awakener* (London: Samson Law, Marston & Co., 1930), p. 56.
29. M. D. George, *London Life in the Eighteenth Century* (London: Kegan, Paul, Trench, Trubner & Co., 1925), pp. 22, 314. See also her *England in Transition* (London: Methuen & Co., 1928), p. 93.
30. G. V. Portus, *Caritas Anglicana* (London: A. R. Mowbray & Co., 1912), p. 7.
31. *Works*, VII, 454. Wesley here speaks of Deists, Arians, and Socinians being "too infamous among us to do any great service" to unbelief, but inveighs against "those accounted the pillars of our church, and champions of our faith; who . . . betray that Church," and includes Tillotson in his charge.
32. Law, *op. cit.*, p. 8.
33. *Sermons*, I, 266.
34. Joseph Butler, *The Analogy of Religion, Natural and Revealed* (London: Pr. for J. J. & P. Knapton, 1736), advertisement to First Edition, p. b2.
35. *Works*, VII, 215
36. Dr. Trapp was the first Professor of Poetry at Oxford, manager for Dr. Sacheverel in the famous trial, participant in the Bangorian controversy, author of translations, poetry, fiction and drama, London rector and chaplain to Lord Bolingbroke.
37. Joseph Trapp, "The Nature, Folly, Sin and Danger of Being Righteous Overmuch" (2nd ed.; London: S. Austen, 1739), p. 19.
38. *Ibid.*, p. 17.
39. *Ibid.*, p. 43.
40. Law, *op. cit.*, p. 80.
41. Anonymous, "The Oxford Methodists" (3rd ed.; London: Oxford Arms, 1738), p. 11.
42. Simon, *op. cit.*, p. 91. Simon describes these "charitable employments" as the work of "philanthropic pioneers," cutting "wilderness roads over the mountains," p. 92.
43. *Journal*, I, 462.
44. *The Letters of the Rev. John Wesley, A.M.*, ed. John Telford (London: Epworth Press, 1931), II, 49.
45. Joseph Trapp, "A Reply to Mr. Law's Earnest and Serious Answer . . ." (London: L. Gulliver, 1741), p. 51.
46. *Ibid.*, p. 53.
47. *Loc. cit.*
48. Wesley published an abridgement of *The Whole Duty of Man* in the *Christian Library*, Vol. XXI, but omitted all defense of a social hierarchy.
49. Gibson, *op. cit.*, p. 11.
50. *Works*, VIII, 65.
51. *Loc. cit.*
52. William Bowman, *The Imposture of Methodism Displayed* (London: Pr. for Jas. Lord, 1740), p. 9.
53. *Ibid.*, p. 9.
54. *Works*, XIII, p. 273.

III

Some Other Ways

Very early in life, it would seem, Wesley began to ask, What is Christianity? The answers furnished by his age which he found unsatisfactory are readily discoverable because of his constant reference to them. They were of four sorts.

The Way of Formalism

That mentioned most frequently was given by official religion: Christianity is assent to doctrine, membership in the church and observance of rites. Wesley's rejection of this conception as incomplete is repeated over and over again. In his discourse on "The Way to the Kingdom," for example, he says flatly that true religion does not consist "in any *outward thing;* such as *forms* or *ceremonies,* even of the most excellent kind." [1]

He granted the value of symbolism, "not only to the vulgar, whose thought reaches little farther than sight, but even to men of understanding, men of stronger capacities." Yet he insisted that "true religion does not principally consist therein; nay, strictly speaking, not at all. . . The religion of Christ rises infinitely higher, and lies immensely deeper, than all these." [2]

Forms are good in their place, just so far as they are "subservient to true religion" and used "as occasional helps to human weakness." "But," he warned, "let no man dream that they have intrinsic worth; or that religion cannot subsist without them." [3]

A state-religion, Christian as may be many of its devout adherents, is always in danger of declining into a religion of mere observance, a way of formalism. Devotion to intermediaries takes the place of devotion to God. Rites degenerate into mechanical performance, and with that spiritual development ends.

Anglicanism owed its very origin to the Protestant remonstrance against the decay of a state religion. The quintessence of Protestantism is its distrust of all intermediaries between God and man, whether they be priest, images, churchly architecture, or ritual.

It builds its doctrine and worship upon its belief in the immediacy of religious experience and the universality of the religious consciousness and declares that the commonest of men may come to a vision of God without dependence upon any human device. Whenever the instruments of liturgy, ecclesiasticism, or theology arise to obstruct this vision, some form of Protestantism inevitably recurs and sweeps them away.[4]

Wesley's warnings against the extreme dependence of the eighteenth century Church upon the sacerdotal and ritualistic agencies mark, therefore, a reassertion of the Protestant spirit. This fact becomes patent at various stages in the Methodist movement, for example, in the controversy which developed over the significance of the rite of baptism. We have already noted the efforts of prominent clergymen to identify the New Birth with this rite. Wesley saw that therein lay a substitution of a liturgical device for personal religious experience. Accordingly, he insisted that for all who have reached the age of accountability the New Birth implies "not barely being baptized or any outward change whatever; but a vast inward change."[5]

Against the pretensions to Christianity made by a great number of unregenerate church members he protested: "Say not then in your heart, 'I was *once* baptized, therefore I *am now* a child of God.' Alas, that consequence will by no means hold. How many are the baptized gluttons and drunkards, the baptized liars and the common swearers, the baptized railers and evil-speakers, the baptized whoremongers, thieves, extortioners? What think you? Are these now the children of God?"[6]

Viewing the ineffectiveness of sacramentalism in and of itself, Wesley reached the realistic conclusion that its importance had been much over-rated by church-members whose behavior differed in no way from that of non-Christians. He went so far as to attribute the growth of infidelity to those who "think going to church and sacrament will bring them to heaven, though they practise neither justice nor mercy...."⁷ No amount of church attendance can take the place of good works.

Yet even good works may become a component of the Way of Formalism and a substitute for the vision of God. If the virtuous place their faith in the efficacy of good works they miss real Christianity. Wesley made this discovery after long and baffling experiences. In his sermon on "The Almost Christian" he was painting a portrait of himself when he described a man who sincerely and uniformly endeavored to do good to all men. "I did go so far for many years," he said, "yet finally discovered that all this time I was but *almost a Christian*." ⁸

If such high endeavor is to be condemned as semi-Christianity, what could be said for that great host of church members, as common in our day as in Wesley's, who believe that Christianity consists in a respectable, harmless sort of life? They were jolted out of their complacence by Wesley's declaration that there is no particular virtue in mere harmless living. "... many birds and beasts do no harm," said Wesley, "yet they are not capable of religion." ⁹

His assault upon the religion of the respectable aroused great animosity. Often, after a sermon on the real nature of Christianity, Wesley would be told by the resident vicar that his services in the parish were no longer desired. At first he could not understand why a logical presentation of the distinctive claims of Christianity should produce such consequences. The minister who had engaged him might even admit that all that Wesley had said was true, that it was actually the doctrine of the Church of England, yet would dismiss him as the fomenter of "enthusiasm."

Wesley finally concluded that the way of formalism had been so fully accepted as the only alternative to fanaticism that insight into the real teaching of the Bible on the Christian way had been virtually lost. A method of Biblical exegesis, he said, had been adopted for explaining texts on the nature of the Kingdom "so that they shall mean just nothing; so that they shall express far less of inward religion, than the writings of Plato . . ." [10]

"The real state of the case is this," he said, "religion is commonly thought to consist of three things—harmlessness, using the means of grace, and doing good. . . . Accordingly, by a religious man is commonly meant one that is honest, just, and fair in his dealings; that is constantly at church and sacrament; and that gives much alms. . . ." Hence it followed that when Wesley preached that "true religion, the consequence of God's dwelling and reigning in the soul . . . . does not properly consist in any or all of these three things; but that a man might both be harmless, use the means of grace, and do much good, and yet have no true religion at all," [11] his listeners were shaken out of their false security and filled with fear. Their discovery of the real nature of the Christian way, Wesley saw, created such a tension that true religion was identified with dreaded "enthusiasm." The Revival was "enthusiasm from end to end," he said, "to those who have the form of godliness but not the power." [12]

Still another source of false security to the formalist was his reliance upon doctrinal soundness. Through all Wesley's sermons resounds the iteration, Real religion is not mere orthodoxy. He was much misunderstood when he declared that assent to doctrine is no more than the faith of the devil; but his meaning is clear when he explains that ". . . even the devils believe that Christ was born of a virgin; that He wrought all kinds of miracles, declaring himself very God; that, for our sakes, He suffered a most painful death, to redeem us from death everlasting; that He rose again the third day; that He ascended into heaven, and sitteth at the right hand of the Father . . . These articles of our faith the devils believe. . . ." [13]

Every age needs to be reminded that faith is not barely a speculative, rational thing, not simply an act of the understanding, but a "disposition which God hath wrought in the heart."[14] Wesley had to make very plain the psychological fact that Christian faith requires an act of the whole man. A "train of ideas in the head," however right, does not necessarily change the disposition or conduct, a fact amply demonstrated in every congregation of Wesley's time. "A common swearer," he declared, "a Sabbath-breaker, a whoremonger, a drunkard, who says he believes the Scripture is of God, is a monster upon earth, the greatest contradiction to his own, as well as to the reason of all mankind."[15]

This monster contradiction, created by an age that had rested the whole case for Christianity upon an appeal to reason, could be corrected only by an appeal beyond reason and nature to the "true, living, Christian faith, which whosoever hath is born of God."[16] This is more than an "assent to divine truth, upon the testimony of God, or upon the evidence of miracles . . .";[17] this is the life of God breathed into the soul of man.

Official religion, which had become the Way of Formalism, did not satisfy Wesley. This is not to say that he knew no Christians in the Anglican Church. He knew many. Neither does it follow that the absence of vital Christianity within the Church of his day led him to withdraw from the Church. He remained an Anglican until his death, but he had to reject the Way of Formalism to find an answer to his question, What is Christianity?

The Way of Sectarianism

It was not likely that Wesley, even when failing to find satisfaction in the church of his upbringing, should turn for an answer to the Dissenting sects. A deep repugnance to their ecclesiastical polity, their modes of worship, their predilection for Calvinistic doctrine, and their concern about particularities of practice had been bred in him by his High Church Tory parents.

Like most converts to a new faith, the elder Wesleys were excessively biased in their devotion to their adopted church.

From them probably Wesley received the impression that all sectarianism was an un-Christian "religion of opinions." The controversies that had raged from the sixteenth century into the time of Wesley's boyhood had inevitably created this reaction among Anglicans. They failed to see in the sects the logical outcome of the Protestantism of which they themselves were a part.

The Protestant theory of the right of private judgment had been considerably modified by institutional checks in Anglicanism. These modifications seemed to the radical Protestant the very "dregs of Romanism." The root principle of Protestantism, as we have seen, was the removal of all the intermediaries that Catholicism had erected between man and God. To the radical the retention of some of these intermediaries marked Anglicanism as a form of "arrested Protestantism"; it had simply "swept the rubbish behind the door."

Out of the shock of the disappointment produced by this compromise had sprung the Puritan sects.[18] The exercise of private interpretation of the Word was given free course among them; society was reorganized "on the basis of a Bible reading populace"; and the removal of intermediaries proceeded to its inevitable end.[19] The Bible as "the people's book" became an open treasury of truth to every man, whatever his grade of intelligence. It is not surprising that wide variation of interpretation resulted when every one from the cultivated upper middle-class Presbyterian to the illiterate lowly Ranter was given an opportunity to formulate his own view of holy things.

Neither is it surprising that extreme dogmatism accompanied the exposition of these views, for the theory of the right of private judgment implies not only faith in human reason but also belief in Biblical authority. The result was bitter controversy over doctrine, modes of worship, sacramental rites, forms of church polity, and codes of conduct. Seen from the perspective of the twentieth century, this controversy was only one element in a mighty revolution whereby freedom for religious thought and personal religious experience was guaranteed for all men, and like every revolution it had its right, left, and center, as determined by social, economic and cultural differences.[20]

It was a revolution with inestimably valuable results, but the Churchman of the early eighteenth century lacked the needed perspective for recognizing them. It was inevitable that a young High Church man of Wesley's breeding and social rank should dismiss sectarianism as an unchristian "religion of opinions."

Later, when he had gained perspective, he said of Presbyterians and Independents: "I cannot but have a widely different opinion, from that I entertained some years ago." He had by that time "conversed with many among them" and found in them "the root" of Christianity and an earnest endeavor "to keep a conscience void of offence, both toward God and toward men."[21] But during the period when he was asking, What is Christianity? nonconformity, in general, seemed to him to have substituted opinions about peripheral matters for the core of Christianity. The sects, he believed, had originated in controversies over these peripheral elements, and although most of them had once possessed spiritual vitality, their first fervor had now passed and they now tended to equate Christianity with the retention of these opinions.

Was there any truth in Wesley's contention that nonconformity had settled down into a religion of externalities? Had they, too, after a half century of protest against the intermediaries that had separated men from God, drifted away from the heart of Christianity? Those who know this period, whatever their religious bias, tell of the rapid declension of the sects from their original insight into the nature of Christianity. Over-emphasis upon doctrine, in particular, had become the foe of inward religion, and, paradoxically, had produced confusion rather than clarity in belief.

The devastating effects of exclusive attention to beliefs were most fully apparent in Presbyterianism. Coomer points out that, whereas there were some 500 Presbyterian churches in England at the beginning of the eighteenth century, there were not more than 300 by 1770, and worse than that, only half of these were orthodox.[22]

Arianism, with its heretical theory of the person of Christ, had first penetrated Presbyterian academies and thence had entered their pulpits.[23] It was followed by Socinianism, which denied the doctrines of original sin and the atonement and exalted man's natural capacity for virtue. The whole structure of orthodoxy was shaken, and before the century was over Unitarianism had claimed many chapels for its own and divorced Christianity from belief in the miraculous. So complete was the triumph of heterodoxy that the term, Presbyterian, Coomer says, came finally to be identified with all three heresies—Arianism, Socinianism, and Unitarianism—and not until 1876, when the Evangelical movement had brought about a separate organization, namely, the Presbyterian Church of England, was the title for orthodoxy regained in this group of believers.[24]

The decline of Presbyterianism continued throughout Wesley's lifetime. William Watson in his survey of Dissenting Churches of London, made in 1806, reported that the Presbyterians had "either deserted to the world or sunk under the influence of a lukewarm ministry."[25] They had come to form the greater portion of upper middle-class Dissent. Perhaps their rise in the social scale had had as much influence upon their desertion "to the world" as had an heretical ministry.

Slightly lower down in the social scale were the Independents, who seem to have been less troubled by the "deceitfulness of riches" and the problems of belief. Coomer attributes their ability to withstand the assaults of deism and Arianism in great part to their adoption of a Church Covenant, by which all members "separated from all wrong doers and promised to choose God alone."[26] They were a "gathered church" made up of individuals "convincedly Christian," who testified to personal religious experience. Their pattern of doctrine and conduct was maintained by a monthly Church Meeting which exercised severe disciplinary powers.[27]

Much the same type of Church Meeting enforced similar standards among the Baptists, who were a step or two below the Independents socially and economically. This method for preserving purity of doctrine and practice appealed to Wesley, in spite of his devotion to the national church. He commended its effectiveness, saying to the Baptists: "The smallness of your number, compared to that of either the Presbyterians, or those of the Church, makes it easier for you to have an exact knowledge of the behaviour of all your members, and to put away from among you every one that 'walketh not according to the doctrine you have received.'"[28]

Yet by 1745 laxity in the exercise of this function of the Church Meeting had crept in and Wesley observed: "There are unholy, outwardly unholy men in your congregations, also men that profane either the name or the day of the Lord; that are intemperate, either in meat or drink, gluttonous, sensual, luxurious; that variously offend against justice, mercy or truth, in their intercourse with their neighbour, and do not walk by that royal law, 'Thou shalt love thy neighbour as thyself.'"[29]

The reason given by Wesley for this inconsistency between profession and practice is their growing reliance upon correct opinions. "Many of you," he said, "have unawares put opinion in the room of faith and repentance." This for him was a fatal mistake! "Supposing your opinion to be true, yet a true opinion concerning repentance is wholly different from the thing itself; and you may have a true opinion concerning faith all your life, and die an unbeliever."[30]

All this spelt decline in the spiritual power of the various sectarian groups. Even among the Quakers, those ardent seventeenth century exponents of practical Christianity, a satisfaction with mere outward religion was supplanting their first deep thirst for the vision of God. Margaret Fox Fell as early as 1698 had occasion to warn that "legal ceremonies . . . are far from Gospel freedom. . . . It is a dangerous thing," she said, "to lead young Friends much into the observation of outward things, which may be easily done, for they can soon get into an *outward garb to be all alike outwardly,* but this will not make them *true Christians.*" [31]

Barclay, in 1879, after sketching the decline of orthodoxy and practical piety among the Presbyterians, Baptists, Independents and Friends, concluded that "the darkest period in the religious annals of England was that prior to the preaching of Whitefield and the two Wesleys." [32]

There was apparently good reason for Wesley's rejection of the Way of Sectarianism and his reiterated statement that Christianity is not distinguished "by actions, customs, or usages, of an indifferent nature . . . does not lie in doing what God has not enjoined, or abstaining from what he hath not forbidden . . . does not lie in the form of our apparel, in the posture of our body, or the covering of our heads. . . ." [33]

As a consequence of this mistaken emphasis, the Way of Sectarianism did not afford an answer to Wesley's question, What is Christianity? Yet it did offer valuable negative instruction, for it warned him to beware of the controversies which inevitably arise when theories about belief or practice push to the fore in a movement. As Barclay says, Wesley was not "led away by controversy from his one great mission of saving souls." He had learned, "where controversy was needed to set forth truth which had been obscured," to handle it " with a stronger perception of its dangers." [34]

---

1. *Sermons,* I, 149.
2. *Loc. cit.*
3. *Loc. cit.*
4. Ralph Barton Perry, *Puritanism and Democracy* (New York: The Vanguard Press, 1944), p. 88.
5. *Sermons,* I, 281, note.
6. *Ibid.,* p. 295

7. *Letters*, II, 59.
8. *Sermons*, I, 60.
9. *Works*, VI, 498.
10. *Journal*, II, 321.
11. *Loc. cit.*
12. *Loc. cit.*
13. *Sermons*, I, 63.
14. *Ibid.*, p. 284.
15. *Works*, VIII, 15.
16. *Sermons*, I, 284.
17. *Loc. cit.*
18. William Haller, *The Rise of Puritanism* (New York, Columbia University Press, 1938), p. 8.
19. *Ibid.*, p. 178.
20. Perry, *op. cit.*, p. 70.
21. *Works*, VIII, 180.
22. Duncan Coomer, *English Dissent under the Early Hanoverians* (London: Epworth Press, 1946), p. 79.
23. *Ibid.*, p. 11. Coomer describes the custom of having a young assistant from one of the academies preach on the new ideas in the afternoon, after the older minister had preached on high Calvinism in the morning. When the older man died, the younger man followed, having ingratiated himself with the prominent seatholders. In time such a church became completely Unitarian.
24. *Ibid.*, p. 66.
25. Quoted from William Watson in Coomer, *op. cit.*, p. 119.
26. Coomer, *op. cit.*, pp. 16, 19.
27. *Ibid.*, p. 18.
28. *Works*, VIII, 183.
29. *Loc. cit.*
30. *Loc. cit.*
31. Robert Barclay, *The Inner Life of the Religious Societies of the Commonwealth* (London: Hodder and Stoughton, 1879), pp. 500-1.
32. *Ibid.*, p. 596.
33. *Works*, VIII, 341.
34. Barclay, *op. cit.*, p. 597.

IV

Still Other Ways

THE WAY OF HUMANISM

The history of the Christian religion records the difficulties of charting a middle course between sectarian bigotry and doctrinal chaos. It is surprising that Wesley was not driven by his dislike of the sects into the camp of the liberals. Socinianism had become a pervasive force, felt as powerfully in Anglicanism as in Presbyterianism. Hence the errors of the Way of Humanism were not so easily recognizable as those of the Ways of Formalism and Sectarianism, especially to an intellectual of Wesley's type, who had been taught that the final appeal must be made to Reason.

This appeal in Wesley's century was as universal as the appeal to scientific data in ours. Frequently the century has been labeled The Age of Reason. Although this term is too narrow to do justice to the whole complex of tendencies, it is true that the prevailing temper of the first half of the century was rationalistic. Every thinker, whatever his subject—art, science, commerce, politics or religion—supported his position by a demonstration of its reasonableness.

Wesley, when addressing the "intelligentsia," always made this approach. His greatest polemic was entitled *An Appeal to Men of Reason and Religion.* And when addressing humble audiences he explained the term, "reason," and endeavored to bring their views and practices into alignment with this universal criterion.

Popularly used, the term was equivalent to our expression, "common sense"; but it had a much more highly specialized meaning, for back of it lay a theory of reality that had been developing ever since the Renaissance. It was believed that a certain body of truths is given by nature to all men and, hence, may be recognized simply by the exercise of the reason. Because these truths belong to reality they make their appeal and are known intuitively.

In the sphere of religion the foundation for rationalism had been laid in the seventeenth century by Hooker, the great defender of Arminianism. He had argued that so uniform and universal are the pronouncements of reason that it may be considered the dictum of God. The universality of certain truths would suggest that "Nature herself must have taught" them to mankind. And, since God is "the author of Nature," He must use "her voice as His instrument" to give men without the aid of revelation a knowledge of reality. To a large degree, therefore, reason is capable of finding in itself and by itself the essential truths relating to the nature of God and the duties of man.

Hooker, of course, had no notion that he was undermining the foundations of revealed religion, but his efforts to confute the Calvinistic doctrine of total depravity prepared the way for eighteenth century humanism. Ultimately even the Arminian theory of original sin became adulterated or abandoned through the exaggerated emphasis upon the sufficiency of reason, and after that came the rejection of revelation.

Scientific discovery in the seventeenth century also greatly strengthened the belief that man lives in a universe that can be measured by his reason. The work of Newton, for example, seemed to demonstrate that all principles, whether mechanical, social, ethical, or religious, commend themselves to man's mind.[1] Unlike the scientific movement of the nineteenth century this discovery did not breed atheism nor hostility to religion. It seemed rather to strengthen belief in God by its evidences of a general harmony of all nature under the government of the Maker.

But it did raise questions concerning revelation, for in making man the measure of all things it asserted his independence of the supernatural, and reduced the authority of the Scriptures. The church of the eighteenth century became the battleground between the defenders of Revealed Religion and the proponents of the religion of reason, or Natural Religion, as it was called.

The first great speaker for Natural Religion was John Locke, who toward the end of the seventeenth century won the respect of both deists and liberal Churchmen by a simple, rational statement of a minimal creed which was designed to appeal to all men. It reduced Christianity to a common denominator with all religions. Locke believed that the ethical ideals and religious experiences of the best men of all ages, from Plato to Luther, were essentially the same. Reason had not "failed men, even outside the Christian dispensation."

With Locke reason became the final arbiter even of the authenticity of Biblical statement. "There can be no evidence," he said, "that any traditional revelation is of divine origin, in the words we receive it, and in the sense we understand it, so clear and so certain, as that of the principles of reason; and therefore nothing that is contrary to, and inconsistent with, the clear and self-evident dictates of reason, has a right to be urged or assented to as a matter of faith, wherein reason hath nothing to do." [2]

He conceived of the Christian religion as simply a scientific statement of rational propositions. These in their minimal form could be reduced to three, namely: there is an omnipotent God; God demands virtuous living; there is a future life with rewards and punishments.

All the doctrines emphasized by the sects in their cultivation of personal religious experience, such, for example, as the doctrines of free grace, original sin and justification by faith, were dismissed as no more convincing than the Catholic doctrine of transubstantiation. Assurance was among the "enthusiastic" notions founded "neither on reason nor divine revelation, but rising from the conceits of a warmed or over-weening brain." [3]

What room was left for revelation in a system so largely

humanistic, so divested of the miraculous element inherent in Christianity? Does Natural Religion leave any necessity for Revealed Religion? This was the question that engaged all Churchmen in the eighteenth century. It was answered in two different ways by the exponents of Natural Religion. Within the Church revelation was described as "natural religion enlarged"—a restatement of truths discoverable by the cultivated reason, but not so easily recognized by the common man, whose superstition, passion and prejudice obstruct the activity of reason.

Outside the Church and bitterly attacked by Churchmen as unorthodox or even atheist were the deists, who followed the theory of Natural Religion to its logical end and rejected the supplementary assistance of revelation as both unnecessary and unreliable. Their rationalism led them to an abandonment of the Bible, the church and all doctrine.

Actually, there was little difference between the basic beliefs of deists and those of the Church advocates of Natural Religion. In the anti-Methodist pamphlets we have seen the drift within the Church away from supernaturalism. The desire to avoid enthusiasm, to objectify religion, to agree with the latest scientific thought, to conform to the age doctrine of reason led farther and farther away from true Christian faith.

Their close proximity to the deists is repeatedly seen in the priority given in their writing to Natural Religion. Often clergymen professedly orthodox treated Revealed Religion as a sort of appendix to their treatises on Natural Religion. Scripture, too, was examined by the touchstone of Natural Religion; if it did not accord with reason, then it was adjudged inaccurate.

The boundary line between the Church spokesmen for Natural Religion and the socially ostracized deists is so uncertain that today many historians describe them all as deists, distinguished only by their differing relationship to the Church. Yet the church spokesmen assumed that they were serving the cause of Christianity in the most effective way possible by proving to the deists and all doubters that revelation is essentially acceptable to reason.

The credibility of the Bible became the most stressed feature of Christianity. It finally appeared that Christianity had come into existence "for nothing else but to be proved." Christianity as a way of life was hardly thought of. This was the state of things when Wesley came upon the scene. Butler had published the *Analogy of Religion, Natural and Revealed* in 1736 in an endeavor to show those who accepted only Natural Religion that it possessed as many difficulties and mysteries for the reason as did Revealed Religion. The logical outcome for this kind of apologetics could be only further doubt of the validity of reason.[4] Butler in exposing the weakness of deism had really demonstrated the fallacy of the major hypothesis upon which the eighteenth century had built its intellectual system, the sovereignty of reason.[5]

Law had warned the Church in 1732 when he published *The Case of Reason* that "those who make their own minds the measure" of God often land on the "rock of *Atheism*," for the reason that inbred evil has impaired man's reason as much as his other faculties.[6] He saw no historical basis for the trust in reason and shrewdly pointed out the lack of empirical proof: ". . . he that asserts the sufficiency of . . . reason to guide men in matters of religion, is not only without any positive proof from fact or experience on his side, but has the history of all ages . . . fully demonstrating quite the contrary."[7]

The age had built an elaborate intellectual structure upon an hypothesis that had nothing to do with fact. Eighteenth century theology finally discovered to its dismay that the very method used to support revelation could be used just as effectively to destroy it. Butler had simply paved the way for a thorough-going skepticism and Hume followed, disposing of both Natural and Revealed Religion by showing the unreliability of reason, the outcome which Law had foreseen.[8]

The survival of the Christian faith in the eighteenth century was not due to the apologists. This fact is acknowledged now by all the historians. The Way of Humanism proved to be a dead-end road.

The Way of Secularism

The ethical aspect of "the religion of reason" furnishes the last category under which we shall discuss the religion of Wesley's time. Under the corrosive force of rationalism Christian ethics suffered as great a change as did Christian theology. Humanism in syncretizing Christianity with all religions obliterated all its distinguishing ethical features. The Bible was made nothing more than a sanction for humanly conceived morality, a divine fiat needed mainly by "the illiterate bulk of mankind."

The notion that the Christian life is merely "the good life" perpetually recurs in the history of the church for the reason that the distinction between Christian ethics and purely secular ethics has never been clearly apprehended. But this notion was virtually forced upon the eighteenth century when the opposition to "enthusiasm" had closed the door to personal religious experience and the battle over revelation had destroyed faith in the supernatural. If a man could neither consciously know God, nor be sure of doctrine or the Bible, he could at least lead a good, decent life.

This is the reason why discussions of morality were so very common in and out of the pulpit. The age is known for its excessive interest in conduct, and the interest was created, by and large, by uncertainty about faith. A typical discussion of the comparative claims of morality and faith occurs in the *Spectator Papers*. Addison gives morality the pre-eminence over faith because "the rule of morality is much more certain than that of faith," and he bases this certainty upon the fact that "all the civilised nations of the world" agree in "the great points of morality, as much as they differ in those of faith." *

Obviously the ethical code which Addison here has in mind is no more Christian than are the ethics of Confucius. The type of preaching which we have previously mentioned, done often by men of such prominence as Archbishop Tillotson, had left the masses with no clear demarcation of Christian duties. Some of Wesley's contemporaries recognized this fact and protested against the tendency of the sermon to become a mere moral disquisition. Bishop Gibson was one of these, and even in his Pastoral Letter attacking Methodism he turned aside to warn young preachers of his diocese against confining their discourses to the ethics of the Greek philosophers.[10] But when he goes on to advise that they include the improvements made in "the moral scheme" by the Holy Scriptures we discover that actually he regards the Bible much as had Locke, simply as a supplementary re-enforcement to Natural Religion.

Eighteenth century humanism by divorcing Christian ethics from both Biblical authority and Christian faith ushered in an age of secularism. Up until this time man, because of his imperfect reason and his diseased will, had been considered unable of himself either to apprehend his whole duty or to perform it. The religion of reason, however, taught him that moral principles do not derive from God, but rather from the moral constitution of the universe. Man should choose good, not because God commands it, but because good is a necessary element in the great universal harmony and because his reason convinces him that it is essential to his well-being. In the realm of ethics, as in the realm of doctrine, reason is the primary authority and man need obey nothing that does not appeal to him as reasonable.

Now it is indubitably true that morality is not only made plain in the teachings of Jesus, but is also revealed in the structure of Reality. The universe rewards goodness, because goodness is of the nature of things. But eighteenth century secularism by its limitation of observation to material reality missed the supersensuous. Furthermore, evil as well as good is present in the limited portion of the universe known to us. It taints everything and only the Spirit of God can reveal it. The unaided reason cannot be trusted to give a full account of ethical truth. What the secularist defines as a virtue may be only a mixture of good and evil, or even a vice.

Furthermore the fundamental distinction between the secularist and the Christian is that the secularist makes the betterment of self his final goal while the Christian organizes his whole scale of values around the supreme value, the love of God. The major difference between the Way of Secularism and "the Way" taught and exemplified by Christ has been well stated by E. Stanley Jones: "Know thyself, accept thyself, develop thyself—that is pagan. Surrender thyself, discipline thyself, obey Another Self—the Spirit of God—that is Christian." [11]

Wesley's refusal of the secularist's ethical code was unhesitating and his condemnation of it stern. The drastic criticism of contemporary Christianity which he made to his nephew, Samuel, who was considering entrance into the Roman Catholic Church is typical: "I care not a rush for your being called a Papist or Protestant. But I am grieved at your being a heathen. Certain it is that the general religion both of Protestants and Catholics is no better than refined heathenism." [12]

The austerity of the way of life advocated by Christ had been toned down to meet the demands of unregenerate human nature until it was commonly assumed that any man could of himself live the Christian life. The code of conduct for "the good life" was little different from the ethical systems devised before the advent of Christianity.

Wesley attacked repeatedly the almost universal assumption that Christianity is identical with secular morality. In his sermon on "True Christianity Defended" he asked his audience, "Are there not many present here . . . who believe that a good moral man and a good Christian mean the same thing? that a man need not trouble himself any further, if he only practices as much Christianity as was written over the Heathen Emper-

or's gate—'Do as thou wouldest be done unto. . . . !' " [13]

He did not undervalue the efforts of the virtuous man, but he made very plain the distinction between a humanly attained virtue and the love of God, which comes only by the exercise of faith, and which alone can be the source of the virtues demanded by Christianity. Discussing these severe demands, he remarked: "I do not wonder that one of the most sensible deists should say, 'I think the Bible is the finest book I ever read in my life; yet I have an insuperable objection to it: It is *too good*. It lays down such a plan of life, such a scheme of doctrine and practice, as is far too excellent for weak, silly men to aim at or attempt to copy after.' All this," Wesley admitted, "is most true," [14] unless one knows and accepts the provision made by Christianity. The difficulty for "weak, silly men" vanishes when they see that if "all things are possible with God, all things are possible to him that believeth." [15] The humanly unattainable "goodness" required by the Bible was therefore the feature that distinguished Christian morality from the secular.

He believed that Christianity begins where secular morality ends. ". . . poverty of spirit, conviction of sin, the renouncing ourselves, the not having our own righteousness (the very first point in the religion of Jesus Christ)," he said, "leave all pagan religion behind." [16] To show the character of Christian virtues, he once traced the evolution of new meanings in the word, *humilitas*, under the influence of the Christian ethic.

The Christian meaning of *humilitas* is lowliness of heart, such as springs from a sense of total dependence upon God in the accomplishment of good. In neither the Roman nor the Greek language can be found any such concept; instead the word humble meant "mean-spirited" and "contemptible." [17] This change of meaning under the influence of Christianity furnishes an index to the difference between purely secular and truly Christian virtues. The Christian ethic is built upon a recognition of the supreme authority and power of God and man's dependence upon Him for all his goodness." [18]

Humanism and secularism had destroyed the consciousness of God upon which depend many of the Christian virtues. In his sermon on "The Unity of the Divine Being" Wesley called attention to the fact that ". . . almost all men of letters in . . . all the civilized countries of Europe, extol *humanity* to the skies, as the very essence of religion. To this the great triumvirate, Rousseau, Voltaire, and David Hume, have contributed all their labours, sparing no pains to establish a religion which should stand on its own foundation, independent of any revelation whatever; yea, not supposing even the being of a God. So leaving Him if he has any being, to himself, they have found out both a religion and a happiness which have no relation at all to God, nor any dependence up him." [19]

"It is no wonder," he concludes, "that this religion should grow fashionable, and spread far and wide in the world. But call it *humanity, virtue, morality,* or what you please, it is neither better nor worse than Atheism.... It is a plausible way of thrusting God out of the world he has made. They can do business without him; and so either drop him entirely, not considering him at all, or suppose that since

He gave things their beginning,
And set this whirligig a-spinning

he has not concerned himself with these trifles, but let everything take its own course." [20]

Wesley even objected to applying the term, virtue, to the Christian graces for the reason that in current usage virtue meant a character to be attained by human effort. He likewise objected to the current efforts to Christianize the principle of self-interest by identifying self-love with public good. Altruism thus became nothing but sublimated selfishness.

The adoption of a minimal creed had led to a life of minimal righteousness. The Way of Humanism, in spite of its efforts to reconcile the natural with the supernatural, had led to the Way of Secularism. The result was a "falling church" and a pagan nation. Skepticism pervaded the upper class, worldliness characterized the once Puritan middle class, and raw paganism reduced the lower class to a state of bestiality.

A new way of life had to be found.

---

1. See A. N. Whitehead, *Science and the Modern World* (Cambridge, University Press, 1927), pp. 49-70.
2. John Locke, *Selections*, ed. Lamprecht (1928), p. 316.
3. *Ibid.*, p. 342.
4. C. S. Lewis says of Butler's argument that its effect upon the atheist is to make him despise and defy God for the foolishness imputed to Him by the analogy to Nature. C. S. Lewis, *op. cit.*, p. 141.
5. E. C. Mossner, *Bishop Butler and the Age of Reason* (New York: Macmillan Co., 1936), p. 152.
6. William Law, *The Case of Reason* (London, Pr. for G. Robinson, 1774), p. 147.
7. *Ibid.*, p. 121.
8. Mossner, *op. cit.*, p. 131 et seq.
9. Joseph Addison, *The Spectator*, ed. G. A. Aitken, V, No. 459 (August 16, 1712).
10. Gibson, *op. cit.*, p. 44.
11. E. Stanley Jones, *The Way* (New York: Abingdon-Cokesbury Press, 1946), p. 280.
12. *Letters*, VIII, 218.
13. *Works*, VII, 456.
14. *Ibid.*, p. 298.
15. *Loc. cit.*
16. *Sermons*, I, 326.
17. *Loc. cit.*
18. *Ibid.*, p. 328. Humility begins "where a sense of guilt and of the wrath of God ends; and is a continual sense of our total dependence on him."
19. *Works*, VII, 270.
20. *Ibid.*, p. 271.

V

The Seeking

The most powerful formative influences upon Wesley's early life came from the Anglican Church—the Anglican Church at its best. Yet until he was twenty-two he apparently was satisfied with the Way of Formalism. His home training under parents, once Puritan, now High Church, had been positive enough to give him a very clear idea of the outward marks of Christian life. Toward these he became more or less indifferent during his public school days at Charterhouse, excusing himself for habitual sins and taking refuge in the defense that he was not "so bad as other people."[1] His religion consisted of attention to private and public devotion, assent to doctrine, and general harmlessness in behavior.

This moral and spiritual complacency continued until late in 1724, when, having received the B.A. degree from Oxford, he began to think seriously upon a profession, and, influenced to some degree by his father, decided to enter the ministry. Immediately his attitude toward pleasure seeking seems to have undergone a change. He lost his relish for it as he came to recognize the value of time for Christian service.

His correspondence with his mother, an important index to Wesley's development during this period, exhibits a new moral intensity, a determination to bring religion from the circumference to the center of life. At her suggestion he undertook a serious self-examination, to find whether he had "a reasonable hope of salvation." This could be determined, she said, by his "state of faith and repentance," which are "the conditions of the gospel covenant on our part"[2]; that is, assurance of salvation is measurable in terms of human attainment, rather than divinely given.

Another piece of motherly advice much emphasized by biographers was her preference for "practical divinity" rather than "critical learning." Her husband, with whom she says she rarely agreed, and whom she considered "a casuist," had recommended the latter, wishing his son to be fully prepared to understand and to defend the Scriptures. In this, of course, he was following the current speculative trend and perhaps hoping for some able controversial writing from his son. Allowing for the necessity for some critical training, she still urged him to place major stress upon the ethical aspects of religion.[3] Wesley followed his mother's advice.

This must not be interpreted, however, as indifference on the part of either mother or son toward the intellectual problems of the day. These were thoroughly and intelligently discussed in the Epworth vicarage from his earliest years. *Mrs. Wesley's Conference with Her Daughter*,[4] written by her in 1711-12 for lack of proper books to be used in the training of her children, shows her acquaintance with the ruling ideas of her time. Its treatment of various aspects of eighteenth century religion and its estimate of the proper sphere of natural religion probably gave Wesley insight into the fallacies of the Way of Secularism. While recognizing the existence of a religion of nature outside of revelation she points out that those who neglect revelation abandon the greater strictness and purity of life demanded by Christianity and also exhibit a humanistic "pride of intellect" that would make them a law unto themselves. This leads them to an abandonment of the doctrine of original sin, a fatal error, for upon this doctrine stands the whole system of the Gospel, and its distinction from natural religion.[5]

During the period under discussion, Wesley had a proneness to the casuistry which distinguished his father. As late as 1732 William Law criticized him for his resort to a "philosophical religion."[6] But efforts to reconcile religion with current philosophy were, of course, to be expected of a young man of Wesley's acumen. For a time he was engulfed in the intellectual confusions that harassed all thoughtful students as they endeavored to find a satisfactory religion within the limits of reason. Later he described the melancholy defeat which met his efforts: "After carefully heaping up the strongest arguments which I could find, either in ancient or modern authors, for the very being of a God, and . . . the existence of an invisible world; I have wandered up and down, musing with myself . . . What if that saying of a great man be really true: 'Post mortem nihil est; ipsaque mors nihil?' . . . And I have pursued the thought, till there was no spirit in me; and I was ready to choose strangling rather than life." [7]

His mother gave him wise counsel, assuring him that truth is its own defender, if the seeker is utterly sincere and willing for his personal life to be measured by it. "I highly approve," she wrote, "of your care to search into the grounds and reasons of our most holy religion, which you may do, if your intention be pure, and yet retain the integrity of your faith." She believed he would in time "discover the congruity . . . between the ordinances and the precepts of the gospel and right reason." [8]

With these facts before us we cannot agree with those biographers who discount Wesley's intellectual power. Throughout his life he kept in the thought current of his time, reading so widely and commenting so wisely that a good annotated bibliography of eighteenth century literature might be compiled from his record. He made, as we shall see, a significant contribution to the literature of the deistic controversy, offering the testimony of religious experience as a solution to the dilemma created by too exclusive an appeal to reason.

In 1725, after he had begun his preparation for the ministry, the question as to what Christianity really is arose. *The Imitation of Christ*, by Thomas á Kempis, had been recommended to him by a religious friend, probably Betty Kirkham. Although he had frequently seen it, he had never responded to the piety of the author. Now he was impressed, even while refusing Kempis' asceticism. "I was angry," he writes, "at Kempis for being too strict ... yet I had frequently much sensible comfort in reading him, such as I was an utter stranger to before...." He began to alter the whole form of his "conversation and to set in earnest upon a new life." [9]

He spent an hour or two each day in religious retirement, and communicated every week. This, to be sure, only increased his zeal in outward religion, but he also began "to aim at, and to pray for, inward holiness." This he saw "in a stronger light" than ever before, and with it the need for "simplicity of intention and purity of affection, one design in all" of life and "one desire ruling" every temper.[10]

At this point in his experience, Christianity for Wesley passed forever out of the realm of pure speculation and became identified with life. Never again was Christianity simply an expression of Truth; it was a Way and a Life, as well. This he clearly saw by 1735 when he published his own translation of *The Imitation of Christ*.[11] In his preface he announced that the book would make no appeal to those who were fond of controversy, nor to those who looked for "an easy and cheap religion" of mere observance. Such persons have "learned to dispute, not to live." They "provoke one another," not "to love and to good works, but rather to wrath, strife, and envy. They are always ready, by starting unnecessary doubts and questions, to turn a spiritual conference upon the most clear, practical truths, into a wholly spiritual debate upon some point of mere speculation."[12]

For a century there had been a long succession of controversialists, first the sectaries, then the apologists for natural and revealed religion, all of them trying to prove Christianity; and what had become of Christianity in the meantime? Where were the Christians? "Show me where the Christians live," Wesley was to say over and over again.

During the same year Wesley read another devotional classic which so influenced him that he recommended it repeatedly to his followers and published an extract of it in his *Christian Library*.[13] This was Jeremy Taylor's *Rules and Exercises of*

Holy Living, with its companion volume on *Holy Dying*. It, too, was brought to his attention by Betty Kirkham, who had come to value it, even though it had "almost put her out of her senses when she was fifteen or sixteen years old," [14] because of some of its impracticable rules.

Wesley agreed that some portions of it were too strict and others illogical, but that its total effect was to stimulate a deep desire to become a "whole Christian." Taylor in his section on "Purity of Intention" insists that all of life must be brought under the sway of Christ. The commonest actions of life then take on religious significance and nothing remains purely secular. Conversely, pious acts are no longer hypocritically performed through wrong motives.

Rules for this way of life were furnished by Taylor with tests for determining the extent of achievement. The *Rules and Exercises* might be described as a manual for attaining moral and spiritual competence and might be compared with modern manuals in popular psychology, Taylor's end being spiritual poise.

His tests for purity of intention were, for example: valuing a religious design more highly than a temporal; being superior to the opinions of others; trusting the consequences of all actions to God; loving virtue wherever seen; despising the world and all its vanities.[15] These directions for singleness of intention Wesley took deeply to heart and from this time forward strove for utter sincerity in his search for truth, a "willingness to know and to do the whole will of God." He refused to be satisfied with the mediocre achievement of the average professing Christian, who he felt never really intended to be wholly Christian.

Taylor and Kempis banished forever Wesley's moral complacency, setting before him the goal of Christian perfection and inducting him into a life of tireless self-discipline and arduous conquest of the flesh. Success in this ascetic effort he believed would make him acceptable with God. Taylor's dedicatory epistle reveals unmistakably the High Church adoption of the ascetic theory of works as an answer to the dissenters' theory of "assurance." His readers were instructed to identify assurance with consciousness of virtuous conduct.

Twelve "signs of grace and predestination" were given by which they might know whether they "certainly belong to God." The first may be taken as representative of Taylor's emphasis throughout upon human effort. A Christian is one who "believes and is baptized into all the Articles of the Christian faith, and studies to improve his knowledge in the matters of God." [16] He cultivates faithfulness in public and private worship, chastity, mercifulness, justice and diligence in business, contentment, obedience to government, superiority to worldly-mindedness, and devotion to God, even to the point of suffering persecution. Virtue and Religion will become "easie and habitual" by the persistent cultivation of these qualities and will give assurance in the "labyrinths" of "uncertain talkings." [17]

It is no wonder that Wesley, eager for religious certainty, adopted this severe regimen, confident of becoming a "whole Christian" thereby. Later on he was to say of this period, ". . . doing so much and living so good a life, I doubted not that I was a good Christian." [18]

Yet Wesley detected a flaw in Taylor's treatment of assurance. He called his mothers's attention to an inconsistency between two passages on the subject. In one Taylor declared concerning sins after baptism: "Whether God has forgiven us or not we know not; therefore be sorrowful for ever having sinned." [19] In the other he seemed to imply an inward witness in saying that "by the Lord's Supper all the members are united to one another, and to Christ the Head. The Holy Ghost confers on us the graces necessary for, and our souls receive the seeds of an immortal nature." Wesley reasoned: "Now surely these graces are not of so little force as that we cannot perceive whether we have them or not: if we dwell in Christ, and Christ in us, . . . certainly we must be sensible of it . . . If we can never have any certainty of our being in a state of salvation, good reason it is, that every moment should be spent, not in joy, but fear and trembling. . . ."[20]

From the very beginning Wesley's logical mind sought reality in religion, but neither Taylor nor his mother gave him much help. His mother in her reply made a "reasonable persuasion of the forgiveness of sins" depend upon a true penitent's reflection upon "evidences of his own sincerity." She argued that "we may surely perceive when we have . . . . in any good degree" acquired the virtues demanded by God. Accordingly she encouraged her son to confirm habits of virtue and maintain an "even tenour of life" and assured him of eventual freedom from "torment, doubts or fears."[21]

Wesley's mother is sometimes blamed for his slavish cultivation of virtues, but she was merely sanctioning the best Anglican teaching she knew. It was Taylor who gave Wesley his fearful uncertainty about his relationship with God and preparedness for death. Consider the effect of the following passage upon an earnest inquirer:

"Every man is to work out his salvation with fear and trembling; and after the commission of sin his fears must multiply, because every new sin and every great declining from the ways of God is still a degree of new danger, and hath increased God's anger, and hath made him more uneasie to grant pardon: and when He does grant it, it is upon harder terms both for doing and suffering; that is, we must do more for pardon, and, it may be, suffer much more. For we must know that God pardons our sin by parts; as our duty increases, and our care is more prudent and active, so God's anger decreases, and yet it may be the last sin you committed made God unalterably resolved to send upon you some sad judgment. . . A true penitent must all the days of his life pray for pardon, and never think the work compleated till he dies. . . ."[22]

The definition of faith as assurance of salvation, which had been ushered in by the Reformation, had been subjected to the subversive influences surveyed in the previous chapter and was almost lost for Anglicanism. What did faith actually mean to Wesley and his mother? In their correspondence Wesley at first accepted unquestioningly Locke's rationalistic definition of faith as "an assent to a proposition upon reasonable grounds." [23] He logically deduced from this conception the conclusion that "faith must necessarily at length be resolved into reason." [24]

Presently, however, he qualified this statement and came over from the camp of natural religion to his mother's position that faith is "an assent to what God has revealed because He has revealed it and not because the truth of it may be evinced by reason." [25] However, he had a long way to go before he was to declare, "Faith (instead of being a rational assent and moral virtue, for the attainment of which men ought to yield the utmost attention and industry) is altogether supernatural and the immediate gift of God." [26] This, according to Wesley, was an almost unknown theory in 1738, Anglicans being for the most part in unconscious agreement with the Catholic doctrine of works.

The only conceivable outcome of a thorough-going adoption of Taylor's pattern of living would be an extreme asceticism, which sought negatively, through self-denial and abstinence, to subdue bodily impulses, and positively, through the cultivation of Christian virtues, to arrive at holiness.[27] Soon Wesley was fasting once or twice a week, communicating as often as possible, observing hourly periods of prayer and uttering frequent prayerful ejaculations. Of great significance was his keeping of a diary, which became a life-long practice. During this period it contained an hourly record of his employments and a minute inquiry into motives and consequences of acts.

Taylor also exerted an incalculable influence upon Wesley's attitude toward leisure. The first section of the *Rules for Holy Living* deals with the use of time and makes it the first and foremost instrument to Christian development. Idleness is "the sin of Sodom and her daughters," and must be avoided, lest there be room for temptation. Considered positively, time must be redeemed from the sinful uses that prevail; life is brief; account must be given for even an idle word. "He that would die well must always look for death every day knocking at the gates of the grave." [28]

Twenty-two regulations for the employment of time are given, including such matters as sleep, business, private devotions, recreation, charity and differentiated employments for rich and poor. Self-examination at the day's end is to point the way to improvement.[29]

That a profound change in Wesley's mode of life during this year was noticeable to all about him is indicated by the criticism that arose when his application for a Fellowship at Lincoln was considered. So severe were the objections to his piety that Dr. Morley, the Rector, made personal inquiry into his conduct, with the consequence, however, that his moral intensity was reckoned valuable for the academic reform that was under way at Lincoln. Both Wesley's father and mother encouraged him in his course, condemning as a "weak virtue" that which "cannot bear being laughed at." [30]

During 1727, Wesley met with a book that was to shape much of his future thinking. Almost immediately after its publication, it would seem, Wesley read William Law's *Treatise on Christian Perfection* and was "seized with an idea that never after that let him go." [31] Later on, in 1732, his visits to Putney to seek counsel from this great English mystic began and continued until Wesley's thought had carried him to an independent position at odds with that of his teacher.

The two men in 1727 had much in common. Similar home backgrounds had disposed them toward religious earnestness and disciplined living. Law upon entering Cambridge in 1705 had drawn up "Rules for My Future Conduct" after the style of Taylor's *Rules*. Eleven years later he had courageously obeyed his political and religious convictions and refused to take the oath abjuring the Stuart Pretender. He was by far the most brilliant mind among the Nonjurors; yet for the sake of his conscience he deliberately cut himself off from his Fellowship and his high prospects of Church preferment. In him Wesley was to find both example and counsel when his own position at Oxford later called for courageous acceptance of persecution.

Wholly different from the typical eighteenth century Churchman, different even from the Nonjurors, who for the most part were more concerned with politics than with theology, Law quietly, yet with ultimate effectiveness, revolted against the main currents of the age, craving to see beyond the mental horizons of the age and protesting against its "purely rational temper."[32]

Capable of rivaling Swift in satire, or Addison in the ethical essay, or Butler in apologetics, he dedicated his literary talents to meeting the deepest needs of the age and produced two of the greatest English classics of Christian devotion. He had already shown his power to perceive and analyze error in a notable work: *Remarks upon "The Fable of the Bees,"* 1721, an answer to Mandeville's satire upon Christian morality. His disposal of the self-interest theory here demonstrates the power and originality of his ethical insight.

Perhaps his excursion into contemporary ethics brought Law in sight of the *cul de sac* toward which religion was moving.[33] Profound thinker and erudite scholar that he was, he recognized how futile were the efforts of those who had placed their faith in reason alone. "Human learning," he granted, "is by no means to be rejected from Religion, for it is of the *same good* Use and Service, and affords the *same Assistance* to Religion, that the *Alphabet, Writing* and *Printing* does. But if it is rais'd from this *kind* and *degree* of Assistance, if it is consider'd as a Key, or *the Key* to the Mysteries of our Redemption in Jesus Christ, instead of opening to us the Kingdom of God, it locks us up in our *own Darkness.*"[34]

God, he says, is "an *all-speaking, all-working, all-illuminating Essence*" that becomes the "true light of our Minds here." This belief, he declares, is not Enthusiasm and "it is the running away from *this Enthusiasm*, that has made so many great Scholars as useless to the Church as tinkling Cymbals, and all Christendom a meer Babel of learned Confusion." [35]

The distinctions between the popular religion and the true nature of Christianity had become plain to him by 1726 and led him to the writing of *The Treatise on Christian Perfection*. The same theories and standards were presented in a more popular style in 1729 in *The Serious Call to a Devout and Holy Life, Adapted to the State and Condition of all Orders of Christians*. "Few books have had such a marvellous effect upon a nation as these two volumes," [36] says Hobhouse.

Law's logic is inescapable. Dr. Johnson tells how he picked up *The Serious Call,* expecting to laugh at it, and found Law quite an "overmatch" to his lax talk against religion. For the first time he began "thinking in earnest" about Christianity.[37]

Gibbon, in spite of his skepticism and his feeling that Law's precepts were too rigid, granted that they were "founded on the Gospel." He commented, "His satire is sharp; but it is drawn from the knowledge of human life ... If he finds a spark of piety in his reader's mind, he will soon kindle it to a flame; and a philosopher must allow that he exposes, with equal severity and truth, the strange contradiction between the faith and practice of the Christian world." [38]

This was the secret of Law's power. He had caught the full meaning of Christianity and had made it the touchstone for the religion of his day. No one can read him without "great searchings of heart." To him Wesley came, conditioned by a Puritan and High Church heritage to disciplined reasoning and living, and filled with a great spiritual hunger. The result was a great moral illumination. "Once and for all" his conscience was stabbed wide awake and the way prepared for even greater changes.

In Wesley's case,[39] and to varying degrees in all cases, both an ethical and an intellectual conversion must precede the final spiritual release of the whole personality. Otherwise "a vague uplift" will be followed by moral instability, and a blind acquiescence to truth will be followed by enervating doubt. Wesley's intellectual conversion was to come much later, with Peter Boehler as the immediate agency, but Law became the "human Factor" at this time in determining the sort of ethical conversion Wesley would experience and the "sort of message" he would afterwards proclaim.[40]

After the teaching from Kempis and Taylor he was ready to accept completely Law's insistence that Christianity includes every aspect of life. Viewing the existing chasm between profession and practice, he agreed with Law that nothing is "more absurd" than adding "wise, and sublime, and heavenly prayers" to a "life of vanity and folly, where neither labour nor diversions, neither time nor money, are under the direction of the wisdom and heavenly tempers of our prayers."[41]

Both reason and religion, Law said, prescribe Christian "rules and ends to all the ordinary actions of our life." It is plain that this, and this alone is Christianity; yet it is likewise plain that the general state even of devout people is to add "Christian devotion to a Heathen life full of self-love and indulgence, sensual pleasures and diversions, love of show and greatness" and "gaudy distinctions of fortune."[42]

Christianity, he declared, recognizes no difference between the secular and the sacred, no difference in the standards for priest and people. It holds the same ideal of perfection before all. "It calls no one to a Cloister, but to a right and full Performance of those Duties, which are necessary for all Christians, and common to all States of Life."[43]

In the first chapter of *A Practical Treatise upon Christian Perfection* Law set forth the nature and design of Christianity. This chapter was used by Wesley among students at Oxford, among his communicants in Georgia, and soon after the formation of the Methodist Societies was published as a separate tract and circulated widely. Since it played so great a part in shaping the Methodist conception of Christianity a summary of it is pertinent to our purpose.

Law first raises the perennial question of the nature of man and the world in which he finds himself. The answer, Law says, has never been satisfactorily given by man, even at his wisest. His terrible experiences with misery and his frantic efforts to compensate by moments of happiness only add to the mystery. Man is "a mere Riddle to himself . . . . . A restless Inhabitant of a miserable disordered World, *walking in a vain Shadow, and disquieting himself in vain.*" "

Only God through a divinely given revelation has ever penetrated the darkness that surrounds him. If man is willing to admit his inadequacy and accept revelation he may find an answer and know certainly what his true nature is; what he must do to satisfy his true nature; what real good and evil are; and what his relation to a world of mistaken values should be.

Man's real nature, Law says, is God-like; but, because his will is turned against God, he retains only a faint resemblance to his original self. This perverted self exists now in a dying body and a "drowned world." It is "as if a Person sick of a Variety of Diseases, knowing neither his Distempers, nor his Cure, should be enclosed in some Place, where he could hear, or see, or feel, or taste of nothing, but what tended to inflame his Disorders." "

As a consequence man cannot tell where his happiness lies. His ethical judgment is so vitiated that he attaches supreme importance to such things as honor, rank and pleasure and looks upon poverty, disesteem and persecution as absolute evils. His values are so reversed that what is really evil appeals to him often as good and what is good he blindly dismisses as evil. Yet only unhappiness can follow, when the demands of his true nature are not met.

The purpose of the Christian Revelation is to show man his "lostness," to account for its occurrence, to describe his true nature, to inform him of an eternal existence and eternal values in keeping with this existence, and to assure him that these are his through the redeeming death of Jesus Christ.

What, then, for Law is the end of Christianity? It is to call man back to his true self, to God and to eternal values. Only when man has returned is he prepared to examine good and evil. He finds then that the wisdom of secular ethics is often foolishness. The goals set by it for the good life are often too low and the means used to attain these goals may be entirely wrong, for they may involve a sacrifice of eternal principles. Furthermore, what is called evil by worldly wisdom—poverty or persecution, for example—may be the very means to be used in attaining eternal values."

The ethical code of Christianity is thus seen to be unique. It is not the product of human wisdom; it is not perceived apart from revelation; and it certainly does not appeal to unregenerate human nature. Only a restoration to his original nature can make a man see or accept the values offered by Christ. "Christianity is not a *School,* for the teaching of moral virtue, the polishing our Manners, or forming us to live a Life of this World with Decency and Gentility. It is deeper and more divine in its Designs, and has much nobler Ends than these. It implies an entire Change of Life, a Dedication of ourselves, our Souls and Bodies unto God, in the strictest and highest Sense of the Words." "

The Church was instituted for the instruction of men in this revelation and for their nurture in the Christian way. Men must be made to know that the Christian ethic is not only unique but is accompanied by the inflexible mandate of the Ruler of all things, the Maker of all Law. Both the command of God and the very nature of things require its fulfillment." Hence man cannot escape the consequences of disregarding or rejecting it.

In view of all this, what should be man's relation to the world? He must reject the worldly wisdom of a secularized theology and ethics, he must constantly resist the forces that deny and oppose the supreme good and must cultivate those

Christian virtues which form the scale of true values and belong to his true God-like nature.

It is at once apparent that this conception was very different from that which was engaging the spokesman for the religion of "the good life." It was a conception that challenged the sovereign place that had been given reason. Law eventually went on to a complete disavowal of reason and hence parted ways with Wesley, but the immediate effect of his teaching was to clarify Wesley's thoughts on Christian ethics. From Law Wesley received his fundamental sense of the awful holiness of God, the demand upon man for ethical perfection, and the utter inability of man in his unregenerate state to reach this goal.

---

1. *Journal*, I, 466.
2. Tyerman, *op. cit.*, p. 32.
3. *Loc. cit.*
4. *Proceedings of the Wesley Historical Society*, I-IV (1898), 275.
5. *Ibid.*, p. 34.
6. *Letters*, III, 332. Since he did not meet Law until 1732, the statement may have been made even later.
7. *Works*, VI, 356.
8. John Whitehead, *The Life of John Wesley, M.A.* (Philadelphia: William S. Stockton, 1845), 2nd American ed., I, 245.
9. *Journal*, I, 466-7.
10. *Works*, XI, 366-7.
11. This was Wesley's third publication, undertaken because of his dissatisfaction with the translation by Dean Stanhope. It was prefaced with "an account of the Usefulness" of the treatise and "Directions for reading it with advantage." See Richard Green, *The Works of John and Charles Wesley: A Bibliography* (London: C. H. Kelly, 1896)
12. *Works*, XIV, 222.
13. See John Wesley, *Christian Library*, IX, (1749-55), 137-230.
14. *Letters*, I, 19.
15. Jeremy Taylor, *The Rule and Exercises of Holy Living* (London: Pr. by Miles Fleshner, 1678), pp. 19-22.
16. *Ibid.*, Epistle Dedicatory, A-4.
17. *Ibid.*, A-5.
18. *Journal*, I, 467.
19. *Letters*, I, 19.
20. *Ibid.*, p. 20.
21. Tyerman, *op. cit.*, p. 20.
22. Taylor, *op. cit.*, p. 297.
23. *Letters*, I, 22.
24. *Ibid.*, p. 23.
25. *Ibid.*, p. 25.
26. *Letters*, II, 46.
27. Illustrations of Taylor's asceticism may be found in his section on types of mortification. For instance, he marks off three stages in the attainment of Christian sobriety: first, a declaration against pleasure on the basis of good reason and strong resolution; secondly, opposition to all offers of sensual pleasure by prayer, fasting, cheap diet, hard lodging and laborious exercise; thirdly, development of relish for spiritual pleasures. *Ibid.*, p. 54.
28. Taylor, *op. cit.*, p. 40.
29. *Ibid.*, pp. 6-12.
30. Whitehead, *op. cit.*, pp. 245-6.
31. Cell, *op. cit.*, p. 354. On the influence of Law upon Wesley see: R. New-

ton Flew, *The Idea of Perfection in Christian Theology* (London: Oxford University Press, 1934) Chapter XVIII; John Brazier Green, *John Wesley and William Law* (London: Epworth Press, 1945); Eric W. Baker, *A Herald of the Evangelical Revival* (London: Epworth Press, 1948).

32. Oliver Elton, *A Survey of English Literature*, 1730-1780 (London: Edward Arnold, 1928), II, 212.

33. Green says that "this controversial work . . . marks the beginning of a new phase of Law's thought, an interest in ethical religion . . . a bridge by which he crossed into new territory, where the *Christian Perfection* and the *Serious Call* were to be the supreme landmarks." Green, op. cit., p. 37.

34. William Law, *An Earnest and Serious Answer to Dr. Trapp's Four Sermons against Whitefield*, p. 101.

35. Loc. cit.

36. Stephen Hobhouse, *William Law and Eighteenth Century Quakerism* (London: G. Allen and Unwin, 1927), p. 261.

37. Green, op. cit., p. 43.

38. Loc. cit.

39. Baker, op. cit., p. 66.

40. Ibid., p. 69.

41. William Law, *Works* (London: Private Reprint, 1893), IV, 9.

42. Ibid., pp. 12-14.

43. Law, *Works*, III, 5.

44. Ibid., p. 11.

45. Ibid., p. 12.

46. Ibid., pp. 20-23.

47. Ibid., p. 23.

48. Ibid., pp. 22-3.

VI

The Finding

The first phases of Wesley's quest for Christian Perfection bore a close resemblance to monastic withdrawal for the attainment of mystical union. Although Law takes great pains in his *Treatise* to distinguish his ideal from that of the cloister he relates it so incompletely to the legitimate interests of life that they become obstructions rather than means to the expression of the ideal. Law's later career as well as Wesley's early mistakes demonstrated the ultra-mystical tendency inherent in his teaching.

In March, 1727, Wesley informed his mother that he was considering a post as school-master in the Yorkshire hills where he might achieve the goal of Christian Perfection presented in Law's treatise. He described himself as "so little . . . in love with even company—the most elegant entertainment next to books—that, unless the persons have a peculiar turn of thought, I am much better pleased without them." He preferred a retirement that "would seclude" him from all the world, a place, he said, "where I might confirm or implant in my mind what habits I would, without interruption, before the flexibility of youth is over."[1] He objected to the "impertinence and vanity" to which he was exposed at Oxford.

This proposal was not carried through in Yorkshire, but instead in Lincolnshire, where he served as his father's curate at Wroote for over a year. Law had given him the *Theologia Germanica* and some of the works of Tauler to read; later other mystical writers were added.[2]

However, this aspect of Law's influence came shortly to an end. By 1735 his admiration for these mystical writers was waning, and the next year his objections were so violent that he wrote, ".... all the other enemies of Christianity are triflers; the Mystics are the most dangerous of its enemies."[3] Their chief error was their neglect of the objective intermediaries of religion. Other errors mentioned later by Wesley were their seclusion from men, their individualism, their dismissal of the ordinary elements of Christianity, their search for unique experiences and their use of eccentric language in describing them.

We shall see later that, although Law by discouraging faith in works and outward acts had carried Wesley beyond the influence of Taylor, he had really encouraged faith in "virtuous habits and tempers" more than faith in God himself. Wesley still trusted in his own righteousness[4] and the result finally was bitter disillusionment. In 1738 he wrote to his former mentor that for two years he had been preaching after the model of his two great books and that "all that heard have allowed that the law is great, wonderful, and holy. But no sooner did they attempt to fulfil it but they found that it is too high for man, and that by *doing* 'the works of the law shall no flesh living be justified.'"[5] Law's books convinced and stimulated but they did not conduct him to his goal.

No better index to Wesley's confusion during this period of mystical quest could be asked for than he gave himself in describing his work among his parishioners at Wroote. "I preached much," he recalled in 1746, "but saw no fruit of my labour. Indeed, it could not be that I should, for I neither laid the foundation of repentance, nor of believing the gospel; taking it for granted that all to whom I preached were believers, and that many of them needed no repentance."[6]

What was this experience which he was seeking in solitariness? If he considered the people to whom he ministered in no need of repentance or of the work of God in their hearts, what was the object of his *own* quest but a kind of spiritual luxury to be enjoyed by elect souls, the religious geniuses? His later discovery of this fallacy strengthened his teaching upon the universality of salvation. He came to believe that perfect love is for all.

The first corrective to this ego-centric life came, Wesley says, in the advice of "a serious man" who showed him the importance of "social religion." He said to Wesley, "Sir, you wish to serve God and go to heaven? Remember that you cannot serve him alone. You must therefore find companions or make them; the Bible knows nothing of solitary religion."[7]

The means toward carrying out this counsel was soon at hand in Wesley's recall to Oxford in 1729 to become tutor, moderator and lecturer. To this responsibility for shaping the academic career of young men was soon added the spiritual counseling of members of the Holy Club, a religious society organized by his brother, Charles.

Gradually Wesley swung back from the mysticism of the Wroote period toward a religion of observance. The Club made much of "the duties of the Christian religion, the fasts, the prayers, and sacraments of the Church." Their insistence upon receiving "the blessed Communion as often as there is opportunity"[8] was, in fact, the source for the nickname, "Methodists."

Yet Wesley believed his goal to be inward religion, for he wrote a critic, "I take religion to be, not the bare saying over so many prayers, morning and evening, in public or in private; not anything superadded now and then to a careless or worldly life; but a constant ruling habit of soul, a renewal of our minds in the image of God, a recovery of the divine likeness, a still-increasing conformity of heart and life to the pattern of our most holy Redeemer."[9]

So far, it would seem, Wesley was simply expanding into a group code of conduct his individualistic creed of sacramentalism, asceticism and mysticism. But in 1730 at the instigation of William Morgan, one of the Holy Club, social service was added. By dint of severe self-denial charitable activities of various sorts were carried out. We have seen that this work among the poor and prisoners provoked drastic opposition from students and school authorities. As persecution grew, fearlessness and a new sense of vocation were born in Wesley.

His position as Greek lecturer naturally increased his intimacy with his Greek Testament and in his inquiry into the nature of Christianity he now began "to study the Bible, as the one, the only standard of truth, and the only model of pure religion." This brought into clearer focus the character and conduct of Christ. He says:

> I saw ... the indispensable necessity of having "the mind which was in Christ," and of "walking as Christ also walked"; even having, not some part only, but all the mind which was in him; and of walking as he walked, not only in many or in most respects, but in all things. And this was the light, wherein at this time I generally considered religion, as an uniform following of Christ, an entire inward and outward conformity to our Master. Nor was I afraid of anything more, than bending this rule to the experience of myself, or of other men; of allowing myself in any the least disconformity to our grand Exemplar.[10]

The desire for flexibility of mind which marks this last statement gradually broadened his outlook, but was checked for the time by his predisposition toward High Church asceticism which received fresh stimulus from another quarter. Under the influence of John Clayton, another Oxford Methodist, he began an eager study of the ascetic and liturgical practices of primitive Christianity.

Had he focused upon the character and life of early Christians, as he later did, he might more quickly have reached his destination. As it was, he became even more zealous in his sacramentarianism. The correspondence between the two friends would indicate that they "contemplated the formation of a society, who should observe saint days,"[11] fasts on Wednesdays and Fridays, and other traditional practices, such as auricular confession before the Eucharist, and the addition of water to the wine used for the sacrament.

The ardent young followers at Oxford were cooperative enough in the execution of this program, but later the imposition of such a severe regimen upon Wesley's congregation in Georgia brought trouble and opened his eyes to its inappropriateness for the ordinary worshiper.

In October, 1735, Wesley left England on his mission to Georgia. His efforts to mould a raw pioneer community into a cohesive religious body met with utter defeat; yet the paradoxical significance of this defeat is that within five years he was accomplishing his greatest work in pioneer communities—communities even more degenerate than that at Savannah—shaping them into powerful agencies for personal and national righteousness.

Much more might be said here of his excessive rigor, as well as of his successful experimentation with a religious society designed to nurture Christian life and provide Christian fellowship. We might also describe his personal experiences, which included a devastating love affair, but our present purpose confines us to the account of his quest for the Christian way.

Did he find an answer while in Georgia? The primary cause for his going to Georgia seems to have been the quest. Apparently he was driven by a great sense of personal need, for he wrote Dr. John Burton, of the Society for the Propagation of the Gospel in Foreign Parts, on the eve of his embarkation: "My chief motive, to which all the rest are subordinate, is the hope of saving my own soul. I hope to learn the true sense of the gospel of Christ by preaching it to the heathen. They have no comments to construe away the text; no vain philosophy to corrupt it; no luxurious, sensual, covetous, ambitious expounders to soften its unpleasing truths, to reconcile earthly-mindedness and faith, the Spirit of Christ and the spirit of the world. They have no party, no interest to serve, and are therefore free to receive the gospel in its simplicity. They are as little children, humble, willing to learn, and eager to do the will of God; and consequently they shall know of every doctrine I preach whether it be of God. By these, therefore, I hope to learn the purity of that faith which was once delivered to the saints; the genuine sense and full extent of those laws which none can understand who mind earthly things." [12]

Such a confession of religious uncertainty would brand him with some missionary boards today as an improper candidate for missionary work. But the most notable thing about this statement is not its portrayal of Wesley's personal confusion: it is rather its disclosure of the basic uncertainties of the whole Church, which had been created by the misuse of critical learning, by heterodoxy, by clerical corruption and by accommodation to the spirit of the world. Wesley wished to get away from all this and put the Gospel to the test among a people who could react naturally and spontaneously.

The genuineness and the efficacy of the faith that he had found in the accounts of early Christians he proposed to seek for himself. He longed for reality. Even though he was to continue for two more years to place his hopes in ascetic practices and sacramentalism he had now discovered the root of his difficulty, for he wrote, "A right faith will, I trust, by the mercy of God open the way for a right practice. . . ." [13] To the wilderness, then, he would go, away from the unreality of sophisticated society! There he might discover the faith of the early Christians and live a life of poverty, chastity and charity.

His preoccupation with primitive Christianity is shown in two ways: first, in his selection of reading matter for the voyage across and during his stay abroad; secondly, in his interpretation of the religion of the Moravians. Of the books read during this time seventeen or eighteen dealt with church history and nine more on Christian biography fall in the same category. Harrison, who made a study of this reading, reported that "in some respects the dominant passion of his life seems to have been to try to find out what Primitive Christianity really was, and to put it into practice." [14]

From five to seven each morning he read the Bible and carefully compared it with the writings of the earliest ages. These writers, he believed, had "so perfect a knowledge of the mystery of godliness, as to be judged worthy by the Apostles themselves to be overseers of the great Churches of Rome, Antioch, and Smyrna." "We cannot therefore doubt," he says, "but what they deliver to us is the pure doctrine of the gospel; what Christ and his Apostles taught, and what these holy men had themselves received from their own mouths." [15]

He considered their work done under the direct assistance of the Holy Ghost and worthy, therefore, "of greater respect than any composures that have been made since," even those written with greater art and learning." [16] His quest had reached the point where he was determined to find if possible Christianity in its pristine simplicity, when it was still accessible to the humblest believer, and before it had taken on accretions from Greek philosophy, from liturgical formalism, and from ecclesiastical organization. As Simon says, "He was convinced that a standard of belief and of conduct had been set up that ought to be reached by all churches bearing the name of Christ." [17]

As his study progressed he realized that this ideal could be achieved only as the Church renewed its attention to the doctrines of the New Testament and the formularies of the Church which relate to personal salvation and make a man's membership in the Church wholly dependent upon his moral and spiritual qualifications. He saw that the Church of his day was not a "fellowship of saints . . . built upon the foundation of the apostles and prophets." [18]

The desire to re-establish such a fellowship, keeping as near "to the fountain head of Christianity in the early Fathers as he could," [19] was undoubtedly the primary cause for his later formation of the Methodist societies, and so fully operative in them were the principles of early Christianity that Wesley repeatedly remarked upon the spontaneous appearance of parallel practices as the movement grew.

A second factor intensifying and illuminating this study of Apostolic times was his observation of the unique character of the Moravian missionaries whom he met on shipboard and whom he chose as his close associates upon arrival in Georgia. He fancied at once that he saw correspondences in them to the original church. Their calmness during the stormy passage across, their realistic talk of "knowing" Jesus Christ, the impressive simplicity and solemnity of their meetings made him "forget the seventeen hundred years between," and imagine himself "in one of the assemblies where form and state were not, but Paul, the tent-maker, or Peter, the fisherman, presided, yet with the demonstration of the Spirit and of power." [20]

They exhibited the spirit of Christian Perfection that Law had described and for which he had been seeking. Their meekness in enduring all sorts of ill treatment convinced him that "they had put away all anger, and strife, and wrath, and bitterness, and clamour and evil-speaking; they walked worthy of the vocation wherewith they were called, and adorned the gospel of our Lord in all things." [21]

So eager was he to enter fully into their secret that he learned German in order to talk with them and read their books. He met with them almost every day to sing their hymns, to exchange doctrinal opinions and to seek counsel on problems in his own congregation. It was the Moravians, not the Indians, that brought Wesley to a knowledge of the "right faith," by making actual what he already knew theoretically.

It has been previously seen that Law distinguished Christianity from the popular religion by the "mighty change" which it works, putting "us into a new state," and purifying our Souls. [22] But apparently Law did not make plain enough the act of faith whereby this change is to be wrought. As a matter of fact he had identified the act almost exclusively with the rite of baptism.

"Christian baptism," he says, "is not only an external Rite, by which we are entered into the external Society of Christ's Church, but is a solemn Consecration, which presents us an Offering to God, as Christ was offered at his Death." We are therefore to be dead with Christ to this world and "to *consider* ourselves as new and holy Persons, that are entered upon a new State of Things...." The rite of baptism thus begins "a Life suitable to that State of Things, to which our Saviour is risen from the Dead ... a Newness of Life, such a holy and heavenly Behaviour, as may show that we are risen with Christ ..."[23]

The prominence given by Law to a ceremonial rite concealed the full meaning of "justification by faith." Consequently, Wesley had to broaden his observation beyond the Anglican communion and overcome his bigotry and his prejudice against nonconformist approaches to Christianity. On the other hand, Wesley never reduced the place of the sacraments to the insignificance given them by many nonconformist groups. He would have been appalled at the casualness which characterizes the entire worship services of some of his own followers. He simply relinquished his blind faith in these material intermediaries of grace in order that he might discover the direct approach to God and the faith that unites man with God.

Yet the process of relinquishment was most bitter. His experiences in Georgia had produced complete disillusionment. His analysis of his state as he voyaged homeward may be read in his *Journal*. A few passages will serve to indicate his sense of utter defeat. He wrote: "I went to America, to convert the Indians; but, oh, who shall convert me? who, what is he that shall deliver me from this evil heart of unbelief? I have a fair summer religion. I can talk well; nay, and believe myself, while no danger is near. But let death look me in the face, and my spirit is troubled. Nor can I say, 'To die is gain.'"[24]

The uncertainty that had haunted John Donne and many another Anglican divine, was his.

"I have a sin of fear, that when I've spun
My last thread, I shall perish on the shore."[25]

Having admitted his failure, he proceeded to make a religious inventory. Examining his life he was convinced that "Whoever sees me, sees I would be a Christian." He knew his dedication to be complete, even to the point of death. Reviewing his beliefs, he concluded that he had held the proper correlation between outward and inward religion, as well as a balance between faith, good works, and the means of grace.

Yet a review of his course of doctrinal changes yielded him no satisfaction. First he had been confused by Lutheran and Calvinistic attempts to correct the Catholic doctrine of works. From that he had been swung to the other extreme by Anglican efforts to correct these Reformation views by an appeal to reason and Scripture. Then followed the period when he interpreted Scripture by an appeal to the early Fathers. But in this, he shortly swung into the extreme of "making antiquity a coordinate rather than subordinate rule with Scripture." [26]

His next phase he considered the worst of all. This was his quest for mystical union, which he once described as "the rock on which I had the nearest made shipwreck of faith." [27] Here overemphasis upon internal religion had made good works and the means of grace seem "mean, flat and insipid." After this manner he had gone on fluctuating "between obedience and disobedience, . . . continually doubting" whether he was right or wrong and "never out of perplexities and entanglements." [28]

In another self-examination written during this period he concluded that all his study in theology, philosophy, and languages, in spite of its thoroughness, and in spite of its seeming adequacy for others, had not brought him the peace he sought. He asked, "Does all I ever did or can know, say, give, do or suffer justify me in His sight?" Does even his "constant use of all the means of grace," or his "outward, moral righteousness," or his "having a rational conviction of all the truths of Christianity" give him "a claim to the holy, heavenly, divine character of a Christian"? [29]

He would seem to have reached here a renunciation of all faith in human effort, for he closed this analysis by declaring: "If the oracles of God are true, if we are still to abide by 'the law and the testimony,' all these things, though when ennobled by faith in Christ, they are holy and just and good, yet without it are 'dung and dross,' " . . . [30] He seems clear also concerning the faith he seeks—" 'a sure trust and confidence in God,' that, through the merits of Christ my sins are forgiven, and I am reconciled to the favour of God." This faith, he says, "none can have without knowing that he hath it." [31] He recognizes its psychological consequences: it frees its possessor from sin, fear and doubt.

Such a disavowal of faith in works and a definition of faith in terms of assurance should have accomplished his intellectual conversion. Yet succeeding events proved that remnants of his unbelief still remained. Soon after his arrival in England he met Peter Boehler, a Moravian missionary, temporarily in London before going out to Georgia, a man eminently fitted by his education in German universities and his personal religious experience to understand Wesley's need.

During three months of association with him Wesley had the constant impact of Moravian teaching and through that a clarification of his understanding of the Protestant doctrine of justification by faith. "Step by step," Harrison says, "Wesley was driven from the mediaeval view of salvation to what can best be described as a Protestant view." [32] The Protestant view, it is true, was embodied in the formularies and homilies of the Church of England, and there Wesley discovered it; but it "had never come to life in High Church circles"; therefore "the reality of its personal application came" very slowly to Wesley.[33] Before he could be justified by faith he had to admit to practical unbelief in the doctrine.

At the beginning of his acquaintance with Boehler there were two intellectual hurdles yet to be surmounted. The first was deeply ingrained hatred of dissenting teaching about "assurance." In spite of the fact that he had confessed some time before his longing for calm and freedom from sin, he was amazed at Boehler's insistence that all true faith has two fruits, "dominion over sin and constant peace from a sense of forgiveness." [34] He was ready to grant that in some cases of religious experience this might be true, but he still denied that faith necessarily included these fruits. He disputed this, he says, with all his might, construing away all scriptures relating to it, for so he had long ago been taught to do and to call all those who spoke otherwise "Presbyterian." [35]

The implications are plain. The century-long accumulation of Anglican prejudice against enthusiasm which he had inherited is seen in his use of the label, "Presbyterian." His bias against dissent was still so strong that he could not accept completely the full Protestant view. Rattenbury describes him as "a man of strong intellect and indomitable will" who "was beaten down in every point by irrefutable arguments." [36]

The same bias blocked for a time his recognition of the instantaneous nature of conversion. But his renewed study of New Testament cases finally opened his eyes to his error. He described the process as follows: "I could not understand how this faith should be given in a moment: how a man could *at once* be thus turned from darkness to light, from sin and misery to righteousness and joy in the Holy Ghost. I searched the Scriptures again touching this very thing, particularly the Acts of the Apostles; but, to my utter astonishment, found scarce any instances there of other than *instantaneous* conversions; scarce any so slow as that of St. Paul, who was three days in the pangs of the new birth." [37]

The stubbornness with which his intellect retreated from the High Church position is further shown in his next step. "I had," he says, "but one retreat left, namely, 'Thus, I grant, God wrought in *the first* ages of Christianity; but the times are changed. What reason have I to believe He works in the same manner now?'" [38]

The distinction between the "extraordinary" experiences enjoyed by the early church and the ordinary experiences considered possible to the eighteenth century man was the issue here, and a very important issue it was. Had it not been met and fully settled intellectually and experientially by Wesley the Methodist revival would never have occurred.

One of the earliest and most famous of Wesley's debates with the Anglican bishops was that with Bishop Butler, who had accused him of pretending to "extraordinary religious experiences." The utter confidence with which Wesley answered that he preached only "what every Christian may receive and ought to expect and pray for" [39] came out of a profound intellectual conviction. He had arrived at that conviction, first, through a thorough knowledge of the Word of God and the life of the early Christians, and, secondly, through direct observation of the religious experiences of eighteenth century men and women.

Peter Boehler had an answer to Wesley's doubt of the occurrence of instantaneous conversion in his day. There were, he said, living witnesses to this fact whom he could produce. He accordingly brought in four English members of the Moravian society in London who testified that faith had instantaneously brought them salvation from sin. Wesley, Peter Boehler records, was thunderstruck at their testimony, but contended that four examples were not enough. Boehler then brought eight more witnesses.

The instantaneous conversion of a condemned prisoner had already come within Wesley's personal observation. The man had been so fearful of death that Wesley had instructed him to "believe unto salvation." The result had been that he had gone in perfect peace to the gallows, saying, "I am now ready to die; I know that Christ has taken away my sin, and there is no more condemnation for me." [40]

This testimony and the twelve brought by Boehler drove Wesley from his last "retreat." "Here ended my disputing," he says, "I could only cry out, 'Lord, help Thou mine unbelief!'" [41] Boehler tells how Wesley weeping sang with them,

> "Lost and undone, for aid I cry;
> In Thy death, Saviour, let me die!

Grieved with Thy grief, pained with Thy pain,
Ne'er may I feel self-love again." [42]

Although he had claimed intellectual agreement with the dogma of Justification by Faith, he had resolutely willed partial unbelief, and now he saw why he had not experienced for himself the justification that comes by faith.

For the first time he recognized fully the part that self-righteousness had played during the past years in keeping him from God. During the ensuing weeks he maintained an absolute renunciation of "all dependence, in whole or in part," upon his own works or righteousness, on which, he says, "I had really grounded my hopes of salvation, though I knew it not, from my youth up." [43] He later saw that in this respect he was no different than a Papist in his trust in his own "works."

His weeks of constant, faith-filled prayer and use of other means of grace brought him finally, as everyone knows, to that evening of May 24, when, listening to the reading of Luther's *Preface to the Epistle to the Romans* at the Aldersgate Society meeting, he felt his "heart strangely warmed." He then testified to trusting in "Christ alone for salvation. An assurance," he says, "was given me that He had taken away *my* sins, even *Mine*, and saved me from the law of sin and death." [44]

Luther's description, based upon his own experience, of "the change which God works in the heart" had brought Wesley "an insight into depths of truth" unplumbed by logic. His imagination was illuminated, his affections aroused. Faith was no longer "a train of ideas in the head," nor simply a strong resolution of the will; it had become a living, growing, purifying principle that organized his personality and brought "spiritual and mental integration." The Methodist revival had begun. [45]

He knew that he had rediscovered the life principle of Christianity. One cannot fully appreciate what this meant to Wesley and to his times unless one realizes the extent to which eighteenth century religion had abandoned the supernatural elements of the Christian faith. Few men any longer knew God as reality and fewer still could say, "The life I now live I live by faith in the Son of God."

Wesley did not experience "the ecstasy of happiness" felt by many converts. His response was more intellectual than emotional, as one would expect from his temperamental inclinations. But what was more important than a transient emotion was the profound and abiding consciousness of the reality of God and spiritual values, which now possessed him and supplied the dynamic that had been missing.

The strong sense of calling which had animated his work in Oxford and Georgia now impelled him to make "the new gospel" known. In it he saw the only hope for his age, and he was soon declaring, "Salvation by faith strikes at the root, and all (errors) fall at once when this is established." This he now recognized as the original dynamic of the Reformation. "It was this doctrine, which our Church justly calls *the strong rock and foundation of the Christian religion,* that first drove Popery out of these kingdoms; and it is this alone can keep it out." [46]

Humanistic faith in reform, of itself, could never cope with moral decadence. Nothing but the supernatural work of God "can give a check to that immorality which hath 'overspread the land as a flood.' Can you empty the great deep, drop by drop? Then you may reform us by dissuasives from particular vices. But let the 'righteousness which is of God by faith' be brought in, and so shall its proud waves be stayed." [47] This is Wesley's answer to a church that had put its faith in social reform and education, rather than in the power of God.

Two consequences attended the proclamation of this message: hostility from the organized Church, and at the same time eager response from the people. Wesley believed that opposition from the Church arose, as it had in the time of Luther, from the substitution of the doctrine of works for vital faith. He said, the "adversary . . . rages whenever 'salvation by faith' is declared to the world . . ." [48] On the other hand, he found that when he made the nature of saving faith the standard topic multitudes began to cry out, "What must we do to be saved?" [49] As success grew he came to believe that it was the peculiar mission of the Methodists "to understand, explain, and defend" this "great evangelical truth" which they had rediscovered by "searching the Scriptures," and then confirmed by their own experience.[50]

It is no wonder then that this doctrine was over-emphasized in Wesley's early ministry and continued to be by some of his followers. This has often produced a mistaken impression, such as that recorded by Piette, that for the Methodists "the chief event of the Christian life is the experience of conversion."[51] Instead Wesley came to see that conversion is only "the gate" to all the rich country of Christian experience, and, furthermore, that the manner of entrance might vary considerably with different individuals.

In 1738, so extreme was his self-condemnation for his previous lack of faith that he shocked some of his friends by declaring that up to May 24 he had not been a Christian. Yet later, after years of observing seekers after God, he modified this statement, saying that before that date he had been a servant of God but not a son. In 1785, writing to a friend who had a problem in faith, he said, "There is an irreconcilable variability in the operations of the Holy Spirit . . . as to the manner of justification." To many He gives "The o'erwhelming power of saving grace," but with others He works "in a gentle and almost insensible manner." [52]

This does not mean that Wesley departed in the least from his original conviction that "the common privilege" of Christians who fear God and obey Him is "a consciousness" of His favor and abiding presence, but it does mean that he finally allowed for variation in degrees of consciousness, and, more important than that, he laid greater stress upon Christ, the object of belief, and less on the mere act of believing.

The flexibility of mind which led Wesley to adapt his preaching on these aspects of conversion to observed facts characterized his entire course as the leader of a great movement. It is manifest not alone in the synthesis which he accomplished in doctrines, a matter which has received much emphasis by Methodist scholars, but may be observed, also, in his continuing receptivity to all the practices which have characterized the Christian way whenever the church has returned to its original piety and power. But always in both doctrine and practice the end and emphasis remained the same—a loving fellowship with God, which will produce Christian character and express itself in Christian living.

As we have surveyed the course of Wesley's inquiry into the nature of Christianity we have seen that at the very beginning he recognized the dead end toward which speculative inquiry was leading. Humanism had created a religion of "the good life," which was nothing more than the observance of a secular ethical code and at its very best made the cultivation of virtues rather than the love of God the supreme good.

Wesley possessed a moral sensitivity not commonly given to men. He saw with terrific clarity that neither he nor his associates were meeting the Christian standards for life. His intellectual power was equal to theirs; he could have become a commanding figure in religious controversy; but his moral insight surpassed theirs. He saw the full meaning of sin in the light of revelation. This is the key to his resolute refusal to stop where his contemporaries had stopped with a "religion within the bounds of reason," with a religion of mere observance, or a "religion of opinions." He knew that only a supernatural solution could ever meet his need.

Kempis, Taylor and Law greatly increased this moral sensitivity and set before him once and for all the goal of Christian Perfection. Yet they did not bring him to the miracle of salvation from sin. He sought for light in the Bible, in the records of the early church, in the biographies of great Christians. In his efforts to find a balance between inward and outward religion he went to extremes in both sacramentarianism and mysticism.

His very hatred of the bigotry of the "religion of opinions" drove him into a counter form of bigotry. But under the Moravian influence all that remained to block his discovery came to light: his hatred of nonconformists, his self-righteousness, his fear of "extraordinary" Christian experience, his deep-seated unbelief.

When these were gone, when he had finally entered into the knowledge and the love of God, he had something to say to his age concerning true Christianity, for in it he saw the answer to the moral problems, the social needs and the intellectual confusions. Even for the deists he had an answer: if they really wanted to test the validity of revelation let them attempt to meet the moral demands of Christianity by faith in the revealed Word.

In his letters to Conyers Middleton[58] on Christian evidences he asks, "What is real, genuine Christianity?" Is it this speculative, hypothetical thing that all the defenders of revealed and natural religion have been discussing? Far from it. It is the creative force through which Christian life and character come into being. Christian doctrine is essentially, then, a description of this creative force and an explanation of the principles and processes which produce Christian personality and conduct. Christian faith is more than an intellectual act; it is the response of the whole being to this creative force, to God Himself, who proposes to bring Christian character into existence. It follows that no amount of doctrinal discussion will establish the validity of Christianity without the evidence from miraculous Christian living.

What, he asks, is the surest and most accessible evidence to know that Christianity is of God? It is the knowledge of the individual that the promises made by God have been fulfilled in his life. The collective evidence from such individuals throughout the history of the Christian church constitutes a living, irrefutable proof of the truth of the Word. It should be noted that

THE FINDING

this evidence is not confined to subjective religious experience, as important as that was to Wesley. He makes clear in a lengthy portrait of a Christian that the distinctiveness of Christianity consists in the actual attainment of the high moral standards demanded and promised by the Word.

He holds, therefore, that Christian evidence presented in terms of experience, conduct, and character far outweighs in value the traditional evidence, about which there had waged such controversy. Wesley grants: "I do not undervalue traditional evidence. Let it have its place and its due honour. It is highly serviceable in its kind, and in its degree." [54] But, he declares, if these contenders for the authority of the Scriptures do not "lay far more stress than they have hitherto done on this internal evidence of Christianity, they will . . . one after another, give up the external, and (in heart at least) go over to those whom they are now contending with . . ." [55] The patent fact is that this had already happened to such an extent that deism was now flourishing within the church.

Wesley did have an answer to the intellectual problems of his day, for as someone has said, he "turned the Acts of the Apostles into English history," [56] and "the Way," the Truth, and the Life spoke again, as it had with the early Christians, in something stronger than argument or speculation. Clemenceau once said: "When a Christian decides to live his Christianity, then a real revolution starts." [57]

---

1. *Letters*, I, 42.
2. Flew mentions Tauler, the Cambridge Platonists, Molinos, Bourignon, Guyon, the Homilies of Macarius, the Egyptian. Flew, *op. cit.*, p. 315.
3. *Journal*, I, 420.
4. *Letters*, I, 239.
5. *Loc. cit.*
6. *Sermons*, I, 270, note.
7. *Works*, VIII, 468.
8. Simon, *op. cit.*, pp. 97-8.
9. *Letters*, I, 152.
10. *Works*, XI, 367.
11. Tyerman, *op. cit.*, p. 95. So zealous was Wesley in his pursuit of this subject that he was nicknamed "Primitive Christianity" by his friends. *Letters*, I, 50, note.

12. *Letters*, I, 188.
13. *Loc. cit.*
14. *Proceedings of the Wesley Historical Society*, XV (1926), No. 5, 113.
15. *Works*, XIV, 238-9.
16. *Ibid.*, p. 241.
17. Simon, *op. cit.*, p. 331.
18. *Loc. cit.*
19. Umphrey Lee, *John Wesley and Modern Religion* (Nashville: Cokesbury Press, 1936), p. 297.
20. *Journal*, I, 170-1.
21. *Ibid.*, p. 142.
22. Law, *op. cit.*, p. 13.
23. *Ibid.*, pp. 31-2.
24. *Journal*, I, 418.
25. *Loc. cit.*
26. *Ibid.*, p. 423.
27. *Ibid.*, p. 418.
28. *Ibid.*, p. 419.
29. *Ibid.*, p. 420.
30. *Ibid.*, p. 423.
31. *Ibid.*, p. 424.
32. A. W. Harrison, *The Evangelical Revival and Christian Reunion* (London: Epworth Press, 1942), p. 39.
33. See Sugden's discussion. The doctrine, though in the homilies, "had been obscured by the Sacramentarian teaching of the Romish Church, and exaggerated by the Mystics." *Sermons*, I, 200, note.
34. *Journal*, I, 471.
35. *Ibid.*, p. 454.
36. J. E. Rattenbury, *The Conversion of the Wesleys* (London: Epworth Press, 1938), p. 75.
37. *Journal*, I, 454.
38. *Loc. cit.*
39. Henry More, *The Life of the Rev. John Wesley, A.M.* (London: Printed for John Kershaw, 1824), p. 21.
40. *Journal*, I, 448.
41. *Ibid.*, p. 455.
42. Henry Bett, *The Spirit of Methodism* (London: Epworth Press, 1937), p. 21.
43. *Journal*, I, 472.
44. *Ibid.*, p. 476.
45. See Bett, *op. cit.*, p. 34; also Rattenbury, *op. cit.*, pp. 59-60.
46. *Sermons*, I, 50.
47. *Loc. cit.*
48. *Ibid.*, p. 51.
49. *Sermons*, I, 270, note.
50. *Sermons*, I, 343-4.
51. Maximin Piette, *John Wesley in the Evolution of Protestantism* (New York: Sheed & Ward, 1937), p. 436.
52. *Letters*, VII, 298.
53. "A letter to the Reverend Dr. Conyers Middleton," *Works*, X, 1-79.
54. *Ibid.*, p. 75.
55. *Ibid.*, pp. 76-7.
56. Quoted by E. Stanley Jones, *The Way* (New York) Abingdon-Cokesbury Press, 1946), p. 327.
57. Quoted by J. Arundel Chapel, *The Supernatural Life* (London: Epworth Press, 1934), p. 145.

VII

"An Highway Shall Be There and a Way"

With the waning of Puritan fervor the eighteenth century had confined itself to the speculative, the ethical, and the liturgical aspects of religion, and in each aspect the pervasion of secularism had tended to obscure the fact that Christianity is primarily redemptive. Christianity originated in the entrance of God into temporal affairs in the person of Jesus Christ for the purpose of bringing *eternal life* to every man. Christ came to a world which cared little for life, a world sunk in pessimism or in stoical resignation. Yet to those who hungered and thirsted for righteousness Christ brought life in abundance and presented a way in which men might walk and enjoy true life forever.

Thus it was that very early in the history of Christianity the followers of Christ were known, not only as Christians, but as those of the "Way." They became "a community which had accepted a distinctive way of life."[1] They had received from Jesus the principles of this Way; they had observed in his life the concrete example of the Way; and at Pentecost they had received the necessary empowerment for their own life in the Way.

In the century that followed the whole church carried on as effective propagandism as the world has ever seen by witnessing in their lives to the supreme excellence of the "Way" over all other ways. Both the principles and the practices that constituted the "Way" became very familiar to Wesley during the long period which he devoted to an assiduous study of primitive Christianity. He became "a specialist" in the subject, says Simon.[2] Few men in England at that time knew the early church so intimately.

As he extended his studies in the history of Christianity to later periods he found that whenever Christ has become known, not simply as a historic personage, but, likewise, as the source of empowerment for living in accordance with his principles, the Way has emerged. He saw running through the "whole seeming maze of history" one supreme, transcendent Way.

But with this perception came also the realization that the Way must be rediscovered over and over again, for the undergrowth from the surrounding jungle of human pride, passion and stupidity is forever crowding in and blotting it out. When again it emerges, clear, unmistakable, witnessing by its own inherent authority that it is *the* Way, a great revival follows. This is a recurrent historical phenomenon which should be easily recognizable when it arrives; yet so gross is spiritual blindness and so deceptive is intellectual pride that more than one generation has succumbed to a philosophy that destroyed its power to perceive spiritual reality.

Many examples might be given of the return of Christianity to its pristine purity. Perry, who makes this the primary explanation for American Puritanism, cites as other instances the Paulicians in fifth century Armenia, the Albigenses of the twelfth and thirteenth centuries, John Wycliffe and his followers in the fourteenth century and the mighty sectarian movements in seventeenth century England.[3]

Sweet says of the early American church as it spread out through the middle West: "Much the same pattern of development which we find in the establishment of the primitive church was followed in laying the foundations of the American Churches. Of necessity in both instances the stress was upon the life rather than upon creed."[4] He points out that "the Apostle Paul, upon whose writings so much of Christian theology is based, was first and last a missionary and his theology grew out of concrete experiences.... So too the builders of the church in America... were bent upon bringing Christianity to bear upon life."[5]

"AN HIGHWAY SHALL BE THERE AND A WAY"   103

As we have seen, Wesley's reading and observation broke down the sectarian barriers that had prevented him from recognizing the Way and accepting the Life that is in Christ. Once this Life was his he knew that he had discovered with St. Paul and Augustine and Luther and Bunyan the heart of Christianity. As a result, his thinking on many matters was clarified.

Doctrine was one of them. He saw that fundamental theology is not fine-spun speculation; it is instead the "fruit of reflection upon *lived and practised*" Christianity. Hence the most important doctrines are those which a seeker for the life in God must necessarily believe in order to reach his goal.

Law, the great agent in Wesley's moral conversion, had convinced him that "all the Precepts and Doctrines of the Gospel are founded on . . . . . two great Truths, the deplorable Corruption of human Nature, and its new Birth in Christ Jesus."[6] Accordingly, the doctrines of original sin and justification by faith became the cornerstones of Wesley's message.

Under the corrosive influence of humanism both of these doctrines had lost their prominence and meaning. For half a century they had been adulterated or dismissed by Anglican pulpits and more recently by many dissenting preachers, as well.[7] Wesley commented on "how many laboured panegyrics . . . we now read and hear on the dignity of human nature!" He refers to a sermon by an eminent preacher which affirms, "first, that men in general . . . . are very wise; secondly, that they are very virtuous; and thirdly, that they are very happy." He has found no one who "has been so hardy as to controvert the assertion."[8]

Resolutely Wesley went to work to restore these evangelical doctrines to their proper places, declaring that departure from the doctrine of original sin had erased the essential distinctions between Christianity and heathenism, that Socinianism is nothing but veiled deism, sapping "the very foundation of all revealed religion."[9] Moreover, the softening of the doctrine of sin had led to the flood of immorality that now submerged the nation,

Speaking on the awfulness of sin and the inevitability of punishment for it, he asserted, "Had all men a deep sense of this, how effectually would it secure the interests of society! For what more forcible motive can be conceived to the practice of genuine morality? to a steady pursuit of solid virtue? to an uniform walking in justice, mercy, and truth?"[10] He saw that faith in man's inherent goodness has never produced national righteousness.

With a return to the doctrines of original sin and justification by faith, the doctrine of the atonement resumed its proper significance, for Christ's death on the cross makes plain the cost of our sin to God and God's willingness to meet that cost. Wesley's soundness on these doctrines gave him disrepute among the "modernists" of his day. Coomer finds him much disliked by those who held "lax views .... of the Person of Christ" and the Atonement. On the other hand he was also disliked by Calvinists, who associated his Arminian views on the universality of salvation with "modernism."[11]

Today it can readily be seen that Methodism was solidly founded upon the Christian doctrines of the great creeds. Wesley had no patience with the doctrinal chaos of the time; "this unsettledness of thought," he called it, "this being 'driven to and fro, and tossed about with every wind of doctrine.' " He considered it "a great curse, an irreconcilable enemy to true tolerance. A tolerant man," he declared, "does not halt between two opinions, nor vainly endeavour to blend them into one." To learn a truly tolerant spirit he advised Methodists to "learn the first elements of the Gospel of Christ" and find "settled, consistent principles."[12]

A critical reduction to principles, the factor which Harnack considers first and foremost in every important reformation movement,[13] was Wesley's dominating concern. This measure is made necessary repeatedly by the attraction of alien matter to religion in the course of its development. For this reason Wesley made a distinction between those doctrines upon which "vital religion" depends and those which "do not strike at the root of Christianity." There are "some truths," he said, "more important than others." [14]

It is interesting to find that he dislikes to call these "fundamental truths" for the reason that fundamental "is an ambiguous word," so ambiguous that "there have been so many warm disputes about the number of 'fundamentals.' " ". . . surely," he pleads, with those who substitute controversy for Christian life, "there are some which it really concerns us to know, as having a close connexion with vital religion." [15]

These, the evangelical doctrines, Wesley chose to emphasize, and so out of the bewildering array of doctrines which for a century had produced bitter controversy and barren speculation emerged once more the Gospel in its simplicity, and the Evangelical Movement was born.

In another area, also, simplification took place. Wesley's critical reduction of theology to basic principles led him to a clarification in the field of ethics. From the beginning he had held a theory that Christian conduct is not obedience to a set of externally imposed laws, but rather action which springs spontaneously from a single internal principle. Kempis, Taylor, Law and various other much read writers had taught him that this principle is love. Love must be, according to Arndt, one of his early mentors, "an active, lively, strong, vigorous principle, seated in the inmost soul" and created by God. [16]

This was Wesley's emphasis even during the Holy Club period. He advised his brother, Samuel, "to labour . . . to convince students" that "Christianity is not a negation or an external thing, but a new heart, a mind conformed to that of Christ, 'faith working by love.' " [17] Yet, despite his seeming comprehension, he obviously never acted fully upon the principle until 1738.

The theory which actually governed him appeared occasionally whenever he described his own practice, as, for example, when writing to Mrs. Pendarves he said: "I would recommend those assistances which I find so necessary for myself. . . if our ultimate end is the love of God, to which the several particular Christian virtues lead us . . ."[19] Here he was making the love of God the goal rather than the *source* of Christian behavior. It was this mistake which led him after his conversion to object, as we have seen, even to the use of the word, virtue, in describing Christian graces.

Wesley's "heart-warming" experience brought not alone a recovery of the Protestant doctrine of justification by faith. Much has been made of this theological aspect of his conversion; but of equal significance was his revival of Christian ethics. Because he placed so much emphasis upon the internal principle of love, he brought to the fore the central and distinguishing ethical feature of the "Way," loving loyalty to a Person, who is able to empower the believer for living "on the level of miracle."

Various aspects of this feature emerged as the full implications of his conversion experience were realized. In the first place, the reason for the current identification of the Way of Secularism with the Christian Way became plain. If Christian morality is nothing but a cultivation of traditional virtues, then there is, of course, little distinction between the two ways; but if loving loyalty to Christ is the essence of Christianity, then the two ways are as wide apart as heaven and earth. Love of any sort makes heavy demands upon the individual, and when directed toward One who is both Love and Goodness itself, the ethical demands reach to their uttermost. Poor human nature is embarrassed by such Love, and hopeless before such Goodness. Truly Christian conduct becomes utterly impossible without supernatural aid.

Much of the persecution from the Anglican clergy arose from their refusal to see that Christian morality can begin only with the experience of God. Their moral compromise and fear of enthusiasm blocked their way. Wesley said of them, "They would have their parishioners moral men—that is, in plain terms, honest heathens; but they would not have them pious men, men devoted to God, Bible Christians." [19] They rejected any preacher who taught that Christians have been "transformed into that 'image of God wherein they were created'" and maintain "a constant 'fellowship with the Father and His Son Jesus Christ.'" [20]

These are high standards. They had been given Wesley by Law and other practical mystics. We have seen that they seemed to Wesley during his Oxford period unattainable—"too high for man"—and that it was the Moravians rather than Law who led him to faith for their attainment. The defect in Law's teaching was not that it set the standard too high, nor that it ignored God's power, but rather that it limited His power by throwing too much emphasis upon man's share in the process. Actually, Law had modified the Protestant doctrine of justification by faith to make room for lingering Roman Catholic belief in self-mortification. He concentrated, Lindstrom says, more on man's love to God and his neighbor than on God's love to man.[21] Hence man must *win* God's love by constantly mortifying the fleshly demands which conflict with the love of God.

To rediscover the full meaning of justification by faith Wesley had to reject Law's belief concerning self-mortification, and he did so with vehemence. But he did not question the primary aspect of Law's ethical teaching, the ideal of Christian perfection. He might conceivably have adopted the position of the early Reformation teachers of justification, namely, that only in the moment of death will "inherent perfection" be given the Christian. But Wesley could not be satisfied to place such a limitation upon the promise and power of God.

The Catholic and Anglican writers who had shaped Wesley's goals ever since 1725 had convinced him that "the work of God in the soul of man" extends beyond forgiveness of sins to the perfecting of love here and now. Furthermore, accepting as completely as he did the Protestant theory of the priesthood of all believers, he could not interpret this idea as merely "a counsel of perfection," given only to those called out of the world to be saints, a conception recurrent in the history of Catholicism.[22] For Wesley the call to Christian Perfection was "an evangelical precept" meant for all who are named Christian. Life lived on this high level was God's purpose for everyone.

This had become the central belief of Wesley's whole religious career. He could not accept the Reformers' restriction of perfection to perfection of faith, nor could he after his "heart-warming" experience and his subsequent observation of the experiences of hundreds of Methodists, agree with the limitations put upon the attainability of the goal by Law and other practical mystics. Eventually he became convinced that no branch of Protestantism had as yet explored the full implications of the Christian ethic.

He held that the greatest distinction between the Old Testament and the New and, likewise, between secular and Christian ethics, is the provision made through Christ's death on the cross for man's ethical perfection. The Old Testament statement, "Thou shalt love the Lord thy God with all thine heart, and with all thy soul, and with all thy might," he believed to be more than a commandment when reiterated by Christ. In the New Testament it is to be taken as both commandment and promise, for the Gospel is "no other than the commands of the law, proposed by way of promise. Accordingly, poverty of spirit, purity of heart, and whatever else is enjoined in the holy law of God, are no other, when viewed in a Gospel light, than so many great and precious promises."[23]

The Christian dispensation thus brought to an end man's futile endeavors to win God's love by conformity to a code of laws, for it made fulfillment possible through a restoration of man to his original nature, which, like God's, is love. Man, if he will believe the promise, may now serve God out of a perfect heart of love.

This transcendent faith in the far-reaching promises of the Gospel is the most notable feature of early Methodism. It laughed at impossibilities and cried, "It shall be done." It was the inspiration of many a hymn, which like the following, declared the availability of God's grace:

> "All things are possible to him
>   That can in Jesus' name believe:
> Lord, I no more Thy truth blaspheme,
>   Thy truth I lovingly receive;
> I can, I do believe in Thee,
> All things are possible to me.
>
> "The most impossible of all
>   Is, that I e'er from sin should cease;
> Yet shall it be, I know it shall:
>   Jesus, look to Thy faithfulness!
> If nothing is too hard for Thee,
> All things are possible to me.
>
> "All things are possible to God,
>   To Christ, the power of God in man,
> To me, when I am all renewed,
>   When I in Christ am formed again,
> And witness, from all sin set free,
> All things are possible to me." [24]

If Wesley's conception of perfect love threw new light upon the full meaning of the Christian Way it is important that we hold a proper understanding of it. His teaching on the subject looks in two directions; positively, toward indwelling love; negatively, toward deliverance from the inward and outward sins which interfere with the operation of love. The fusion of the two points of view has been well described in modern psychological terms as "the expulsive power of a new affection," or "the total inhibition of sinful tendencies by the rule of love in the heart." [25] Wesley says in eighteenth century language: "It is love excluding sin; love filling the heart, taking up the whole capacity of the soul." [26]

He stressed always the positive approach, stating in his sermon, "On Perfection," that salvation from all sin is "the lowest branch" of perfection, and "only the negative part of the great salvation." [27] The influence of Kempis, Taylor, and Law is plainly seen in the positive aspects selected for emphasis. The first and lowest degree of Christian Perfection, he says, is purity of intention, or singleness of motive in dedicating all the life to God. One who has this stands "on the threshold." [28] The next phase is a renewal of spirit, supernaturally given, which restores man to his original nature, to all the mind that was in Christ and enables him to walk as Christ walked. The third phase is the one most stressed by Wesley, the love of "an undivided heart" for God and all mankind. [29]

Over and over throughout his ministry Wesley reiterated his belief that every Christian may be transformed into the "image of God" and be filled with perfect love. This is the central meaning of Christian Perfection as taught by Wesley. The term, "Perfection," it is true, was ambiguous, creating confusion and misinterpretation. Wesley, as well as his followers, recognized this fact; yet he felt that he must use it, as he said, because the Bible uses it. The substance of his thought on the whole subject was summed up in his letter to Dr. Dodd in 1756. [30]

He began by welcoming suggestions, saying that he had adopted the term, "Perfection," only because it is Scriptural, that he had no particular fondness for it, and that he would not contend for it. However, the Scriptural use of the term was beyond dispute. The Bible employed it as another description of holiness, or "the image of God in man." [31]

One implication of the term is freedom from all known sin. Scripture declares that "he that is born of God sinneth not." To Dr. Dodd's objection to this inference he replied that this meaning and "abundantly more than this" is contained in the single expression, "the loving God with all our heart and **s e r v i n g** Him with all our strength," a conception of Christianity commonly held. Wesley said that he had never said nor meant "any *more* by perfection than thus loving and serving God," but he insisted that perfection in this sense is an attainment possible to all who would follow Christ. This he declares, first, upon the authority of the Bible and the ancient writers, and, secondly, upon empirical evidence, which, as we have seen, meant much to Wesley in verification of Scripture. In this case it was furnished by his "own experience and that of many hundred children of God whom" he personally knew.[32]

Wesley met great opposition to what was called "sinless perfection," and said sometimes that it was "not worth disputing about." On the other hand, he was well aware of the destructive effect upon high moral endeavor of the commonly accepted assumption that all men daily break the commandments of God "in thought, word and deed" and cannot by any "grace received in this life" avoid it. This, he believed, built up a mental provision for sin in one's life and created a "doctrine of the necessity of sinning."[33]

He said of those who refused to face this fact: "They will allow all you say of the love of God and man; of the mind which was in Christ; of the fruit of the Spirit; of the image of God; of universal holiness; of entire self-dedication; of sanctification in spirit, soul, and body; yea, and of the offering up of all our thoughts, words, and actions, as a sacrifice to God—all this they will allow so we will allow sin, a little sin, to remain in us till death."[34]

Wesley told Dr. Dodd that this allowance for sin amounted to a direct plea "for looseness of manners" and was "directly subversive to all holiness."[35] Holiness cannot be separated from love. Dr. Flew, in his classic work on the history of the Perfection ideal, points out that in Jesus' teaching there is "no setting love over against holiness as though one attribute were separate from another in the character of God. Both fused together in an indissoluble personal unity." [36] Neither can known sin exist along with perfected love in the Christian believer.

Wesley makes very plain the impossibility of such a situation in a sermon, "On Sin in Believers." Pride conflicts with the humility of love; self-will exalts itself against loving obedience to God's will; love of the world brings in the pleasures of the eye and the flesh to unseat the love of God from its sovereign place. These and other rivals, such as jealousy, malice, hatred and resentment, are as incompatible with love for one's neighbor as with love for God. Dispositions of covetousness, love of money, uncharitable thoughts and conversation must be gotten rid of if good will is to be the ruling temper.[37]

Christian Perfection, therefore, fulfills God's command for holiness insofar as "the humble, gentle, patient love of God and man" rules "all the tempers, words and actions, the whole heart and the whole life." To this degree, Wesley said, a man might through faith in the grace of God live a sinless life.[38]

He granted, however, that perfection can be set "too high"; in fact, he admitted that he himself had at first done so, and retracted some of his early statements. Perfection in the absolute sense is an impossibility, for men are subject to ignorance and mistakes in opinion and practice. But if sin may be defined as "an actual, voluntary transgression . . . of any commandment of God, acknowledged to be such at the time that it is transgressed," [39] then perfect love may be said to take away "all the bent to sinning." In this sense sin cannot exist where "love is the sole principle of action."

Wesley also allowed for those outward and inward imperfections that are due to bodily infirmities. ". . . we may observe," he said, "that, naturally speaking, the animal frame will affect more or less every power of the soul; seeing at present the soul can no more *love* than it can *think,* any otherwise than by the help of the bodily organs." [40] Therefore, constant tranquility, complete thought control, constant degrees of faith, or continual sense of guidance cannot be expected. Neither can freedom from temptation. Indeed, exposure to temptation is the means to greater degrees of love and should enhance his Christian experience.

This r a i s e s acutely the troublesome question of the appropriateness of the term, "perfect." How can one speak of *degrees* of perfection? Wesley, as we have already noted, was fully conscious of the inadequacy of the term. Sangster says that evidently "no small part of Wesley's difficulty in pressing this doctrine on his preachers turned upon his ill-advised use of a name." [41] Yet had their moral aspiration corresponded to Wesley's no mere misnomer could have obstructed their continuing quest for deeper acquaintance with God. Wesley was no blind worshiper of verbal or even theoretical consistency. Labels meant little to him;[42] in fact, he avoided all those terms which become shibboleths and imprison truth. He had set out, like Paul, "to know him and the power of his resurrection" and when new discovery called for revision in statement he made it.

His flexibility in thought is manifest in his attitude toward the schematizing of religious experience. Early in the Revival he had reason to believe that the gift of perfect love is a second and instantaneous work of grace. Yet he never made a completely dogmatic statement to this effect. He said in 1757, "I never knew or heard of any exception; and I believe there never was one," [43] and after forty-five years of observation and close examination of those who professed the experience he stated that he still found no exception and was therefore forced to believe that "sanctification is commonly, if not always, an instantaneous work." [44] Yet in 1765 he wrote to Lady Maxwell: "It may be He that does all things well has wise reason, though not apparent to us, for working more gradually in you than He has done of late years in most others . . . . And it is all one how it began, so you do but walk in the light. Be this given in an instant or by degrees, hold it fast." [45]

His matured views after hundreds of conversations and hundreds more of letters of inquiry were expressed in "The Large Minutes" of 1789, where he urged his assistants strongly and explicitly to exhort all believers to "go on to perfection." To the question, "Is the change gradual or instantaneous?" he answered: "It is both one and the other. From the moment we are justified, there may be a gracious sanctification, a growing in grace, a daily advance in the knowledge and love of God. And if sin cease before death, there must, in the nature of the thing, be an instantaneous change; there must be a last moment wherein it does exist, and a first moment wherein it does not."

His preachers are to insist on both types of change, but most especially on the instantaneous work, for "constant experience shows, the more earnestly they expect this, the more swiftly and steadily does the gradual work of God go on in their soul; the more watchful they are against all sin, the more careful to grow in grace, the more zealous of good works. . . . Whereas, just the contrary effects are observed whenever this expectation ceases. They are 'saved by hope,' by this hope of a total change, with a gradually increasing salvation. Destroy this hope, and that salvation stands still, or, rather, decreases daily. Therefore, whoever would advance the gradual change in believers should strongly insist on the instantaneous." [46]

One must not miss the emphasis here upon faith. The Christian life is growth in love, but it is likewise growth in faith, for growth in love depends upon the maturing of faith. Faith was the means by which the love of God was first planted in the soul at conversion. If growth is to follow, faith must become stronger and stronger. As this work of faith continues the enemies that fight in the soul for supremacy over love become more and more manifest. Gradually the Christian moves toward the crisis where a special act of faith will claim deliverance from these internal enemies. This crucial act of faith *must*, therefore, be preceded by a gradual work of grace, which has perfected faith, inasmuch as only a strong faith can grasp the fullness of the promises.

In the sermon, "The Scripture Way of Salvation," Wesley describes four stages in the exercise of sanctifying faith: first, we must be convinced that God has promised it; secondly, we must believe that God is able to fulfill His promises; thirdly, we must have faith that He is able and willing to do it immediately; and, lastly, we must have the conviction and internal evidence that the work is done.[47]

The last two steps follow logically upon the first two, Wesley believed, for he had found "by long experience" that "it comes exactly to the same point, to tell men they shall be saved from all sin when they die; or to tell them it may be a year hence, or a week hence, or any time but *now*."[48] The seeker must find. The faith which laughs at impossibilities must claim the promise in the now.

Yet the faith of this high moment does not secure holiness for a lifetime. As Sangster says, Wesley believed that "Freedom from conscious sin . . . could be given in an instant, but for the impartation of the rich wholeness of holiness, . . . eternity is too short."[49] Wesley carefully guarded the doctrine against a complacent feeling of final attainment. He issued many warnings that should always accompany the preaching of Christian Perfection. For example, in 1771, he asked, "Does not talking of a justified or a sanctified *state* tend to mislead men? Almost naturally leading them to trust in what was done in one moment. Whereas we are every hour and every moment pleasing or displeasing to God *according to our works,* according to the whole of our inward tempers and our outward behaviour."[50]

Again in 1778 he advised, ". . . you cannot insist too much on that point—that, whatever our past experience has been, we are *now* more or less acceptable to God as we more or less improve the *present* moment."[51] This is an aspect of his teaching to which some of his followers have been unfaithful. They have made a specific religious experience the e n d, even emphasizing exclusively its emotional content. They have failed to keep love in its central place, stressing deliverance from a few bad dispositions rather than the creative love which expresses itself continuously in Kingdom building. They have neglected Wesley's central emphasis upon on-going growth in love and ever-increasing knowledge of the eternal values discovered by maturing faith.

His warning in 1789 needs to be reiterated to all those who profess perfection in love: ". . . those who do already enjoy it (perfect love) cannot possibly stand still. Unless they continue to watch and pray and aspire after higher degrees of holiness, I cannot conceive not only how they can go forward but how they can keep what they have already received. Certainly, therefore, this is a point much to be insisted on . . . that all who have tasted of the pure love of God should continually grow in grace . . ." [52]

Many quotations from Wesley's later writing might be given to indicate his concern lest the ethical ideal should lose its central place in the Revival, for he observed that in places where "Christian perfection is not strongly and explicitly preached there is seldom any remarkable blessing from God." [53] Revival came only where believers expected "full salvation." Conversely, where there was no such expectation, believers became "ripe for levity, tattling, and evil-speaking, which soon destroy all the life of God out of their souls." [54]

This belief, that only in the preaching of perfect love can far-reaching results be achieved for the Kingdom, is supported by the survey made by Dr. Flew of the history of the idea of Perfection. He concludes that "a vast evangelistic advance can only be sustained if the Christian ideal for this life is steadily set forth in all its beauty and its fullness as being attainable "by the grace of God." [55] Early Methodism seems to him comparable to the early Christian community addressed by the apostle John, in w h i c h were many who knew through experience that astounding moral transformation may be the normal issue of the Christian way.[56]

We have devoted considerable attention to Wesley's teaching on perfect love for three reasons; first, because it was the pivotal point in his own religious career; secondly, because it furnishes a key to an understanding of the Wesleyan Way; and, thirdly, because it was one of the principal factors in the spread of the Methodist Revival.

No one can leave a thorough study of Methodism without the realization that the governing principle of the Wesleyan Way was perfect love and furthermore, that the centrality in the movement of this ethical i d e a l accounts greatly for its phenomenal success. Methodist character and conduct were shaped by the teaching that "Christianity is not Christianity unless it is aiming at Perfection." Coming, as it did, at the ebb-tide of seventeenth century Puritanism, it restored to Protestantism "something it had lost," [57] a transcendent faith that life here and now may be lived "on the level of miracle."

---

1. See the excellent discussion of the Way among the early Christians by Frank Bertram Clogg, *Christian Character in the Early Church* (London: Epworth Press, 1944).
2. J. S. Simon, *John Wesley and the Methodist Societies* (London: Epworth Press, 1923), p. 105.
3. Ralph Barton Perry, op. cit., p. 66.
4. William Warren Sweet, *American Churches: an Interpretation* (New York: Abingdon-Cokesbury, 1948), p. 115.
5. *Ibid.*, p. 116.
6. Law, *Works*, III, 13.
7. See discussion in Chapter II, p. 24.
8. *Works*, VII, 336.
9. *Works*, IX, 194.
10. *Sermons*, II, 402.
11. Coomer, op. cit., p. 110. See also Wesley's letter of February 7, 1778: "Nothing in the Christian system is of greater consequence than the doctrine of the Atonement . . . the distinguishing point between Deism and Christianity."
12. *Sermons*, II, 144-5.
13. Adolph Harnack, *What Is Christianity?* (London: Williams & Norgate, 1901), p. 270.
14. *Works*, II, 200.
15. *Loc. cit.*
16. See Wesley's extract of John Arndt's *True Christianity* in *A Christian Library*, I.
17. *Letters*, I, 193.
18. *Ibid.*, p. 66.
19. *Letters*, VII, 391.
20. *Loc. cit.*
21. Harold Lindstrom, *Wesley and Sanctification* (Stockholm: Nya Bokfoilags Akstiegologet, 1946), p. 163.

22. Eric Baker, op. cit. p. 73.
23. *Sermons*, I, 403.
24. *Methodist Hymn Book* (London: Epworth Press, 1933), p. 480.
25. *Sermons*, II, 150, note.
26. *Ibid.*, p. 448.
27. *Works*, VI, 415.
28. *Letters*, V, 81.
29. *Sermons*, II, 150.
30. *Letters*, III, 166 (March 12, 1756).
31. *Ibid.*, p. 168.
32. Loc. cit. See Roy S. Nicholson, "John Wesley's Personal Experience of Christian Perfection," *The Asbury Seminarian*, 1952, VI, pp. 65-89.
33. Loc. cit.
34. *Works*, VI, 423.
35. *Letters*, op. cit., p. 170.
36. Flew, op. cit., p. 15.
37. *Sermons*, II, 360-79.
38. *Letters*, IV, 187.
39. *Sermons*, I, 304.
40. *Letters*, V, 4.
41. W. E. Sangster, *The Path to Perfection* (New York: Abingdon-Cokesbury Press, 1943), pp. 147-53. Sangster prefers the term, perfect love, to Christian Perfection, for the following reasons: it is "positive"; it is social, focusing without rather than within the individual; it includes the element of sternness; it makes room for Wesley's limited definition of sin; it emphasizes the given-ness, the free gift.
42. Note that Wesley called conversion his "heart-warming." In his correspondence he tends to use such fresh descriptive terms rather than cliches. J. B. Green, *John Wesley and William Law* (London: Epworth Press, 1945), p. 209, says ". . . if cold criticism succeeds in discovering some obscure and unessential variations of terms, it is far less remarkable than the central consistency and passionate devotion to a great conception of practical Christianity . . ."
43. *Letters*, III, 212.
44. *Works*, VI, 491.
45. *Letters*, IV, 308.
46. *Works*, VI, 328-9.
47. *Sermons*, II, 475-8.
48. *Letters*, V, 316.
49. Sangster, op. cit., p. 143.
50. *Letters*, V, 265.
51. *Letters*, VI, 297.
52. *Letters*, VIII, 184.
53. *Letters*, IV, 321.
54. *Letters*, VII, 109.
55. Flew, op. cit., p. xiii.
56. *Ibid.*, p. 112.
57. Sangster, op. cit., p. 102.

VIII

The Disciplines of the Way

Perfect love is not static, does not operate in a vacuum, nor is it primarily a religious experience. It is essentially a way of behaving. The perfection commanded by Christ, when he said, "Be ye therefore perfect, even as your Father in heaven is perfect," postulates a way of life in which love and impartiality flow out toward all men, whether good or bad. Perfect love, although an inner principle, finds "expression at every point at which a man touches life." [1]

This aspect has not always been kept to the fore by teachers of Perfection, particularly by those who have leaned toward mysticism. Wesley's early and unhappy experiences with mysticism aided him in preserving an interdependence of character and conduct and a balance between inward and outward religion.

He liked to parallel his own situation with that of Paul, who before conversion had attempted slavishly to obey a ponderous code of 613 laws, and yet after his liberation on the Damascus road had not abandoned Mosaic law, but had loved it the more and submitted to its demands even more happily because it had been the means of bringing him to Christ.

Wesley further valued the law because after bringing us to Christ it "keeps us with Christ. The law says, 'Thou shalt not kill'; and hereby (as our Lord teaches), forbids not only outward acts, but every unkind word or thought. Now," says Wesley, "the more I look into this perfect law, the more I feel how far I come short of it; and the more I feel this, the more I feel my need of his blood to atone for all my sin, and of his Spirit to purify my heart, and make me 'perfect and entire, lacking nothing.'" [2]

Throughout the Christian life there is, therefore, continuing dependence upon the law. ". . . on the one hand, the height and depth of the law constrain me to fly to the love of God in Christ; on the other, the love of God in Christ endears the law to me . . . seeing I know every part of it is a gracious promise which my Lord will fulfill in its season."[3]

Without the law neither faith nor perfect love can be attained. In Wesley's case, for example, the exacting standards of conduct set up by Kempis, Taylor, and Law had first convinced him of the unique and lofty quality of Christian morality and then had driven him after utter despair of human endeavor to faith in the atonement.

In another respect, also, Wesley found his course paralleling that of St. Paul's. The great apostle, convinced of Christ's fulfillment of all contained in the law, had had to apply Christ's principles to problems of conduct that arose in the early church. Likewise, Wesley, made aware through his reading in church history of the continuity of the Christian tradition, had to translate the principles he had rediscovered into terms of practice for the eighteenth century.

Law had given him many of his ideas concerning Christian conduct; but it is one thing for a mystic like Law to outline in his quiet study the high standards of Christian Perfection, and quite another for an evangelist to hold these same standards unflinchingly before audiences of semi-pagans and interpret them with sufficient clarity and urgency to call forth truly Christian behavior. This was Wesley's task, and without question he succeeded in it to a phenomenal degree. An abundance of documents from early Methodist writers testify to the beauty of life that resulted when love found expression in action.

How had this been accomplished? Not alone through *the preaching* of "the full ideal." Not simply through the response of individuals to this preaching. Very early in the Revival Wesley discovered to his dismay the universal human tendency toward antinomianism, that is, the proneness of weak human beings, after their first experience of saving grace, to rest in a static legal fiction that divorces works from faith. He did not have to cope long with new converts who loudly professed on Sunday morning to a state of grace, despite their reversion on Saturday night to drunken sprees, before he saw the necessity for positive specification of what constitutes Christian behavior.

Laws and rules that could be definitely observed had to make principles explicit to men and women void of moral insight. Love continued to be the core of his message, but the *modus operandi* of love in life situations had to be made plain. Even those who claimed the high experience of Christian Perfection were sometimes found resting in mere profession. Wesley came to suspect all testimony to religious experience that was not directly accompanied by positive Christian action. He had no patience with the religious sentimentalist.

The foundation for a code of Christian conduct is laid, he declared, in unhesitating acceptance of eternal values as the only reality. His faith in the spiritual capacities of men and women previously sunk in gross materialism is amazing. In such sermons as, "Walking by Sight and Faith," he expects an immediate comprehension of supersensuous reality, and declares that Christians "regulate all their judgments concerning good and evil, not with reference to visible and temporal things, but to things invisible and eternal. They think visible things to be of small value, because they pass away . . . but, on the contrary, they account invisible things to be of high value, because they will never pass away." [4]

Upon this basis they judge all things to "be good or evil, as they promote or hinder their welfare, not in time, but in eternity . . . They regulate all their tempers and passions, all their desires, joys, and fears, by this standard. They regulate all their thoughts, and designs, all their words and actions, so as to prepare them for that invisible and eternal world to which they are shortly going." [5]

Some test cases make this principle clear. He asks, "Which do you judge best—that your son should be a pious cobbler, or a profane lord? Which appears to you most eligible—that your daughter should be a child of God, and walk on foot, or a child of the devil, and ride in a coach-and-six?" Rejecting all materialistic values, he sternly asserts that one who sets his affection upon earthly things is "as surely in the way of destruction, as a thief or a common drunkard."[6]

This, he adds, "is religion, and this alone. . . . It is not *morality*; excellent as that is, when it is built on a right foundation, loving faith; but when otherwise, it is of no value in the sight of God. . . . Religion is no less than living in eternity and walking in eternity and hereby walking in the love of God and man. . . ."[7] The utter renunciation of all materialistic aims in a life of perfect love is here made plain.

The old scale of values must go. To the Christian the love of God is the only total good; all other goods are partial and secondary, and their value depends entirely upon the contribution they can make to a life of love. The Christian sees the "real evil of apparent good," the danger of resting even in such legitimate satisfactions as delight in the beautiful, honor from one's fellows, success in one's vocation.

We are all materialists, according to Wesley—disbelievers in the eternal—to so great a degree, "that it requires no less than almighty power to counteract that tendency to dissipation which is in every human spirit, and restore the capacity of attending to God, and fixing itself on him."[8] Our indifference to eternal things may arise simply from the "hurry of business," or "seeking honour or preferment." Rivalry with God may be set up merely by love of adornment, or "fondness for diversions" or "any trifle under the sun."[9]

"The vulgar," says Wesley, "confine the character of dissipation to those attached to women, gaming, drinking, to dancing, balls, races, fox-hunting, but it applies to anyone who forgets God by attention to any worldly employment." The gratification of the senses, for instance, may become a major source of happiness, not only in "gross, open intemperance," but often in a "genteel sensuality," that is to be found among the poor as well as among the rich.[10]

The satisfaction of the imagination in "objects grand, beautiful or uncommon," especially in dress, furniture and amusements may supersede the happiness found in God.[11] Desire for the honor of men, which is called by great men "thirst for glory" and by ordinary men "taking care of our reputation," in either instance is an expression of the love of the world and engenders pride and conflicts with devotion to God.[12]

We shall find that the evil in most of the matters denounced by the early Methodists lay as much in their refusal to remain subordinated to the supreme good as in their inherent sinfulness. The drama is a striking example of this in its continual tendency to drift away from high spiritual purpose and moral control. Perry remarks that all aesthetic pleasures, although higher than physical delights, may be "proportionately more dangerous to true piety," for they set up a more subtle claim upon the cultivated mind and gradually dull it to the love of God.[13]

The proper attitude to take toward all legitimate interests is that of stewardship. Wesley believed that "we have no right to dispose of anything we have, but according to His will, seeing we are not proprietors of any of these things; they are all, as our Lord speaks . . . *belonging to another person;* nor is anything properly *our own*. . . . We shall not receive . . . *our own things,* till we come to our own country. Eternal things only are our own: with all these temporal things we are barely entrusted by another, the Disposer and Lord of all."[14]

This principle of stewardship applies to much more than money. Wesley enumerates the human faculties of understanding, imagination, memory, will, affection and emotion, as well as the functions of the senses. Other endowments to be used for eternal ends are personality, strength, health, education and influence over others.[15] It follows, then, that no action, no use of time is indifferent. All have significance in a life of love.

One must be ready at the end to give an inclusive accounting: "Didst thou use thy food, not so as to seek or place thy happiness therein, but so to preserve thy body in health ... a fit instrument of thy soul? Didst thou use thy apparel, not to nourish pride or vanity, much less to tempt others to sin, but conveniently and decently to defend thyself from injuries of the weather? Didst thou prepare and use thy house, and all other conveniences, with a single eye to my glory? in every point seeking not thy own honour, but mine ... ?"[16]

If such questions seem too exacting, too much concerned with minutiae, let us remind ourselves of the high goal set by Wesley. Perry says of Puritanism that it requires "a will that is never wholly committed to any subordinate enterprise, or wholly absorbed by any constituent part of life. ... It implies a centralized and unified control which will bring the whole course of man's actions, feeling, and thoughts into accord with his moral judgment or spiritual faith."[17] If this was true of seventeenth century Puritanism, the subject of Perry's investigation, it was even more characteristic of a movement which claimed Perfect Love as its governing principle.

Methodism was the first movement to bring the doctrine of Perfection and the disciplines for its attainment out of the monastic environment and present it as the norm for all Christians. The Reformation had declared that the full Christian life can be lived in any of the ordinary callings. However, neither Calvin nor Luther worked out the full implications of this revolutionary view of the common life.[18] Law saw these implications and Wesley preached them to the masses.

They lie at the base of all his advices to Methodists, and were never more emphatically stated than in his article on the

"Character of a Methodist," of whom he says, "In all his employments of every kind, he not only aims at this (the glory of God) . . . but actually attains it. His business and refreshments, as well as his prayers, all serve this great end. Whether he sit in his house or walk by the way, whether he lie down or rise up, he is promoting, in all he speaks or does, the one business of his life; whether he put on his apparel, or labour, or eat and drink, or divert himself from too wasting labour, it all tends to advance the glory of God, by peace and good-will among men. His one invariable rule is this, 'Whatsoever ye do, in word or deed, do it all in the name of the Lord Jesus. . . .'" [19]

What criterion, then, should govern our desire for the natural goods, such as food, clothing, or work? Wesley had early accepted Law's principle of temperance in the satisfaction of all natural desires. He believed that, just as in eating and drinking the rule is strict temperance, so "we may *dress,* we may buy and sell, may *labour,* we may provide for ourselves and our Families" as nature demands. But "all Variation from this Rule, is like Gluttony and Intemperance, and fills our Souls with . . . Tempers . . . contrary to the Spirit of Christ. . . ." [20]

Wesley condemns those who vary from this rule upon the pretext of accomplishing more good by increased natural goods. Such persons practice "worldly prudence," which declares as its "grand maxim": "The more power, the more money, the more learning, and the more reputation a man has, the more good he will do." But he observes that "Whenever a Christian, pursuing the noblest ends, forms his behaviour by these maxims, he will infallibly . . . use more or less of conformity to the world, if not in sin, yet in doing some things that are . . . not good to him; and perhaps at length using guile or disguise, simulation or dissimulation." [21] Christian prudence forms its judgments from the Word of God, not from compromise with the standards set by men.

This is the lofty ideal for the use of natural goods which the preaching of Perfect Love placed before the early Methodists. If the law of love places such severe controls upon *legitimate* interests, certainly any matter of conduct that contains in it positive elements of evil must be abandoned. Whatever deteriorates personality or harms society can never be harmonized with love of man.

This principle was applied not only to the gross sins but to the so-called lesser sins as well: not only to drunkenness, sexual laxity, licentiousness and brutality in amusements, but also to covetousness, jealousy, a n g e r, evil-speaking, vanity and worldly anxiety. Each age has its own peculiar sins, great and small. Methodism, because of its deep moral sensitivity, its high estimate of the value and potentialities of human personality, and its acceptance of a wholly Christian scale of values, recognized the sins of its age and made no allowance for them in its way of life.

Many of the evils denounced by Wesley had already been specified by seventeenth century Puritanism. This does not mean that he unthinkingly accepted traditional views. It means rather that there still persisted in the eighteenth century a lack of moral control in the same areas of conduct; for example, in dancing, in the theatre, in the use of spirituous liquors. Wesley recognized, as had Fox and Baxter and Law, the deterioration of personality that accompanied the free expression of impulse in these directions and likewise sought for regulation.

So free did Wesley believe himself from any traditional bias that he looked upon Methodism as something new in the eighteenth century, something called forth by the moral and spiritual needs of the time and not simply a revival of Puritanism or Moravianism.[2] There is indeed ground for accepting this point of view when it is remembered that the Methodist Societies were an organic development within the Church of England, and the Rules of the Societies simply means improvised by Wesley for the restoration of the national church to the Christian Way.

If Puritanism be defined in the generic sense, not as a single historic episode in the seventeenth century, but as the recurrent revival of Christianity in its simplicity, then it will be seen that the pattern of conduct evolved by Methodism, dealing drastically, as it did, with all the symptoms of moral weakness in its age, was bound to have some likeness to all conduct-patterns adopted by such revivals. The insubordinated human will remains the same throughout the centuries, manifesting its enmity to God and good in much the same manner; hence, every revival of Christianity brings with it similar insights into universal evils and opposition to them.[23]

No such conduct pattern is ever popular. It is branded as narrow-minded and fanatical. Perry, analyzing this inevitable accompaniment of puritanism, remarks that unswerving adherence to belief will always seem fanaticism to more balanced minds, just as did the faith of the early Christians to the cultivated pagans of that day. The Puritan, in his "ruthless subordination of every lesser consideration to the one thing needful" is single-minded, and single-mindedness is always likely to seem narrow-mindedness.[24]

Wesley in his advices to Methodists warned them of this inevitable reaction to their way of life. They would give offence to all classes: to bigots by laying so little stress on opinions, to men of form by insisting on the inwardness of religion, to secular moralists by declaring the necessity of faith, to humanists by talk of inspiration and guidance of the Holy Ghost, to open sinners by reproof and separation from their company. It will be said of them, "you are grown so precise and singular, so monstrously strict, beyond all sense and reason, that you scruple so many harmless things, and fancy you are obliged to do so many others which you need not."[25]

The *Rules of the Society of the people called Methodists* seemed in 1743,[26] when they were first published, the very epitome of narrow-mindedness, just as they do today, when cultural influences for a century have carried us farther and farther away from the single-mindedness and simplicity of early Methodism. Wesley is now often condemned as a legalist attempting to cramp the religion of love within a narrow set of regulations.

But before we accept this indictment let us try to place ourselves imaginatively in his situation when in 1743 he was faced with the necessity of making more explicit for a large group of near pagans the meaning of the gospel of Perfect Love. It was in Newcastle that the *Rules* were composed. Nine months had elapsed since his first meetings there, during which time hundreds had responded to the call to a life of Christian Perfection. In the interval the society had lost 149 members. About 800 remained.

Of the 149 departures seventy-six had been voluntary, produced mostly by persecution. The remainder had been due to expulsion, upon what appear to be quite legitimate grounds, in accordance with Wesley's clear teaching on conduct. The charges listed are: swearing, sabbath breaking, drunkenness, selling spirituous liquors, quarreling, wife-beating, wilful lying, railing, laziness, and lightness and carelessness."[27]

It was imperative that some precise regulations be formulated for the 800 members who remained. Otherwise disintegration would continue. Those who had gone constituted the "hysterical fringe" of the revival, the seekers for emotional experiences, rather than for the righteousness that is in Christ. Wesley, by this time had come to recognize this peripheral group, common to all great revivals, whose awakening is not moral, and who are, therefore, unprepared for the stern challenge of Christianity. They are those described by Christ as the stony and thorny places, where seed cannot grow. But the good ground that remained could be made to bring forth fruit if properly cultivated. The *Rules* and the organization into classes were the means devised for nurturing the seed.

As we have noted previously, Wesley's first conversion was ethical and determined the ethical emphasis of his message.[28] Like Paul, he recognized the full significance of the negative demands made by the law and knew that love not only fulfills these but exceeds them in intensity because of Christ's new interpretation of inner principles. It was in this spirit that the *Rules* were written, the same spirit that animated Paul when he applied the principles enunciated by Christ to specific situations and problems faced by the first century church.

It must be noted, also, that Wesley as well as Paul was prescribing for those who wished to be "whole Christians," those who were responsive to all the implications of the Christian ethic and proposed by the power of God to live the life of Christian Perfection. The Methodist, as Wesley envisioned him, was a Christian in fact as well as in name. "He is inwardly and outwardly conformed to the will of God, as revealed in the written word. He thinks, speaks, and lives, according to the method laid down in the revelation of Jesus Christ. His soul is renewed after the image of God, in righteousness and in all true holiness, and having the mind that was in Christ, he so walks as Christ also walked. . . ."[29]

In formulating the *General Rules* Wesley looked first of all to the life of Christ. Here was the Way in its purity, and the Methodist was to ask in every situation, What would Christ do here? This required that one be always spiritually alert, flexible, forever open to new light. The *General Rules* formed only a skeletal outline of problems that might arise; each follower was to seek first the "mind that was in Christ." Wesley urged, ". . . in the name of God, be open to conviction. Whatever prejudices you have contracted from education, custom, or example, divest yourselves of them, as far as possible. Be willing to receive light either from God or man; do not shut your eyes against it."[30]

The whole Bible was to be consulted and its precepts accepted without question. ". . . the Christian rule of right and wrong is the Word of God, the writings of the Old and New Testament; all that the prophets and 'holy men of old' wrote 'as they were moved by the Holy Ghost.' . . ." The Christian "esteems nothing good, but what is here enjoined, either directly or by plain consequence; he accounts nothing evil but what is here forbidden, either in terms, or by undeniable inference." On the other hand, "whatever the Scripture neither forbids nor enjoins, either directly or by plain consequence, he (the Christian) believes to be of an indifferent nature; to be in itself neither good nor evil; this being the whole and sole outward rule whereby his conscience is to be directed in all things." [31]

It is very evident from many passages that Wesley proposed to unite in a way never attempted before religious experience at its highest and Christian practice at its best. As he surveyed the practices of the various religious groups of his day, Wesley felt that none of them had acted fully upon this principle. He said: "When we look into the Bible with any attention, and then look round into the world, to see who believes and who lives according to this book; we may easily discern that the system of practice, as well as the system of truth, there delivered, is torn in pieces, and scattered abroad like the members of Absyrtus. Every denomination of Christians retains some part either of Christian truth or practice; these hold fast one part, and those another, as their fathers did before them." [32]

This may be a debatable indictment, but we must remember that Wesley was looking for "whole Christianity" in practice just as he had looked for it in doctrine and experience. Accordingly he concluded that "the duty . . . of those who desire to follow the whole work of God" is "to 'gather up' all these 'fragments' that, if possible, 'nothing be lost'; with all diligence to follow all those we see about us, so far as they follow the Bible; and to join together in one scheme of truth and practice what almost all the world put asunder." [33]

This statement is of great significance, because of the information which it gives: first, concerning the sources of the *General Rules,* and secondly, concerning the claim made by Wesley to the uniqueness of the Methodist movement. While the Bible was his original source, and the practices of the early church, as recorded by the historians, furnished a helpful commentary upon the Biblical directions, Wesley drew also upon practices among contemporary religious groups. For example, the influence of the Quakers, the Independents and the Moravians upon such matters as personal adornment, diversions, and use of money were all acknowledged by him.

It has been generally held that the major source of the Rules was Anglican authorities upon the practices of the primitive church, such as Cave and Fleury.[34] While it is true that they did shape his early thinking, the statement just quoted, as well as others that might be given, indicate a wide eclecticism in his treatment of the problems of Christian behavior. The synthesis between the Catholic theory of Christian Perfection and the Protestant doctrine of Justification by Faith which Wesley is said to have formulated in the realm of doctrine is paralleled by a far-reaching synthesis in the realm of Christian practice. He sought to bring together in the *General Rules* whatever in the practices of early Christians or contemporary believers seemed to conform to Biblical standards.

This is the reason for Wesley's claim that Methodism was something new. Within the State Church groups had voluntarily come together who were so concerned about "whole Christianity" that they were willing to take upon themselves *all* the disciplines that historical Christianity had found helpful. They saw the interdependence of character and conduct more clearly than did their fellows in the State Church. Their uniqueness in religious experience led inevitably to uniqueness in practice.

The extent of these disciplines and the seriousness with which they were adopted is manifest in Wesley's "Advice to the People called Methodists," 1745, when he said to them:

"Your strictness of life, taking the whole of it together, may likewise be accounted new. I mean, your making it a rule, to abstain from fashionable diversions . . .; your plainness of dress; your manner of dealing in trade; your exactness in observing the Lord's day; your scrupulosity as to things that have not paid custom; your total abstinence from spirituous liquors (unless in cases of necessity); your rule, 'not to mention the fault of an absent person,' . . . may justly be termed new." [85]

Wesley believed that these practices occasioned by Methodist emphasis upon perfect love set his followers apart from all eighteenth century religious groups. He said that although some groups were "scrupulous in some of these things" and others were "strict with regard to other particulars," yet he did not find "any other body of people who insist on all these rules together." Methodists might, therefore, be considered a "new people" with respect to their "name, principles, and practice." [36]

The significance of Methodism, Wesley believed, lay in its comprehensive inclusion of the elements which have characterized Christianity, whenever it has returned to its fundamental doctrines, principles and practices. It had discovered what is common to Christianity whenever and wherever it has appeared in its simplicity. In spite of all the seeming diversity in historic Christianity, at the core is uniformity, for the dictates of love remain much the same from age to age.

For this reason he believed the rules would carry their own verification and appeal to every man's judgment. He confidently declared their universal acceptability, saying, "all these we know His Spirit writes on every truly awakened heart." [37] This seems an amazing assumption; yet Harnack has pointed out that Protestantism reckons upon "the Gospel being something so simple, so divine, and therefore so truly human, as to be most certain of being understood when it is left entirely free, and also as to produce essentially the same experiences and convictions in individual souls."[38] Wesley reached this conclusion after years of thought upon the ethical demands of Scriptural Christianity, and, with the rise of the Evangelical Movement, his conclusion was accepted in the main by thousands of Christians within and without the Church of England and on both sides of the Atlantic during the nineteenth century.

To the early Methodists the *Rules* were entirely acceptable. They were immediately adopted by the Manchester Society. We may assume that the withdrawals and expulsions had rid the Society of all those who were not seeking perfect love. Those who remained were glad to submit to rigid disciplines, for they agreed with Wesley that "these outward signs" are the consequences of love of God, which precludes everything that will interfere with right tempers, communion with God, or dedication to His will; and also everything that interferes with love of the neighbor and devotion to his good.

The *Rules* were for them an objectification of principles which had already been filled with meaning by their experiences in their search for God. The *Rules* simply elucidated the way of life which they wished to adopt. They were not a superimposed code of laws; they were a chart of the way of perfect love.

If one understands the spirit in which the *Rules* were written and adopted, one can also understand the spirit which prompted expulsion of those who refused to be governed by the *Rules*. Such persons had not caught the full implications of the Methodist message; they were still too close to the worldliness of the great mass of Anglicans who rested in opinions, church attendance, assent to creed or other false assurances condemned by Wesley. Their way was not the Christian way and their continuance in the movement would soon obscure its high goal and weaken its power.

Wesley attributed the inefficacy of current Christianity to this very lack of discipline in the Church. He agreed with the belief held by the primitive Church that "none could be real

Christians, without the help of discipline." [39] The fact that no such discipline now existed "in any part of England" seemed to him to account for the scarcity of English Christians.

He was very severe with those clergymen who accused him of destroying the order of the Church, replying that if by order were meant "true Christian discipline, whereby all the living members of Christ are knit together in one, and all that are putrid and dead immediately cut off from the body" he would agree to reverence it. "But," he asked, "where is it to be found? ... Your parishioners are a rope of sand ... few (if any) of them are alive to God; so they have no connexion with each other, unless such as might be among Turks or heathens." The clergy had neither the power nor the courage "to cut off from that body, were it alive, the dead and putrid members." [40] They dared not repel the greatest men in their parishes from the communion table, even though they might be drunkards." [41]

Wesley's view of the dependence of Christianity upon discipline for its spread and, likewise, his severity in expelling from the societies all those who did not obey the *Rules* indicate plainly the original nature of Methodist Societies. They were very definitely a "gathered church," who had chosen "the more excellent way." They did not impose their conduct pattern upon those who did not know their principles: this will become evident as we discuss in fuller detail particular rules. But, for themselves, they were convinced that a life of complete dedication to God required acceptance of all the disciplines proposed by Wesley.[42] They agreed with him, likewise, that the moral state of the world would not be greatly bettered until "the more excellent way" was understood and generally followed; hence, while avoiding censoriousness, they were continuously evangelistic.

Wesley's administration of "true Christian discipline" was, therefore, firmly and fearlessly carried out.[43] He advised one of his preachers facing the problem of smuggling among his members, "Begin in the name of God and go through with the work. If only six will promise you to sin no more, leave only six in the Society. But my belief is an hundred and fifty are now clear of blame; and if you are steady, an hundred will amend." "

Direct and sympathetic dealing with the offender always preceded expulsion. In the early days of the Societies Wesley himself met every member at least once in three months. He knew "not only their names, but their outward and inward states, their difficulties and dangers." "How otherwise," he asked clergymen who made no pretense to pastoral work, "can I know either how to guide them aright, or to commend them to God in prayer?" "

As the revival spread, class-meetings were organized and served the purpose of both better counseling and closer discipline. The prospective member was first placed in a class for a quarter and then given a ticket of admission if he had proven himself. The class-leader kept in weekly contact with the members of his class and once a quarter Wesley or one of his preachers examined all members and renewed the tickets of those who had been faithful. Those who had not been were admonished and again put upon probation. This was done in the most quiet and inoffensive manner, and very often the unruly member finally became a faithful Methodist. Only in cases where the offence was great was any announcement of dismissal made. Wesley felt that the plan was simple, rational and scriptural."

He said also that this plan was unusual, that the exclusion of "the disorderly, without any respect of persons" was a method used by few religious communities. He felt that Presbyterians, Baptists, Independents and Friends had close kinship with Methodism in their insistence that Christian principles be translated into action; but he believed that they had all grown lax in enforcement of their position.

One of his principal objections to the Baptists of the time was that, while still maintaining high requirements for admission, they allowed those who had lapsed from their Covenant to remain. He argued that "if no man ought to be admitted into a church or congregation, who has not actual faith and repentance; then neither ought any who has them not, to continue in any congregation." To allow this, he said, was a practical renunciation of the Baptists' main principle.[47]

The *General Rules* close with an injunction that the Societies took very literally: "If there be any among us who observe them not, who habitually break any of them, let it be made known unto them who watch over that soul, as they that must give an account. We will admonish him of the error of his ways: we will bear with him for a season. But then if he repent not, he hath no more place among us." [48] There can be no question that the early Methodist Societies, while remaining an adjunct to the Church of England, were organized like many of the sects of the seventeenth century.

They had rejected "a natural ethic, whose standards differ greatly from those of Christianity"; they had evolved their social ideal from the Gospel and the history of the early church.[49] They had banded together to demonstrate to the world the truth of "whole Christianity" by a consistently followed way of life.

---

1. Baker, *op. cit.*, p. 86.
2. *Sermons*, II, 55.
3. *Loc. cit.*
4. *Works*, VII, 260.
5. *Ibid.*, p. 261.
6. *Loc. cit.*
7. *Ibid.*, p. 263.
8. *Works*, VI, 445.
9. *Ibid.*, p. 448.
10. *Loc. cit.*
11. *Works*, VI, 438-40. Speaking of those things that appeal to the imagination, Wesley says: "The generality of men, and more particularly men of sense and learning, are so far from suspecting that there is, or can be, the least harm in them, that they seriously believe it is matter of great praise to *give ourselves wholly to them.*"
12. *Ibid.*, p. 441.
13. Perry, *op. cit.*, p. 236. Perry remarks that those who "confuse piety with what they call 'the beauty of the service,' . . . testify to the power of this seduction, especially over more cultivated minds."
14. *Sermons*, II, 464.
15. *Ibid.*, pp. 464-7.
16. *Ibid.*, p. 476.
17. Perry, *op. cit.*, p. 253.
18. See Flew, *op. cit.*, p. 250 *et seq.*
19. *Works*, VIII, 345.
20. Law, *Works*, III, p. 76.

21. *Letters*, IV, 63.
22. Umphrey Lee, *op. cit.*, p. 201.
23. See Perry, *op. cit.*, p. 266.
24. *Loc. cit.*
25. *Works*, VIII, 354.
26. Simon says that the dismissals showed Wesley the necessity for an explicit statement of a conduct pattern "in accordance with the gospel." John S. Simon, *John Wesley and the Methodist Societies* (London: Epworth Press, 1921), p. 99.
27. Luke Tyerman, *op. cit.*, p. 403.
28. See Chapter V, p. 80.
29. *Works*, VIII, 346.
30. *Works*, XI, 467.
31. *Sermons*, I, 226.
32. *Works*, XI, 466.
33. *Loc. cit.*
34. Cave is the source given by Simon, *op. cit.*, p. 105 *et seq.* Lee, *op. cit.*, pp. 64, 65 adds Fleury and the *Apostolic Constitutions*.
35. *Works*, VIII, 354.
36. *Loc. cit.*
37. See Appendix.
38. Harnack, *op. cit.*, p. 275.
39. *Works*, VII, 285.
40. *Works*, VIII, 225.
41. *Ibid.*, p. 175.
42. See Wesley's sermon on the "More Excellent Way," *Works*, VII, 29-36, and also his letter to the Earl of Dartmouth on the two different ranks of Christians, *Letters*, V. 173.
43. *Ibid.*, p. 252.
44. *Letters*, VI, 236.
45. *Works*, VIII, 226.
46. *Works*, VII, 209.
47. *Works*, VIII, 183.
48. See Appendix.
49. See Ernst Troeltsch, *The Social Teaching of the Christian Churches* (London: George Allen & Unwin Ltd., 1931), II, 461 *et seq.*

IX

The Christian Use of Time

Most of the disciplines adopted by early Methodists for the purpose of living effectively the life of perfect love had to do with the stewardship of two talents: namely, time and money. The conserving of leisure and wealth in order to give the greatest possible service to one's fellows is at the very heart of the negatives that compose the first division of the *General Rules,* and to fail to recognize this positive goal that lies beyond the self-denials required in the Wesleyan way is to miss their author's major emphasis and purpose. Not asceticism, not world-flight, but such a thorough stewardship of goods as would lead to the speedy building of a Christian world was the end proposed.

Wesley saw that these two gifts afford channels through which the Christian's love of God and man must flow out over all the world, and that not until those who profess Christ's name have recognized this fact and have disciplined their use of them with the same wholeheartedness as characterized the early church is there any hope for the establishment of a Christian society. The Christianizing of leisure activities and the use of money thus became for early Methodists the first practical step toward the goal which they had set.

With this fact in mind, let us seek first an understanding of the disciplines whereby Wesley sought to Christianize the use of time. This is not an easy thing to do when secularized theories of leisure dominate the thought of our day. In the eighteenth century a latent sense of the sacredness of time still remained with most of the religious groups. Wesley received his teaching on the subject largely from Anglican sources.

Taylor, we have seen, taught him that a clearly outlined plan for the day can become a major instrument toward holy living.¹ The sins produced by idleness will thereby be automatically eliminated, the maximum amount of good works will be accomplished and the Christian will be ready at any moment for Christ's sudden coming. Furthermore, the days lost in sin can be, in a sense, redeemed, for God requires as strict an accounting for the use of this talent as for the use of money or any other gift.

The day should begin with the thought of God. The hours spent in sleep should be strictly limited by the needs of nature, a practice fully followed by Wesley up to the day of his death, and expected of his preachers as well. His letters and sermons are punctuated with exhortations to early rising.

A man's vocation need not take him "off from religion," if pursued moderately and "according to the rules of Christian prudence," with the proper allowance of "time for prayer and retirement." But in the midst of employment he should practice the presence of God. Intervals away from employment should be spent in devotions, charities, neighborly activities and recreation.²

The persons of quality for whom Taylor wrote these instructions were advised to devote much time and money to charity, avoiding luxury and idleness to the same degree as was expected of the poor. They were not to engage in idle conversation or useless, trifling labors. Their recreation should be healthful, brief, refreshing, but should never make lavish demands upon their interest or time. They were to "fly from all occasions" such as "Balls and Revellings, indecent mixtures of wanton dancings, idle talk . . . garish and wanton dressings . . . banquets and perfumes." ³

The reiteration of this teaching by Law in his two devotional works served to intensify Wesley's conviction that one of the chief causes of the flagrant evils of his age was the misuse of time. In this he was not mistaken. Many secular writers of the mid-century were as concerned as were the divines over the consequences of idleness among both rich and poor.

Henry Fielding declared that "To the upper part of mankind, time is an enemy and . . . their chief labour is to kill it." His satiric pen interprets the political measures of the ruling class as largely efforts to prevent idleness "from spreading to the useful part of mankind" whose "labour and industry . . . administer to their pleasures and furnish them with the means of luxury."[4]

But no legislation can long prevent the vices of the rich from becoming the vices of the poor, and contemporary records are full of references to idleness as the cause of increasing crime among the lower classes. Autobiographers tell story after story of tradesmen with good businesses who lost them through dissipation and gambling, and died finally in workhouses or on the streets. Their sons, likewise, and often their daughters came to the same bad ends.[5]

In 1744 the grand jury of Middlesex County made the complaint that "the advertisements in the newspapers were seducing the people to places for the encouragement of luxury, extravagance, and idleness; and that, by this means, families were ruined, and the kingdom dishonoured; and that unless some superior authority put a stop to such riotous living, they feared it would lead to the destruction of the nation!"[6]

Law's satiric character sketches of the idle rich who impeded the progress of the national church were not exaggerated, nor was he too severe in placing upon them the responsibility for the low moral standards and the state of the poor. In fact, the popularity of *The Serious Call* must have been due in part to the compelling realism of his skillful character sketches.

Using this novel method for presenting his message, Law made very clear that no Christian, whatever leisure might be his, would ever allow himself to be idle "whilst others are in want of anything that" his "hands can make for them," nor will he engage in amusement "to get rid of time." This is the act of a child, he says, and for grown-ups is "poor, vain or impertinent."[7] He will spend most of his spare time with those who increase his love for God and his compassion toward the world.

Wesley eagerly responded to these counsels from Taylor and Law, announcing to his mother in 1726, "Leisure and I have taken leave of one another: I propose to be busy as long as I live, if my health is so long indulged to me." [8] In 1727, on the eve of finishing his reading for the Master's degree, he drew up a scheme of studies for several years to come, carrying out the principle of strictly useful employment by excluding from the list of books all those which appealed only to his curiosity. "Curiosity," he says, "might be a sufficient plea for our laying out some time upon them, if we had half a dozen centuries of life to come; but methinks it is great ill-husbandry to spend a considerable part of the small pittance now allowed us in what makes us neither a quick nor a sure return." [9]

Ever afterward, his own need and the need of the world for righteousness furnished him his criterion for the use of time. His strong intellectual curiosity was subdued by the argument that it could wait for satisfaction. "Yet a little while," he said, "and we shall all be equal in knowledge, if we are in virtue." [10] This procedure might not produce extensive intellectual discovery, but it did have much to do with producing the Methodist revival.

It should be added however that Wesley's reading, in spite of this curtailment, covered a wide scope of interests, because of his disciplined management of study time. The rules which he early adopted might advantageously be followed by anyone who desires the utmost returns from books. They were: First, to consider what knowledge you desire to attain to: Secondly, to read no book which does not some way tend to the attainment of that knowledge; Thirdly, to read no book which does tend to the attainment of it, unless it be the best in its kind; Fourthly, to finish one before you begin another; and, Fifthly, to read them all in such order that every subsequent book may illustrate and confirm the preceding." [11] Is it any wonder that Wesley's discussions were characterized by logic and thoroughness?

Wesley's early valuation of time naturally intensified as the spreading revival made almost superhuman demands upon his energies. Moore tells how "one day his chaise was delayed beyond the appointed time. He had put up his papers, and left his apartment. While waiting at the door, he was heard to say, by one that stood near him, 'I have lost ten minutes for ever.' "[12]

Yet, in spite of this driving sense of life's brevity, Wesley never allowed himself to be in a hurry. This would have broken his carefully cultivated Christian poise and resulted in a misuse of time. Moore tells how Wesley, when told on one occasion that he need not hurry, retorted, "A hurry! No; I have no time to be in a hurry."[13]

Another instance of his sane point of view was his slowness in writing. The same biographer considered him the slowest writer he ever knew, but, he adds, Wesley never had to revise. Brevity, too, was a studied art with him, and he once whimsically observed, "I believe, if angels were to write books, we should have very few folios."[14]

So effective in Wesley's ethical development had been certain disciplines in the use of time that he considered them essential to any design for Christian living. It is no accident, therefore, that five regulations[15] relating directly or indirectly to the subject appear in the *General Rules*. They specify the misuses of time most flagrant in his day: unprofitable and harmful talk, improper use of the Lord's day, indulgence in diversions which offered no contribution to Christian growth or gravitated toward evil associations. Time spent upon these employments, he believed, was not only squandered but was positively inimical to the founding of a Christian order. The Methodist was to redeem time from these evil uses and make it "distilled opportunity" for accomplishing this end.

In view of this positive goal, the Rule which forbade "uncharitable and unprofitable conversation" was no less important than the Rules dealing with unchristian diversions; in fact,

Wesley preached much oftener on evil speaking than on dancing or theater attendance. He saw the theory of stewardship in all its inclusiveness.

He quotes from his favorite poet, George Herbert, in support of the belief that man has no more right than has nature to consider time his own.

> "If so thou spend thy time, the sun will cry
> Against thee; for his light was only lent."

This principle he applies to time "thrown away" on "dressing, visits of form, useless diversions, and trifling conversation." [16]

This was the reason why Wesley placed the same limitation upon his love for good talk as he placed upon his wish to satisfy his intellectual curiosity. He enjoyed cheerful, free and unaffected conversation and condemned "a stern, austere manner of conversing." [17] Religion, he said, is "the happiest, cheerfulest thing in the world, inconsistent with moroseness, sourness, contrary to all preciseness, affectation, stiffness." [18] Yet time for Kingdom-building is too brief to spend much of it in mere gratification of this enjoyment.

No criticism of Wesley is more famous than that made by Dr. Johnson, the greatest purveyor and lover of enlightened conversation that ever lived. There are indications that the two men talked frequently, but never long enough to suit Johnson, for he told Boswell: "John Wesley's conversation is good, but he is never at leisure. He is always obliged to go at a certain hour. This is very disagreeable to a man who loves to fold his legs and have out his talk as I do." [19]

Conversation of this sort would at least have been beneficial to the persons engaged. What, then, did Wesley think of the vapid, trivial chit-chat of the secularist, the man who does not live in eternity? He warned Ebenezer Blackwell, a very successful London banker, and a very devoted friend and follower, to whose home he often retreated for quiet, against being "carried away with the stream into frequent conversation with

THE CHRISTIAN USE OF TIME

harmless, good-humoured, honest triflers," who would "soon steal away all ... strength and stifle all the grace of God" in the soul.[20] In fact, he suggested that Blackwell converse no "more than is necessary with men that are without God ... ,"[21] lest he be infected with the spirit of materialism.

If unprofitable conversation is so dangerous, then certainly uncharitable talk is a positive menace to both our union with God and our compassion for our neighbors. It proved also to be the most subtle sin afflicting the early Methodist. Although he had resolutely separated from trifling talkers because of the necessity for a complete break with all his past associations, if he had not seen all the implications of perfect love, he might become guilty of this more harmful practice.

The increase in uncharitable talk in the Societies, in spite of the adoption of the Rule and Wesley's clear interpretation of the nature of neighborly love, became so marked that in 1752 he preached a sermon on "The Cure of Evil-speaking." It was first delivered in Bristol,[22] where a serious outbreak of gossip had militated against the teaching of Christian Perfection. The sermon presents the procedure recommended by Christ in Matthew 18:15-17 for dealing with a wrong doer.

This sermon, preached many times afterward by Wesley, and read thousands of times since to Methodist congregations, condemns all forms of uncharitable conversation—slander, backbiting, tale-bearing and mere insinuation—any talk to another of the "fault of a third person, when he is not present to answer for himself." The sin is so common, Wesley says, even among persons who "really desire to have a conscience void of offence toward God and toward man" that it enters into most conversations of any length and cannot easily be avoided. Yet there is "scarce any wrong temper ... which may not occasionally be gratified by it ... We commit sin from mere hatred of sin!"[23]

Wesley expounds the three directions given by Christ. First, go to the offender in a fully Christian spirit, avoiding "everything in look, gesture, word, and tone of voice, that savours of pride or self-sufficiency," dogmatism, arrogance, or disdain, and speak to him of his fault with gentleness and love. Or, if speech is impossible, write him a letter in the same spirit.

If this measure has no effect, then go once more, accompanied by two or three others who are actuated by the impulse of love. This step failing, the only recourse left is action by the elders of the church, who are accountable for the spiritual state of its members. If the offender is unresponsive, he is still to be treated with courtesy, good-will and humanity, though close fellowship is impossible. There is still no room for evil-speaking, for he is to be left "to his own Master."

Christ's direction and the General Rule, as interpreted by Wesley, condemn also listening to uncharitable talk. If Methodists would earnestly practice the Rule, Wesley concludes, a distinguishing mark of a Methodist would be that "He censures no man behind his back: by this fruit ye may know him." [24] This, he believed, would convince "the wild unthinking world," for it would be a real demonstration of love in action. No one will deny the truth of this assumption. It is regrettable that there have been so many occasions among the believers in Perfect Love for the repreaching of this sermon.[25]

Wesley was particularly severe with those who spoke evil of Magistrates or Ministers. The earliest recorded instance of expulsion from a Society involved "scoffing" at the "ministers of God," [26] and, as a rule, he advised his people to refrain from criticism of all men in public office. He considered it "difficult and frequently impossible" for private men to judge fairly since they "do not see many of the grounds" for action.[27]

It would hardly seem necessary to have mentioned profanity in a list of rules for people who profess to love God. In fact, one who has united himself with the Christian church and still takes God's name in vain is a strange anomaly. Yet swearing has probably always been the commonest sin among professing Christians. The reiteration of the third Commandment in the first General Rule is a lamentable testimony to the persisting gap between the profession and the practice of Christianity.

Wesley's denunciation of swearing church members is a recurrent feature in most of his early sermons. He felt it to be a key sin, created by the wide-spread secularism. Secularism produces universal ignorance of God and culminates in contempt of God. He asserted that the English, "high and low .. do not speak of God. God is not in their thoughts." In neither personal nor national schemes is God given a place. "They do not take God into their account: they can do their whole business without him; without considering whether there be any God in the world; or whether he has any share in the management of it." [28]

The contempt of God which logically follows this ignoring of the Eternal finds expression in perjury and profanity. Perjury, according to Wesley, was almost universal in Courts of Justice, among public servants, among voters, and even tacitly taught in the schools. Furthermore, when the name of God meant so little in official use, it was subjected to complete scorn in ordinary conversation. "Some wretched gentlemen (so-called)" set the example and the masses readily follow.

In "A Serious Advice to the People of England" Wesley declared: "We daily curse and swear, and blaspheme the Most High, merely by way of diversion, almost from the highest to the lowest. Nobility, Gentry, tradesmen, peasants, blaspheme the worthy name whereby we are called, without provocation, without remorse! Sloth and luxury we allow are general among us; but profaneness is well nigh universal. Whoever spends but a few days in any of our large towns, will find abundant proof, that senseless, shameless, stupid profaneness is the true characteristic of the English nation." [29]

A latent social force still existed, however, to which Wesley could appeal. Remaining on the statute books were laws against swearing, together with other legislation against more flagrant forms of vice. These statutes had long ago been made and at intervals enforcement of them had revived. The most recent effective execution had occurred in the last decade of the seventeenth century, when Queen Mary, under the urgency of Archbishop Tillotson, had secured the cooperation of the Lord Mayor and Aldermen of London in a thorough-going attempt at suppression of all forms of vice.

This was the great period of activity for the Society for the Reformation of Manners, which was then composed of eminent lawyers, and Parliamentary members, justices of the peace, and influential citizens of London, who took seriously their appointed responsibility for the secular and religious life of the nation.[30]

But during Wesley's young manhood this Society had practically ceased to function. The social conscience which it represented was dead and the glaring sins of the Restoration, such as sexual immorality, drunkenness, gambling were again rampant and accepted without remonstrance; along with them went profanity and its attendant evil, indecent talk. Belden says in his study of Whitefield that any visitor to the British Museum may see "a huge portfolio of broadsheets and handbills such as were commonly distributed . . . so foul and obscene that anyone repeating them today would be arrested."[31] The indecencies of coffee-house talk and even of the occasional verse of the best known poets of the time is known to all who have made any extensive study of Pope, Swift, Gay or others of their circle.

These are the reasons why the first Rule lists among evils generally practiced "The taking of the name of God in vain." So active was the conscience of early Methodists in regard to this sin that they aroused other morally awakened Anglicans and Dissenters to revive the Society for the Reformation of Manners. Sir John Fielding, then Bow Street police magistrate, gave them his full support, and for several years effective enforcement of the old laws was carried out, producing phenomenal improvement in some London areas, especially in Moorfields, the city center for the Methodist revival.

As the widening circles of influence from the revival cleansed the moral thought of the whole nation the imposition of civil laws became less necessary. A profound dissatisfaction with materialism and secularism grew, reverence for the name of God returned, and we shall see in the nineteenth century a widespread adoption of a new attitude toward swearing that condemned it not only as unchristian but also as contrary to good taste—a remarkable change when one recalls the frequency of oaths and loose talk even among women in the eighteenth century.

The misuse of the Sabbath day was another evidence of the universal dismissal of God from human affairs and hence mention is made in the *General Rules* of "The profaning the day of the Lord, either by doing ordinary work thereon, or buying or selling." [32]

Here again Wesley was awakening a dormant public conscience to an evil which had been nationally recognized not so long before. It was less than seventy years since a Parliamentary Act had been passed forbidding the pursuit of all occupations on Sunday, except a few specified food services, and greatly restricting all recreation of a public nature. [33]

Anglican even more than Puritan sentiment had been responsible for the enactment of this law and for the wholehearted support given to officials in enforcing it. English monarchs up to the Georges showed favor toward the efforts of the Religious Societies to bring about reforms of this sort. Whitaker finds that State and Church were at that time united in an attempt to secure a suitable atmosphere for the performance of religious duties and the rest and quiet requisite to the social well-being of the State. [34]

In Wesley's childhood the best of Anglican leaders were as strict sabbatarians as were the Puritans. Bishop Stillingfleet, in offering advice, founded his position upon the long-tested tradition of the Church: " 'These things I have more largely insisted upon to show that the religious observation of the

Lord's day is no novelty by some late sects and parties among us, but that it hath been the general sense of the best part of the Christian World and is particularly enforced upon us of the Church of England, not only by the Homilies, but by the most ancient Ecclesiastical Law among us.'"[85]

Early in the reign of George I the decline in moral conviction, which we have had occasion to note frequently, showed itself in increasing violation of the Sunday Law. With the regulations still remaining on the statute books and a pretense of regard for Sunday still persisting among the law-making classes, absurd inconsistencies developed. William Law describes Flavia, who spends most of Sunday in frivolous or scandalous talk, and yet turns a poor old widow out of her house for mending her clothes on Sunday night.

Defoe in 1729 comments upon the strict enforcement of the law against meatsellers, which results in the loss of valuable food, and the utter failure to regulate public-houses, where the common people observe Sunday as a day of debauchery, becoming so drunken that " 'they cannot work for a day or two following.' "[86] He complains that " 'Instead of a day of rest, we make it a day of labour, by toiling in the Devil's vineyard; and but too many surfeit themselves with the fruits of gluttony, drunkenness and uncleanness.' "[87]

Such pictures of Sunday among the lower ranks became more and more frequent as well as more and more dark after 1725 when spirituous liquors came into universal use. In 1750 the Bishop of London declared that " 'the neglect and profanation of the Sabbath is become the reproach and scandal of the nation.' " The masses spent the day in lewdness, drunkenness, and gaming, while the few who attended the church were, for the most part, inattentive and irreverent.[88]

This was the state among the poor to whom Wesley began to preach in 1739. In certain sections of London and in communities, such as the Newcastle collieries, which had sprung up like mushrooms with the coming of industrialism, and which knew little of either Church or civil regulation, Wesley found that Sunday observance was scarcely known. It was not only a day of low pleasures but of trade as well.

These were the areas to which Methodism went in particular, changing first the inward life of the individual, educating him in the use of time, and finally through the social pressure of this transformed group reforming the Sunday activities of the whole community. Many were the converts who at first faced the prospect of loss of employment when they refused to work on Sunday, but no true Methodist ever placed a material consideration above a moral compunction, and usually his employer had respect for his courage and sincerity.

That the communities reached by Methodism lived up to their convictions and exercised a leavening influence upon community attitude is proved by the data gathered by Whitaker in his study of the eighteenth century English Sunday. By the year 1757, a change in sentiment had become so widespread that, for the first time since Queen Anne's reign, Parliament again gave attention to the matter. Agitation continued, gathering an increasing body of support, until in 1781, ten years before Wesley's death, a new act was passed, which again restricted forms of Sunday entertainment and trade, and which proved enforceable.

By the end of the century during the period of the Napoleonic Wars the Methodist Revival had so strengthened Sabbatarianism in the State Church as well as in Nonconformity that exceptions were made for all those who had conscientious objections to military training on Sunday. While this influence was not strong enough to prevent all Sunday drilling it was sufficient to modify the purpose of Parliament to make Sunday "a general time of military activity." [39]

No better evidence of the triumph of Methodism over the secularism of the early eighteenth century can be found than in the Sabbatarianism that characterized the next century and which led a French historian to say of the Englishman that he was distinguished from the continental European in "his strict observance of the Sabbath" and, more than that, was proud of the distinction. This Sabbath observance, Halevy says, "was unquestionably a direct result of the Methodist and Evangelical revival." [40]

---

1. See Chapter V, p. 77.
2. Taylor, op. cit., p. 6 et seq.
3. Ibid., p. 83.
4. Henry Fielding, An Enquiry into the Causes of the late Increase of Robbers (London: Pr. for A. Millar, 1751), p. 11.
5. M. D. George, London Life in the Eighteenth Century, p. 272.
6. Quoted by Tyerman, op. cit., p. 216.
7. Law, Works, IV, 300.
8. Letters, I, 34.
9. Ibid., p. 39.
10. Ibid., p. 118.
11. Ibid., p. 104.
12. Moore, op. cit., II, 432.
13. Loc. cit.
14. Works, XIV, 301.
15. See Appendix: "The taking the name of God in vain; The profaning the day of the Lord, either by doing ordinary work thereon, or buying or selling; . . .
    Uncharitable or unprofitable conversation, particularly speaking evil of Magistrates or of Ministers . . .
    The taking such diversions as cannot be used in the name of the Lord Jesus.
    The singing those songs, or reading those books which do not tend to the knowledge or love of God . . ."
16. Letters, III, 44.
17. Letters, I, 218.
18. Ibid., p. 217.
19. James Boswell, Life of Samuel Johnson (New York: A. S. Barnes & Burr, 1860), p. 361.
20. Letters, III, 118.
21. Ibid., p. 119.
22. This outbreak led the Wesleys and eleven preachers to draw up a document agreeing,
    "1. That we will not listen, or willingly inquire after any ill concerning each other.
    2. That, if we do hear any ill of each other, we will not be forward to believe it.
    3. That, as soon as possible, we will communicate what we hear by speaking or writing to the person concerned.
    4. That, till we have done this, we will not write or speak a syllable of it to any other person whatever.
    5. That neither will we mention it, after we have done this, to any other person.
    6. That we will not make any exception to any of these rules, unless we think ourselves absolutely obliged in conscience so to do." Sermons, II, 296, Introduction.
23. Sermons, II, 297-8.
24. Ibid., p. 307.
25. See Proceedings of the Wesley Historical Society, IV, 6-8. In his later years Wesley not only used this sermon but also borrowed from the Moravians a device which he hoped would supply a corrective and preclude the fatal tendency to gossip. This was a game played with Scripture cards. References to this game have sometimes led to the mistaken conclusion that Wesley approved of playing cards.
26. Journal, II, 431.
27. Works, XI, 155.
28. Ibid., p. 160.
29. Ibid., p. 148.
30. See E. Sykes, op. cit., p. 193 et seq.; J. B. Botsford, English Society in the

Eighteenth Century (New York: Macmillan, 1924), pp. 201-2; Garnett V. Portus, *Caritas Anglicana* (London: A. R. Mowbray, 1912), p. 15 *et seq.*
31. Albert D. Belden, *George Whitefield—The Awakener* (London: Samson, Low, Marston & Co., 1930), p. 54.
32. See Appendix.
33. W. B. Whitaker, *The Eighteenth-Century English Sunday* (London: Epworth Press, 1940), p. 13.
34. *Ibid.*, p. 33.
35. *Ibid.*, p. 43. Quot. from Edward Stillingfleet, *Ecclesiastical Cases* (1702), p. 138.
36. *Ibid.*, p. 76. Quot. from Daniel Defoe, *Augusta Triumphans*, 2nd edit. (1729), p. 50.
37. *Ibid.*, p. 74. Quot. from Defoe, *op. cit.* p. 41.
38. *Ibid.*, p. 95. Quot. from A Supplement to the Bishop of London's Letter . . . on the occasion of the late Earthquakes (3rd edit., 1950), p. 9.
39. *Ibid.*, p. 166.
40. Elie Halevy, *A History of the English People in 1815* (Harmondsworth: Penguin Books Ltd., 1938), III, 75.

X

"Time in Masquerade"

William Cowper, who found inspiration for great poetry from his experience in the Wesleyan way, regarded the popular amusements of the eighteenth century as nothing more than contrivances "to fill the void of an unfurnish'd brain." The early Methodist needed no such "contrivances," for there were never enough hours in the day for doing what he most loved to do. Hence, he was filled with contempt for the man or woman so void of inner resources as to think of time as something to "fill" or "kill."

The world's time is "Time on Masquerade," said Cowper, Time hiding his real face under the mask of popular diversions, such as gambling, dancing, and theater-going. Time in this guise

> ". . . charms a world whom fashion blinds
> To his true worth, most pleas'd when idle most,
> Whose only happy are their wasted hours."[1]

There is no doubt but that the Restoration generation was pleasure-mad, nor that this form of insanity was inherited by their eighteenth century children. As in all post-war periods, moral controls had relaxed and the diversions that pander most to the passions were indulged in by high and low.

Illustration of the moral degeneration that characterized the first decades of the eighteenth century can be found in every history of the time; the more thorough the documentation, the blacker the picture. Such a series of studies is that recently conducted by Dr. George. Her conclusion, drawn from reading the life-histories of the time, is that economic ruin among the middle and lower classes was "fatally easy" and very "common" and that the causes for it were more often social than economic. It was "drink, thievery, gambling, relations with women, brawling" that brought men to poverty and the workhouse. The picture is further heightened by its contrast with the good social and economic conditions which she discovers among the same classes a century later.[2]

The immorality of the courtly classes is notorious. A shocking but illuminating illustration of evil in high life comes from the literary war in which Pope was usually engaged. In his "Epistle to Dr. Arbuthnot" he had slurred Colley Cibber, popular playwright, actor, and poet Laureate, by the line, "And has not Colley still his Lord and Wh—?" Cibber's reply was: "Don't you think to say a *man has his Wh—e* ought to go for little or nothing? Because *defendit numerus*, take the first ten thousand men you meet, and I believe you would be no loser if you betted ten to one that every sinner of them, one with another, had been guilty of the same frailty."[3]

If one thinks Wesley's pictures of his generation morbid and overdrawn, or his denunciation of sin fiery and ill-balanced, if one considers his thunderings against the complacency and compromise of the average clergyman inappropriate, let him read the drama, the biography, the letters—any of the secular records that bring him into the moral climate of the time—and he will conclude that Wesley's message is characterized by remarkable restraint. Wesley was not the high-powered, emotional revivalist, known to older Americans; his power lay in his cool, logical presentation of facts all too well known among his hearers.

Earnest clergymen like Bishop Gibson, although misunderstanding Wesley's efforts to restore religion to spiritual reality, still shared fully his views on national morals. We shall find, for example, in our discussion of dancing how strenuously Gibson while Bishop of London exerted himself to do away with the masquerade, which had become the shield of vice, even at court.[4]

Each of the diversions condemned by Wesley had evil

associations familiar to his audiences, which we shall describe in the ensuing discussion. We have already noted the confidence with which Wesley declared of Methodist regulations: "All these we know His Spirit writes on every truly awakened heart." He made this statement knowing well that the masses whom he was reaching, though their lives were pagan, had a clear perception of the moral quality of their amusements.

It is characteristic of a return to the principles enunciated by Christ for the moral insight to become so fully alive that the compromise with the admixture of good and evil in current diversions which has been tolerated and even justified by the church is no longer possible. It is further characteristic that this clarified perception of the full implications of the Christian ethic will demand a subordination of all amusement to a minor role in life. Wesley did not emphasize exclusively, therefore, the moral aspect of diversion. This constituted only one of the determining principles in his analysis. His oft reiterated statement that Christianity is not mere morality is as applicable here as elsewhere and needs to be fully comprehended.

An age dominated by pleasure-madness offers a very serious threat to the Christian scale of values. Even the realization of what is meant by a Christian scale of values may be so lost by the professing Christian that when he is told that his love of pleasure interferes with his love of God he will remonstrate that his pleasures do not conflict with moral standards and therefore should not be condemned.

This was probably Wesley's own position when he first met with Kempis, and it was not until he had seen the logic of Law's theory of Christianity that he adopted completely Christian criteria for his amusements. Quite rightly he refused to accept Kempis' ascetic condemnation of all pleasure. After his first thorough reading of the *Imitation* he wrote: "I can't think that when God sent us into the world He had irreversibly decreed that we should be perpetually miserable in it. If it be so the very endeavor after happiness in this life is a sin. . . .

What are become of all the innocent comforts and pleasures of life, if it is the intent of our Creator that we should never taste them?"[5]

Wesley at this time loved the theater and dancing[6] and classified them among the innocent comforts and pleasures of life. He had not yet seen harm in them and could not accept a theory that identified Christianity with renunciation of all joy. Throughout his life he insisted upon enjoyment of all legitimate things, and he and his followers are now pictured as the happiest people of the eighteenth century.

Late in life he wrote: "I dare not add Monsieur Pascal's rule—Avoid all pleasure. It is not possible to avoid all pleasure, even of sense, without destroying the body. Neither doth God require it . . . it is not his will concerning us. On the contrary, he 'giveth us all things to enjoy,' so we enjoy them to his glory. But I say, avoid all that pleasure which anyway hinders you from enjoying him; yea, all such pleasure as does not prepare you for taking pleasure in God."[7]

Frequently Wesley had to answer charges that the Methodist held an ascetic view of pleasure. But he did not, like Law, consider the body evil nor "a prison into which we" have fallen. He could not believe that the Christian has "nothing to do but to get out" of this world.[8]

The Christian's state, in Wesley's thinking, is much like that of Adam's in that his happiness in the love of God is "increased by all the things that are round him." He sees "with unspeakable pleasure, the order, the beauty, the harmony, of all creatures; of all animated, all inanimate nature; the serenity of the skies; the sun walking in brightness; the sweetly variegated clothing of the earth; the trees, the fruits, the flowers, 'and liquid lapse of murmuring streams.' "[9]

The chief difference between Adam and the Christian is that the Christian's happiness is interrupted by the presence of evil in the world. The essence of Adam's perfection had been his "continually seeing and loving and obeying" God, a happiness only increased by the unalloyed goodness of his surroundings. But now evil limits man's power of seeing God, corrupting his faculties so that they are used in disobedience to Him, and entering into the nature of things to taint good with evil. However, when the love of God becomes the supreme end of life, the Christian possesses a criterion for discovering that which interferes with his vision of God and lures his faculties into disobedience, and to some degree he can win back the happiness which Adam enjoyed.

Applying this criterion to amusements, Wesley makes pronouncement upon all that were popular in his day. In these pronouncements may be discovered three principles: First, Amusement must always be a secondary source of happiness; Secondly, Amusement must not only be kept subordinate to the love of God, but it should also prepare one for greater enjoyment of God; Thirdly, Amusements that contain an intermixture of good and evil must be avoided. These principles might be restated very simply in the form of questions: First, Does my love for this amusement surpass my love of God and does the time spent upon it rob me of time or energy I should spend in His service? Secondly, Does this amusement contribute directly or indirectly to the development of my Christian character? Thirdly, Does this amusement have in it any element that will harm either myself or another? Let us observe Wesley's application of these principles.

The first criterion leads the Christian to use "the world as not abusing it." Amusement is not to be regarded as something to be made the most of, not the serious business of life. It is, in the basic sense of the word, to be a diversion, and, in comparison with pleasures that are eternal, "a poor, empty, insignificant trifle." The joy found in private or public devotion, for example, will always surpass that found in diversion and, as a consequence, will determine the arrangement of the time at one's disposal. The reasons given by the Oxford Methodists for their withdrawal from fashionable diversions was not disapproval of them, but the need for the time and money spent upon them for doing work among the poor and the prisoners.[10]

The second principle was also adopted during Wesley's Oxford days under the influence of Law, who convinced him that "no one can *truly* fulfil, or live up to the two first and greatest of all Laws, that of loving God with all our Hearts, all our Strength, and all our Mind, and that of loving our Neighbour as ourselves, unless he be willing and glad in many Instances, *wholly* to *abstain* from Things in themselves indifferent and innocent, and also to make Things that in themselves are indifferent, to be Matters of Duty."[11] Christian amusement contributes to "a greater Purity and Perfection of Heart."[12]

This insistence upon positive value in all our employments Wesley believed to be the essence of Paul's teaching to the early church: "Whether, therefore, ye eat, or drink, or whatsover ye do, do all to the glory of God." It is not sufficient justification of an amusement to say of it, "I can see no harm in it, for it is a good means of passing time." All amusement should make us more like God. Wesley argues: ". . . to be happy I must love God; in proportion to my love of whom my happiness must increase. To love God I must be like Him, holy as He is holy."[13]

This calls for a careful selection of life interests, but it does not exclude those which make an indirect contribution to Christian growth. Wesley recognizes many things only remotely conducive to holiness, which yet relate to our "usefulness in the world" or which are "necessary as means to higher ends."[14] Among these are music, travel and wide reading. Another of his diversions which received increasing attention as he grew older was gardening.

The third principle calls for an examination of the moral quality of the amusement. The Christian must be on his guard against all intermixture of good and evil, for even a slight element of evil hinders one in enjoyment of God. Wesley illustrates this by an analogy in his sermon, "On Public Diversions." He describes one about to drink a cup of wine containing a drop of poison. "You see the wine when it sparkles in the cup and are going to drink of it. I tell you there is poison in it! and, therefore, beg you to throw it away. You answer, 'The wine is harmless in itself.' I reply, 'Perhaps it is so; but still, if it be mixed with what is not harmless, no one in his senses, if he knows it at least, unless he could separate the good from the bad, will once think of drinking it.' "[15] And no more will a Christian enter into a diversion which breaks into his union with God by inflaming passions, rousing impulses and thoughts irreconcilable with a Christian temper.

Another fault with diversions which contain evil is their possible effect upon someone else. Wesley raises the question in this same sermon. "If you add, 'It is not poison to me, though it be to others'; then I say, 'Throw it away also.' Why should thy strength occasion thy weak brother to perish, for whom Christ died?"[16]

He applies both principles to attendance at horse-racing, commenting upon the lying, cheating, gambling and cursing which accompany this form of amusement, degrading those who actively participate in them, and squandering the time which is needed by the Christian for business or for charitable work.[17]

No amusement which has in it any element of harm for one's self or another can properly be called "innocent." In a sermon which deals with types of business in which the Christian can engage Wesley condemns some of these so-called "innocent" diversions, and mentions "taverns, victually-houses, opera-houses, and play-houses" as places of public, fashionable diversion which minister either directly or indirectly to unchastity or intemperance. His criterion is, "If these profit the souls of men, you are clear; your employment is good." But if these are "either sinful in themselves, or natural inlets of sin of various kinds," they cannot be defended."[18] That which is an inlet of sin is condemned along with that which is inherently evil.

The Methodists, because of their exclusion of these so-called "innocent" amusements were met, as they would be today, with the argument, "Relaxation, Amusement, or Diversion of one kind or other, is absolutely necessary to the Human Mind, as it is indispensably requisite to the Health of the Body."[19] The answer given by Law in defense of the Methodists states adequately their position: if a diversion is "right and proper in itself, it needs no Excuse; but if it be *wrong*, and *dangerous* to Religion, we are not to use it *cautiously*, but to avoid it *constantly*."[20]

A glaring example of an amusement that had become inextricably entangled with evil was the dancing of the day. That Wesley saw some value in dancing lessons is undeniable, for he said, "If I had convenience, I would be glad to have our preachers taught, even by a dancing-master, to make a bow and to go in and out of a room."[21] Distressed with the gaucherie of many of the lay ministers, he recalled the benefits he had received from direct training in poise and physical grace.

However, the definite distinction between dancing as an educational device and dancing as a public amusement was early impressed upon Wesley by his mother's practice. He said: "My mother never would suffer one of her children to 'go to a dancing school.' But she had a dancing-master to come to her house who taught all of us what was sufficient *in her presence*."[22]

His mother must have allowed social dancing as well at home, for Curnock found references in the cipher diaries to Wesley's dancing "with his sisters almost every available evening during his visits to Wroot and Epworth." Other references indicate that he danced with friends on visits to various parts of the country and that in his early years he considered this a harmless diversion.[23]

However, by the time the *Rules* were written Wesley had

placed it in quite a different category, for no Methodist who engaged in dancing was allowed to continue in a Society. He still saw no evil in the act of dancing and regretted that it could not be used as a means toward cultivation of social grace, but it seemed inevitably an inlet to evil and must therefore be refused by the Christian.

He wrote to Mary Bishop, a young teacher whose chief trouble with the parents of her students arose from her exclusion of dancing from her school program, that she had chosen "the more excellent way" in doing so and remarked, "If dancing be not an evil in itself, yet it leads young women to numberless evils."[24]

This was its difficulty: it never remained an educational device nor an innocuous form of recreation; it was too susceptible to corrupting influences. The masquerade of the day was an example of this and many of the converts to Methodism knew from personal experience its devastating effect upon moral character.

The masquerade of the upper classes was a kind of epitome of all the licentiousness that had been passed on from the Restoration to the courts of the Georges. It was immensely popular and enjoyed royal patronage. Gibson described it as "a particular example of the looseness of morals at the Court," the occasion of drunkenness, brawls and libertinism. He complained that the mingling of the sexes under the screen of masks encouraged lewdness, while retiring rooms furnished a place where they might " 'fall into any profane discourse or lascivious behaviour to which their inclinations should lead them.' "[25]

Hogarth's satiric eye saw in the masquerade a proper subject for exposing the follies of the time, and in one of his pictures he portrayed the loose gestures and acts that too often accompanied it and suggested its immoral atmosphere by a pair of lecherometers which presumably measured the rise and fall of passion.[26]

Efforts made by the Bishop of London to bring about reform met with no permanent success and even with opposition from some of the higher clergy. A promise given by the King to end the court masquerade was kept for only a few months, and Gibson's continuing criticism led to the King's dislike of him.

The popularity of the masquerade spread until hosts and hostesses " 'vied with each other in the production of gorgeous spectacles, each intended to exceed its predecessor in lewdness . . . as well as finery.' " [27] The lower classes followed suit, indulging in the same practices in the less spectacular setting of public halls and gardens.

The objections voiced by the religious minority through the Society for the Reformation of Manners and other organizations proved utterly ineffective. Not until the foundations for a new moral viewpoint on diversions had been laid by the Methodist revival did the masquerade lose its vogue or its vicious character. Without any doubt the strength of these foundations was determined in great part by the firm refusal by the early Methodist converts to have anything to do with a form of amusement which had associations with evil. Bready compares the amusement problem of early Methodists with that faced by the early Christians, saying, "a complete and peremptory *break* was imperative." [28]

If dancing had become impregnated with evil in the eighteenth century, then card-playing had suffered even greater corruption, for c a r d s were universally associated with gambling, and gambling had become a threat to national well-being. As a symptom of the moral and economic insecurity it has been discussed by every social historian of the period. Economic causes, particularly the increase in wages, have sometimes been given as the sole explanation for the spirit of wild speculation, but the causes lie deeper in the moral and social dislocations of the time. Mrs. George, after denying that gambling was occasioned by higher wages, says that "temptations to drink and gamble were interwoven with the fabric of society to an astonishing extent," and were greatly responsible for producing the "sense of instability, of liability to sudden ruin, which runs through so much eighteenth century literature." [29]

From early in the century gambling was carried on to a shocking degree among the rich, great fortunes often being lost over night at clubs and coffee-houses. Women, too, risked and lost not only money but virtue. Bath is known as the center of the pastime under the reign of Beau Nash, its unique master of ceremonies. Even the government succumbed to the spirit and sponsored huge lottery schemes, such as the scandalous South Sea Bubble.

During the rule of George III betting on horse-racing was legalized and the craze to "make something for nothing" reached the lower classes. Botsford says that this became the "prime objective of the age." [30] "The acquisition of a fortune, preferably without the expenditure of creative effort, the absence of fair play in its pursuits, and the failure to regard wealth as a sacred trust, to be used primarily for the betterment of one's self and of men in general, were all symptoms of a new morality based on a false philosophy, or perhaps a lack of philosophy." [31]

To the true philosophy, which regards money and time as a dual trust, Wesley recalled the age. His penetrating insight into moral values led him to see that the root error in gambling is not really the possibility of losing. He said, "We cannot, if we love everyone as ourselves, hurt any one *in his substance* . . . by gaming." [32] More evil than losing that which belongs to ourselves is taking from another that for which we have given no service.

The man of the world may refrain from gambling because he might lose, but the Christian refrains because he might win and thereby injure his neighbor. Again we are reminded of the profounder moral standard inspired by Christianity. "The spirit of something for nothing," says Lawson, "is the very opposite of the ideal of stewardship."[33] The full adoption of the religion of love is a sure remedy for the evils of gambling in all its forms.

Because playing-cards were an inlet to sin and a symbol of the totally unchristian spirit of the age they were condemned among Methodists. Yet, since only an awakened Christian conscience can recognize the evil in a practice so generally accepted, Wesley gave caution against censoriousness. His treatment of one who quibbled about the matter is described in a letter in 1787: "I say . . . to one that asks, 'Can't I be saved if I dance or play at cards?' . . . 'Possibly you may be saved though you dance and play at cards. But I could not.' "[34] This, he says, is as far as one may "safely speak."

He would not unchristianize one who plays cards, but he could not associate card-playing with "the more excellent way" of perfect love. The reasons? First, like dancing, it is often "an inlet to sin," the sin of gambling. Secondly, it is usually a misuse of time. Wesley pointed out that the rubrics of the Church of England state that "no ecclesiastical persons shall spend time idly, by day or by night, playing at *dice, cards, or tables.*"[35] Now a diversion unfit for a clergyman, to Wesley's mind, was equally unfit for a layman, for in Methodism all were priests unto God. If the Anglican *clergy,* which had become notorious for its misuse of time at patrons' card-tables, had aided in bringing about the existing state of affairs, perhaps an Anglican *laity,* which used leisure time only in diversions that nurture Christian character, might restore the nation to moral soundness.

Still another reason for refraining from card-playing was the tremendous hold which the diversion often had upon many people; devotion to the card-table competed with devotion to God and the church. Dr. Church tells in his history of *The Early Methodist People* of a typical case. A woman "who had been influenced by the preaching of Mr. Romaine, . . . confessed to him that though she could accept his doctrine, she could not 'give up cards.' To his question, 'You think you could not be happy without them?' she replied, 'No, sir, I could not.' 'Then, Madam, they are your god; they must save you,' " he said. The consequence of his honest reply was her conversion.[36]

Botsford sees in the gambling craze of the eighteenth century an unnatural "craving for artificial excitement," which deadened the fondness for the natural pleasures of home and out-of-doors. This in turn led to a general looseness of conduct. The reason for a passionate demand for pleasure always lies within; inner resources have disappeared; "the well is dry."[37] Restore the inner springs of joy and the problems of entertainment are simplified. In fact all of life is simplified. Methodism recalled men, women and children to simple, homespun, uncommercialized pleasures, and the genuine happiness of their lives is revealed in dozens of life stories and hundreds of hymns that throb with joy.

Another General Rule dealing with diversions specifies "reading those books which do not tend to the knowledge or love of God" as one of the evils "most generally practised."[38] No writer, however great, can rise very far above the people for whom he writes. He is bound, by the very nature of things, either to express the ideals of their inner life or to portray their outward behavior. If morals have declined, then literature of necessity mirrors this state of affairs: it may pander to the public taste for the pornographic, or it may seek honestly to portray the life that exists, or, if the moral judgment of the writer is deeply stirred by the enigmatic inconsistencies of the human animal, he may express his indignation in bitter satire.

The early eighteenth century, like the twentieth century, saw all of these kinds of writing and little of note beside. The powerfully original minds found expression in stark realism and savage, often coarse, satire. This created a very complex problem for the morally awakened reader. If he were a highly intelligent, broadly read student of literature he might approach realism and satire analytically and thereby understand his times the better. But early Methodist converts did not belong to that class. What little reading they had done had been done for the sake of pure entertainment, and to find *amusement* in books which depicted the lewdness, profanity and irreligion of the time was surely irreconcilable with their newly accepted standards.

The dangers of this form of entertainment had been clearly set forth by Law in *The Practical Treatise on Christian Perfection,* and Wesley probably received from him the opinion that abstaining from "reading plays, romances, or books of humour" should characterize those of "the more excellent way." He names this practice as one of the singularities of the Methodists.[39]

The sort of books Wesley had in mind in this rule becomes clear when one reads Law's discussion of them. He tells of a father who has feared that the conversation of his daughter with a lewd rake will cause her to lose her virtue of mind; yet the same father allows his daughter to read by the hour poems full of indecency, poems in which the poet's finest skill is expended upon lewdness and immodesty, "as if Profaneness, Blasphemy, the grossest Descriptions of Lust, and the wildest Sallies of impure Passions, were made good and useful for a Christian, by being put into Rhyme and Measure."[40]

It is evident that Law and Wesley are speaking particularly of books of coarse, satiric humor, or of the utterly trivial romances which were devoured by women of fashion, or of the many plays that were the very epitome of all the sensuality of upper class society. It would seem from contemporary comment that the taste for obscenity was very general and determined the character of books in circulating libraries.[41]

Law comments on this kind of entertainment to his fashionable audience: ". . . you entertain your mind with evil Thoughts, you read, relish, and digest the Lewdness, Profaneness, and Impurity, of these Books (not for lewd purposes) but only as it were in jest, and to have a little Pleasure from them." But such books can no more be defended as means of entertainment than can drunkenness be justified as mere gaiety of spirits. Since Christ made virtue to reside in right attitudes, delight in bad books, is "as truly a Temper and Disposition of the Heart" as is covetousness or pride."

Wesley became very serious about his choice of books at the end of his college course. He even questioned the advisability of including voluptuous classical poetry in the reading list for school boys, saying, "Let any man but consider human nature, and tell me whether he thinks a boy fit to be trusted with Ovid?" For himself he determined to read henceforth nothing but what would promote "piety and the good life."

This decision, however, did not lead him into an obscurantist confinement of his reading to religious literature, a policy sometimes adopted by his later followers. In the fifty volumes of the *Christian Library* he made available to his people abridgements of many of the great classics, and in the three volumes of *Moral and Sacred Poems* he collected his choice of the best English poems. His selection (and revision, which seems a bit presumptuous) were made with the aim of excluding everything "contrary to virtue" or offensive to "the chastest ear."

For himself he interpreted very freely his self-imposed limitation to books promoting "the good life." In view of the severe restrictions which he had placed upon his people his own wide sampling of current literature may seem inconsistent and even autocratic. But one wonders if here again he was following the example set by leaders in the early church, who influenced so greatly his formative period.

Fleury says that the converts to Christianity were advised not to read the books of the heathen, but to find all types of reading in the Scriptures. "Yet," says he, "the Bishops and Priests found it to their purpose, to read the profane Authors, and made good use of them in their Contests with the Gentiles, Fighting them with their own Weapons, the Authorities of their Poets and Philosophers. They professed to embrace all Truth, whence soever it came; and wheresoever they found it, they challenged it for their own, as being the Disciples of Jesus Christ, who is the Word, that is to say, the sovereign Reason." [44]

The General Rule which specifies books which "do not tend to the knowledge or love of God" includes songs as well. It is easy to understand this if by it is meant songs which had the faults attributed by Law to popular poetry, but it is more difficult to interpret Wesley's reference to "innocent songs" in his "Advice to People called Methodist." [45] If by this he meant songs popularly called "innocent," but really vulgar, which is the frequent meaning of the word as used by Wesley, we can see reason for associating them with harmful books. If he does not mean this, we must conclude that a disinclination toward all secular music led him into a narrow-mindedness that he did not show toward other forms of art.

It may seem strange that Wesley felt called upon to deal in the *Rules* explicitly with songs and books and yet not to mention forms of amusement opposed even more outspokenly by early Methodists—specifically, card-playing, dancing and theater attendance. Perhaps it was lack of agreement upon such seemingly innocuous employments as indiscriminate reading and singing that made mention of them necessary. Certainly the very universality of objections among serious Christians to card-playing, dancing and the theater took them out of the category of "innocent diversions."

The writings of Wesley and the early Methodists assume without any question that these three forms of amusement belong in the general classification used in the *Rules,* namely, diversion that "cannot be used in the name of the Lord Jesus." Like all unwritten laws this interpretation was the more binding because it was implicit in the very principles of stewardship upon which Methodism had been founded. These diversions simply did not belong in "the more excellent way." When a later generation of Methodists found it necessary to add a rule specifying these diversions they had lost this original unanimity of opinion and, one fears, a clear insight into the underlying principles of the Wesleyan way. Multiplication of rules is usually a sure indication of drift away from original principles.

One of the earliest causes for bitter attack upon the Methodists was their attitude toward the theater. It is true that the first public utterances were made by Whitefield and were, like so many of his utterances, perfervid. After declaring that "the Playhouses are the Nurseries of Debauchery in the Age," he told his readers, ". . . if you have tasted of the Love of God, and have felt his Power upon your Souls, you would no more go to a Play than you would run your Head in a Furnace." [46]

But Wesley, while never indulging in such bombast, condemned the English theater as "the sink of all profaneness and debauchery" and said that he could not attend it "with a clear conscience." [47] The agreement between the two great leaders of the Evangelical revival on this question swept literally thousands on both sides of the Atlantic into united opposition to the theater during the nineteenth century.

Many influences had combined to wean Wesley away from his youthful enthusiasm for the theater. There is no doubt but that drama read or acted had been a favorite pastime for him until his moral conversion. He apparently had inherited no aversion to the stage from seventeenth century Puritanism; in fact, his early antipathy to the seventeenth century sects would have led him to reject their opinion as "enthusiasm." He came to the problem with unbiased mind and continued to make the kind of discrimination that comes only from independent thinking. What, then, were the influences that brought him to a belief that the eighteenth century theater was the foe of Christianity?

One of the most potent agencies was the point of view held by the early church fathers. To understand their opinion and so follow Wesley's line of reasoning we must first know something of the theater in the first centuries after Christ. More than any other form of amusement the stage for the early Christian was "the invisible representative" of his old pagan life. The myths used by the plays and pantomimes preserved for the masses the superstitions and immoral content of the old religion; the songs, dances and spectacles lured them back to the emotional abandon of paganism. Because of this hold upon the common people the theater was the most subtle enemy with which Christianity had to cope.[48]

It had become so decadent that it had none of the sublimity that we associate with the great Greek dramas; in fact, it was often nothing but "an indecent means of stimulating the senses."[49] Moreover, as the inevitable opposition between the spirit of Christianity and the spirit of the theater grew, the plays began to ridicule the Christians, depicting in burlesque even martyrdom. Tunison says that Christianity for three centuries "had to endure this double punishment, to see the faithful driven in crowds a sacrifice to the demon of heathenism, and then to know that all this vast self-devotion was greeted with malicious, artificial laughter. The words of St. Paul, 'We are become a spectacle to the world, to angels, and to men,' epitomized the history of nine generations of Christians."[50]

These are a few of the reasons for unanimous opposition to the Roman theater among the greatest of the early church fathers. Those most familiar to Wesley were Tertullian, Clement of Alexandria, Cyprian, Chrysostom, Jerome and Augustine. When the church became strong enough to influence the state, actors were often denied both the sacraments and their civil rights. Not until a period of compromise between the orthodox and the liberals, who had been making some use of drama to enliven the church service, was the drama legitimatized by the church and even then the secular actor enjoyed little favor.

Fleury, to whom Wesley had turned repeatedly at the beginning of his quest for true Christianity, and to whom he sent his followers for information on the Christian pattern of conduct, gives considerable attention to the objections to the stage held by the early Christians. These may be summarized as follows:

1. The theater was inextricably associated with paganism.
2. It was the source of debauchery and dissoluteness, "a School of Immodesty."
3. It was an expression of the luxury condemned by Christian simplicity in its lavish expenditure of money.
4. It encouraged idleness.
5. It led to immorality in the promiscuous association of men and women.[51]

These tendencies in the early theater discovered by Wesley in his study of primitive Christianity were familiar also to his mentor on Christian conduct, William Law, and had influenced his well-known attack upon contemporary drama. Law shared with a small group of non-jurors, for example, Jeremy Collier, very extreme views, which he first presented in 1726 in the pamphlet entitled, *The Absolute Unlawfulness of Stage Entertainments fully Demonstrated*. Soon afterward these were repeated in the eleventh chapter of *The Practical Treatise on Christian Perfection*. Whether Wesley read the original pamphlet is not known, but the chapter in the *Practical Treatise* undoubtedly aided in bringing him to a decision on diversions that up to that time he had defended as innocent and harmless.

To Law the stage was hopelessly bad, quite beyond redemption. It was married to evil, and the only attitude toward it possible to the "complete Christian" was separation. The "almost Christian" might seek some of his diversion there, but that was due only to his lack of moral enlightenment. The first argument by which Law sought to awaken such a reader was that the language of the current plays should be offensive to the Christian. It was inconsistent to forbid one's self indecent talk and yet "hire Persons to entertain" with "impure Discourse." [52]

The action of most plays should also give offense to a person of genuine modesty. If modesty is a "real Temper and Disposition of the Heart," it can no more tolerate the indecencies of contemporary stage performance than could early Christians endure pagan drama. [53] In view of the disrepute of the acting profession it is also inconsistent for Christians to delight in "any thing that they dare not do themselves." If the actor and his mode of life are so objectionable that parents disapprove of the occupation for their children, does not the theater-goer make himself "a Partaker of other Men's Sins?" [54]

The environs of the theater, Law asserts, are "the general Rendezvous of the most profligate Persons of both Sexes," turning "the adjacent Places into Public Nuisances." [55] These conditions, he believed, were not the result of "the accidental Abuse" of a harmless diversion. The play-house was so inherently evil that it served "the Cause of Immorality and Vice, as the House of God" served the "cause of Piety." [56] It was altogether inconsistent for Christians to bewail the lewdness and debauchery of the age and yet go to the very "Fountain-Head of all Lewdness." He declares to the protesting play-goer: "I tell you that you go to hear *ribaldry* and *profaneness*; that you entertain your mind with extravagant *thoughts,* wild *rants, blasphemous speeches, wanton amours, profane jests, and impure passions.*" [57]

What in the character of the eighteenth century stage would call forth such an indictment? English drama had reached its greatest decadence in the years following the Restoration. The over-simplified explanation for this state has usually been the opposition from the Puritan dissenters. In every age the argument has been given that drama, the art form most susceptible to the evil influences of an age, must look to Christians for its support, if it is to be kept pure.

But the fact is that Puritans early in the seventeenth century had attempted to do this very thing and had met with nothing but opposition to their endeavors for reform. In the years before the theater had been closed by the Puritans as the irreconcilable foe of Christianity there had been support of the best type of plays by men like Milton, and continued attempts had been made to purge drama of its evils and to bring theaters under civil regulation. Yet in the face of these efforts plays had become more and more pagan in spirit and themes, more and more detached from moral reality, more and more hostile to Christianity, satirizing, in fact, all that it stood for.[58]

The Puritan was not hostile to art itself, a fact very clearly proved by much evidence collected by recent scholars.[59] He was opposed to materialism and immorality and, therefore, to the prostitution of art to these ends. In his efforts to release religion from its worship of material symbols he would seem to have gone too far, particularly in his destruction of church architecture; but it is doubtful whether in his efforts to cleanse amusements from their association with evil he exceeded the bounds of sound judgment. Haller, who approaches the subject without bias, concludes that "much that the Puritan condemned would have made a stench in any decent nose."[60]

Crouch, in his analysis of Puritanism and art, says that the "secret" of the quarrel between the two was really that the theater gave "a false estimate of life." The Puritan's conception of art was expressed by Milton when he declared that one who would "write well . . . ought himself to be a true poem; that is, a composition and pattern of the best and honourablest things." This, says Crouch, is not a moralistic aim, but a belief that "the highest achievements in art" can be reached only by those who have "a lofty conception of life."[61]

The closing of the theater in 1642 was therefore a proscription of an art form that had gone completely into the service of evil. It was one of those outbreaks "derisively described as Puritanism" which recur over and over again when "normally constituted people" protest against "abnormal developments in art." [62] When the theater reopened in 1660 there was again reason for the same, if not greater, remonstrance.

Charles II, returning with his dissolute court from his Continental exile, gave support to reproduction upon the stage of the profligacy that characterized his own life and that of his followers. The moral code that ruled the plays as well as the lives of the actors and that determined even the environs of the theater was again flagrantly pagan and a disgrace to any Christian nation.[63]

Flirtation and amorous intrigue, conducted with grace and cleverness, had become the proper pastime of gallants and became in turn the favorite dramatic theme. Seduction was disapproved only when clumsily accomplished, and the stratagems of the seducer became for years the chief source of plot interest in both the play and the early forms of the novel. By the end of the seventeenth century, when Jeremy Collier published his *View of the Immorality and Profaneness of the English Stage*, indecency was so much a part of the action "that ladies, if they were bold enough to go to a new play, were forced to wear masks, presumably to hide their blushes, or the fact that they could not blush." [64]

The extent to which disregard for moral law now ruled the stage was recognized by only a few critics of insight. Swift was one of these; he complained, "I do not remember that our English poets ever suffered a criminal amour to succeed upon the stage until the reign of Charles II. Ever since that time, the alderman is made cuckold, the deluded virgin is debauched, and adultery and fornication are supposed to be committed behind the scenes as part of the action."[65]

Naturally the life of actors and actresses, which had never been above reproach, became especially dissolute at this time.

Actresses had been admitted into companies only in 1662, and were, almost without exception, of easy virtue. Peg Woffington, famous as Polly Peachum in Gay's *Beggars' Opera*, said after numerous affairs that included even the great David Garrick that she would never allow her sister, if she could help it, to become an actress, because of the life that went with it.[66] The farther one reads in stage biographies of the day the less extravagant seems Whitefield's famous assertion, "When you see the players on the stage, you see the Devil's children grinning at you."[67]

Because of their irregularities traveling companies of actors were classified as vagabonds and banned by a law, declaring, "All common players of interludes, and all persons who for hire or reward, act or cause to be acted, any interlude or entertainment of the stage . . . shall be deemed rogues and vagabonds, and be punished accordingly."[68]

The environs of the theater inevitably took on the character of the people of the stage. Contemporary records show the change that quickly occurred in any neighborhood when a theater moved in. *The Gentleman's Magazine* of April, 1735, stated that, "Whereas the street in which the theatre is built used formerly to be inhabited by silk throwsters, ribbon weavers, and others . . . now there is a bunch of grapes hanging at every door besides an adjacent bagnio or two." A new playhouse meant a new set of houses of ill fame.

The theater apparently continued to be a public nuisance throughout the eighteenth century, for Sir John Hawkins, friend and biographer of Dr. Johnson, wrote in 1789: "Although of plays it is said that they teach morality, and of the stage that it is the mirror of human life, these assertions are mere declamation . . . on the contrary, a play-house and the regions about it, are the very hot-beds of vice: how else comes it to pass that no sooner is a play-house opened in any part of the kingdom, than it at once becomes surrounded by a halo of brothels?" From his observation he cites one instance where to his knowledge "the sum of 1300 pounds" had been expended "for the purpose of removing those inhabitants, whom, for the instruction in human life, the play-house had drawn thither." [70]

Prostitutes even carried on their solicitation within the theater, and W. C. Sydney in his *England and the English in the Eighteenth Century* goes so far in his comment upon vices accompanying the stage as to say: "The reader would err . . . were he to suppose that it was the attractions of the stage that induced the majority of fine gentlemen in the last century to resort to the three principal theatres of London . . . it was the attractions presented by the saloons of the playhouses (establishments which partook as much of the nature of brothels as they did of taverns); which filled the benches of the theaters with visitors, and the purses of those who kept them with coin of the realm." [71]

In 1704 Congreve and Van Brugh, the leading dramatists, were appointed by Queen Anne to form a company for bringing the stage under stricter regulation, but in a short time Van Brugh himself was prosecuted for objectionable passages in "The Provoked Wife." The real character of Congreve's plays, the most brilliant stage offerings of the time, was truly perceived by Dr. Johnson fifty years later, when he wrote: "It is acknowledged with universal conviction that the perusal of his works will make no man better; and their ultimate effect is to represent pleasure in alliance with vice, and to relax those obligations by which life ought to be regulated." [72]

A relaxing of "those obligations by which life ought to be regulated"—there is the recurrent tendency in the theater, which in turn must provoke the recurrent remonstrance from Christianity. Already those obligations had been relaxed in eighteenth century society, and in the theater the masses found encouragement toward further relaxation. It was a vicious circle which moved ever downward. Portus observes: "the plain truth was, and is, that the stage reflects national manners. If the reformers wanted to raise the tone of the stage they would have to raise the tone of contemporary London life. Short of this there was no way of restraining the writing and acting of plays like those of Wycherley, Congreve, and Van Brugh without returning" to control resembling that of the Commonwealth."

But how could the tone of London life be raised? Certainly not by continuing patronage of the theater, nor by a return of state control over the theater. Under the widened separation between the powers of state and church no such control would again be attempted. Therefore, Law and Wesley were convinced that the individual Christian, and particularly the member of the State Church, must exercise his private judgment and chart his own independent course in a diversion that was no more lawful than it had been under the Commonwealth.

The position taken by the early Methodist on the theater was not understood and brought upon him satiric treatment in current drama. His way of life was held up to malicious laughter upon the stage just as the early Christian way had been. At Newcastle in the same year as the *General Rules* were issued a farce was announced to follow the performance of *The Conscious Lovers,* entitled *Trick upon Trick, or Methodism Displayed.* " Through the years various satires followed, *The Minor,* by Samuel Foote, being the most popular.

Painful as these public misrepresentations must have been, Wesley never met them with tirades against the theater. In fact, he was quite above that kind of defense of his position. Rarely did he offer any criticism of the theater to non-Christians, and when he did it was always in the spirit of "sweet reasonableness."

In 1764, when he learned that proposals had been made for the building of a play-house in Bristol, a city where Methodism had become very strong, he decided to make known to the city officials the concern felt by his followers and himself. The arguments presented were of three sorts: religious, moral and economic.

The one religious objection which he selects is very significant: "the present stage entertainments . . . tend to efface all traces of piety and seriousness out of the minds of men." Thus "the foundation of all religion"[75] is gradually weakened and national life is de-christianized. That is to say, in its subtle assault upon virtuous and disciplined living the theater is still, as in early Christian days, the representative of paganism rather than of Christianity.

However, this religious objection, Wesley takes pains to emphasize, is only one of the arguments against the building of a theater in Bristol. ". . . drinking and debauchery of every kind are constant attendants on these entertainments."[76] He is using here Law's most repeated criticism, the play-house is "the inlet to sin," but he goes on to broader implications. Law had directed his remarks mainly to Christian individuals who in patronizing the theater encouraged the attendant evils. Wesley calls attention also to the social and economic consequences which follow in the wake of these evils.

The "indolence, effeminacy, and idleness," which accompany drunkenness and debauchery affect trade. They give a "wrong turn to youth" and are "directly opposite to the spirit of industry and close application to business."[77] The theater is a link in a chain of evils which are bound to demoralize even the economic life.

The social historians from whom we have been quoting show the strangle hold which this chain of evils had gained upon London life. Mrs. George finds, from her study of eighteenth century families, that most of the lower class youth were loose livers, who, though receiving higher wages than ever paid before, saved nothing, but spent all upon drink, gambling and vice.[78]

From the distance of two centuries we can see more clearly than could men of that day the forces that were undermining English life. But Wesley had the unusual opportunity of observing these facts first-hand in hundreds of homes. He had, through his moral awakening, not only a true insight into the decadence of his age, but he had also possession of a wealth of facts known to no other man. He knew that he must awaken England to all the destructive influences which popular amusements exercised upon the spiritual, moral and economic well-being of the nation.

This insight into the ramifications of eighteenth century paganism was undoubtedly one of the causes for the broad outreach of the Methodist revival. Complete Christianity meant "total obedience in the total life." The application of this principle first revealed to the individual his moral inadequacy and then exposed the social and economic areas of national life that were pagan. As a consequence, the nineteenth century saw a host of movements designed to Christianize every aspect of personal and national life.

We have noted that Wesley when addressing non-Christians never entered into a tirade against the theater; neither did he when speaking to Methodists. He assumed that a full understanding of the implications of perfect love to God and man would dispose automatically of their patronage of the stage. He granted that there were Christians who did not hold this point of view. As in the case of dancing and card-playing, he made "allowances for *those that are without*" the Methodist Societies." They sought pleasure from such sources because of their lack of moral sensitivity and their failure to see the need of time for Kingdom-building. Perhaps, too, they had never found the happiness that perfect love brings.

There is a very important distinction here between a *principle* applied to conduct and a *rule* superimposed upon conduct. The *Rules* were voluntarily adopted by Methodists because they saw and accepted the full meaning of the principle of love; but they had no intention of imposing them upon others who had not seen the principle. As we have said before, Wesley believed that where there is moral insight there is no desire to compromise with any intermixture of good and evil. Hence the application of the principle of love to specific problems becomes clear to "every awakened heart." For this reason in his public services he rarely preached on popular diversions.

He advised his ministers not to speak of them to unawakened people. "It will anger, not convince them," he said. "It is beginning at the wrong end." He illustrated this by quoting from a London preacher who said: "If you take away his rattles from the child, he will be angry; nay, if he can, he will scratch or bite you. But give him something better first, and he will throw away the rattles himself.' " [80]

In his attitude toward the play itself, it would seem that Wesley was less severe than Law. He did not approve of reading the objectionable current plays, but he himself read Shakespeare and many other dramatists. His own much perused and annotated copy of Shakespeare, which was mistakenly destroyed by an obscurantist follower, would be a rare treasure today. He was so tolerant as to comment favorably upon a play which had brought about the resignation of its writer, a clergyman, from his church in Scotland. Praising *Douglas* as one of the finest tragedies he had ever read, he regretted that a few lines had not been omitted.[81]

He was especially fond of tragedy. He even went so far as to say that a good deal might be said "in defense of seeing a serious tragedy," but added, "I could not do it with a clear conscience; at least not in an English theater." [82] He did go to see the boys at Westminster school present the *Adelphi* of Terence and described it as "an entertainment not unworthy of a Christian." [83]

It is quite clear, however, that the theater, like the dance, was condemned, first of all, because it was inextricably associated with evils; secondly, because it so rarely contributed to the growth of Christian personality; thirdly, because it often threatened the supremacy of God's will in the life, a fact particularly applicable to the actor; and, fourthly, because, by and large, the building of a Christian world leaves little time for any sort of diversion.

"TIME IN MASQUERADE"   183

Wesley's general statement concerning diversions in his sermon on "The More Excellent Way" furnishes a fitting summary and comment on all that we have said on the subject of amusements. After dismissing cudgelling, bear- and bull-baiting, cock-fighting and other like sports as "foul remains of Gothic barbarity," and passing over fox-hunting and horse-racing with a word of censure, he speaks more favorably of tragedy, as we have indicated above, and then continues:

> I cannot say quite so much for balls or assemblies, which, though more reputable than masquerades, yet must be allowed by all impartial persons to have exactly the same tendency. So, undoubtedly, have all public dancings. And the same tendency they must have, unless the same caution obtained among modern Christians which was observed among the ancient Heathens. With them, men and women never danced together, but always in separate rooms. . . . Of playing cards I say the same as of seeing plays. I could not do it with a clear conscience. But I am not obliged to pass any sentence on those that are otherwise minded. I leave them to their own Master: to Him let them stand or fall.[84]

"But," he suggests, "suppose these . . . quite innocent diversions, yet are there not more excellent ways of diverting themselves for those that love or fear God?" He then proposes outdoor exercise, gardening, visiting with neighbors, reading in history, poetry and natural philosophy. Music is also recommended and scientific experimentation, which to Wesley was a fascinating diversion. All entertainment was to be innocent, free from questionable association, and contributory to social and spiritual well-being.[85]

---

1. William Cowper, "The Task," Poetical Works, p. 169, 11. 223-5.
2. George, op. cit., p. 314.
3. F. D. P. Senior, The Life and Times of Colley Cibber (London: Henkle, 1928), p. xiv.
4. Sykes, op. cit., p. 186 et seq.
5. Letters, I, 15.
6. Journal, I, Introduction, pp. 19-25.
7. Works, XI, 462.
8. Elton, op. cit., p. 206.
9. Works, VI, 243.
10. Anonymous, The Oxford Methodists, p. 8.

11. William Law, *An Earnest and Serious Answer to Dr. Trapp's Discourse* . . ., p. 20.
12. *Loc. cit.*
13. *Letters*, I, 92.
14. *Letters*, III, 125.
15. *Works*, VII, 504.
16. *Loc. cit.*
17. *Works*, VII, 504.
18. *Sermons*, II, 319.
19. Anonymous, *The Trial of Mr. Whitefield's Spirit* (London: Printed for T. Gardner, 1740), p. 44.
20. Law, *Works*, III, 179.
21. *Letters*, VI. 47.
22. *Loc. cit.*
23. *Journal*, I, Introduction, p. 19.
24. *Letters*, VII, 228.
25. Edmund Gibson, "Mischief of Masquerades," Gibson MSS iv, 26, as quoted in Sykes, *op. cit.*, p. 187.
26. Sykes, *op. cit.*, p. 187.
27. *Ibid.*, p. 188.
28. J. Wesley Bready, *England Before and After Wesley* (London: Hodder & Stoughton, 1939), p. 160.
29. George, *op. cit.*, p. 272. Dr. George found life stories of many men who came to ruin through drink and gambling.
30. Jay Barrett Botsford, *English Society in the Eighteen Century* (New York: Macmillan, 1924), p. 249.
31. *Loc. cit.*
32. *Sermons*, II, 316.
33. Lawson, *op. cit.*, p. 268.
34. *Letters*, VIII, 12.
35. *Works*, VIII, 34.
36. Leslie F. Church, *The Early Methodist People* (London: Epworth Press, 1948), p. 213.
37. E. Stanley Jones, op. cit., p. 293. Dr. Jones says to those in The Way: "Your world of entertainment has become simple. When there is nothing to entertain you from without, you can do what the ancient scripture says, 'draw waters out of your own well.' The reason for the passionate demand for entertainment and diversions is that the well within is dry."
38. See Appendix.
39. *Works*, VIII, 354. Wesley says that the Methodists may be accounted new in abstaining from "fashionable diversions, from reading plays, romances, or books of humor, from singing innocent songs, or talking in a merry, gay, diverting manner . . ."
40. Law, *op. cit.*, p. 151.
41. See Bready, *op. cit.*, p. 163.
42. Law, *op. cit.*, p. 153.
43. Tyerman, *op. cit.*, p. 367. Quoted from Wesley's abridgement of Norris' *Reflections upon the Conduct of Human Life.*
44. Claude Fleury, *An Historical Account of the Manners and Behaviour of the Christians: and the Practices of Christianity throughout the Several Ages of the Church* (London: Printed for Thomas Leigh, 1698), pp. 54-5.
45. *Works*, *op. cit.*, p. 354.
46. George Whitefield, *A Preservative against Unsettled Notions, and Want of Principles in regard to Righteousness and Christian Perfection* (London: Globe, 1739), p. 13.
47. *Works*, VII, 34.
48. Joseph S. Tunison, *Dramatic Traditions of the Dark Ages* (Chicago: Chicago University Press, 1907), p. 13.
49. Joseph Crouch, *Puritanism and Art* (London: Cassell & Co., 1910), p. 280.
50. Tunison, *op. cit.*, p. 7.
51. Fleury, *op. cit.*, pp. 68-9.
52. Law, *op. cit.*, p. 171.
53. *Ibid.*, p. 175.
54. *Ibid.*, p. 172.
55. *Ibid.*, p. 177.
56. *Ibid.*, p. 173.
57. Law, *Works*, II, 6.
58. Crouch, *op. cit.*, p. 147.
59. See Percy Scholes, *The Puritans and Music* (London: Oxford Press, 1934); Haller, *op. cit.*; Perry, *op. cit.*; Perry Miller-Thomas H. Johnson, *The Puritans* (New York, American Book Co., 1938).
60. Haller, *op. cit.*, p. 221.
61. Crouch, *op. cit.*, p. 171.
62. *Ibid.*, p. 26.
63. Harrison quotes from Evelyn's criticism that "foul and indecent women now . . . are permitted to appear and act . . . become mistresses or wives of noblemen." Among those named are the Earl of Oxford, Sir Robert Howard,

Prince Rupert, the Earl of Dorset, "and another greater person than any of them, who fell into their snares, to the reproach of their noble families, and the ruin of both body and soul." A. W. Harrison, *Liberal Puritanism* (London: Epworth Press, 1935), p. 16.
64. Senior, op. cit., p. 36.
65. Jonathan Swift, "Project for the Advancement of Religion," I, 161, as quoted by Bready, op. cit., p. 164.
66. *Ibid.*, p. 166.
67. T. B. Shepherd, *Methodism and the Literature of the Eighteenth Century* (London: Epworth Press, 1940), p. 189. Shepherd quotes from a biography of a converted actor, John Dungett, whose opinion of the stage is pertinent: "He had been behind the scenes, and knew well the abominations of the theatre, and especially its utter inadequacy as a medium of moral instruction. He had seen the monster without its mask, and he was not backward to declare its features to be awful and hideous."
68. T. B. Shepherd, "Methodists and the Theatre in Eighteenth Century." Proceedings of Wesleyan Historical Society, XX, 166.
69. Quoted in *The Gentleman's Magazine*, April, 1735, pp. 191-2.
70. Sir John Hawkins, *The Life of Samuel Johnson* (London: Pr. J. Buckland et al., 1787), pp. 75-6.
71. W. C. Sydney, *England and the English in the Eighteenth Century* (London: Ward & Downey, 1891), I, 161.
72. Quoted by Norman Marshall in Introduction, *The Comedies of William Congreve* (London: John Lehmann, 1948), p. 11.
73. Portus, op. cit., p. 177.
74. Tyerman, op. cit., I, 404.
75. *Letters*, IV, 279.
76. Loc. cit.
77. Loc. cit.
78. George, op. cit., p. 314.
79. *Letters*, VIII, 12.
80. Loc. cit.
81. *Journal*, IV, 218.
82. *Works*, VII, 34.
83. *Journal*, V, 294.
84. *Works*, VII, 35.
85. *Ibid.*, p. 36.

XI

"The World Is too Much With Us"

"The world is too much with us," Wordsworth complained in 1806.

> ". . . late and soon,
> Getting and spending, we lay waste our powers:
> Little we see in Nature that is ours;
> We have given our hearts away, a sordid boon!"[1]

More than half a century before, Wesley had recognized the soul-blight of materialism and had issued a call back to "plain living and high thinking." But the road had lain, not through a return to Nature, but through utter commitment to Christ, who is the Way to the solution of every problem. The result was a simplification of life that finally appealed to many otherwise untouched by the Methodist Revival and quite unaware that this simplification had to a considerable degree been brought about by the leavening influence of Wesley's teaching on the Christian use of money.

His thought on the subject, like his thought on leisure, had been shaped by his home training and his reading at Oxford. Bebb thinks his mother largely responsible for his early views[2] and Baker gives evidence of later influence from Law.[3] The fact is that Wesley's belief that the use of wealth is the *most* important criterion of practical Christianity was based, first of all, upon his thorough knowledge of New Testament teaching, and secondly, upon the reiteration of this teaching by the early Church fathers.

Law's convincing interpretation of the essential nature of Christianity enforced this point of view, and his observations of developments within the Societies when the economic status of

Methodists improved afforded factual evidence. Just as his views on justification and Christian Perfection were clarified by observed Christian experience, so his original theories on wealth found substantiation in fact as time went by.

Had Wesley followed Taylor he would have held a view more Catholic than Protestant, for Taylor condemned wealth *per se,* asserting that poverty is better because it throws men upon God and develops faith.[4] But to Law money was not inherently evil. It was a good which is susceptible to corruption. When not spent for the good of others it must be spent to the hurt of one's self. Law taught Wesley to view wealth, like all other gifts, in the light of stewardship, and, more than that, to single it out in particular as "both a responsibility and an opportunity for the practice of Christian Perfection."[5]

Law's treatment of the arguments commonly offered for the accumulation and retention of riches is so searching as to expose the fundamental insincerity of most professed followers of Christ. In the form of a prayer he satirizes the real intent of those who seek for more than natural needs require:

> O Lord, I thy sinful Creature, who am born again to a lively Hope of Glory in Christ Jesus, beg of thee, to grant me a *thousand* times more Riches than I *need,* that I may be able to gratify Myself and Family in the Delights of Eating and Drinking, State and Grandeur, grant that as the little Span of Life wears out, I may still abound more and more in Wealth, and that I may see and perceive all the best and surest Ways of growing Richer than any of my Neighbours: this I humbly and fervently Beg.[6]

Those who recoil from this prayer may be sure "that the same Things which make an unchristian Prayer, make an unchristian life."[7]

To observe this quest for superior wealth, power, and sensual gratification, Law says, we "need not go amongst Villains and People of scandalous Characters." It is professing Christians who "catch at all Ways of Gain that are not scandalous, and who hardly think anything enough, except it equals and exceeds the Estate of their Neighbours."[8]

Law dismisses brusquely the time-worn plea for the social and economic benefits that accrue from an amassed fortune, driving home his argument by an illustration drawn from the parable of Dives. "The *rich Man* in Torments could have alleged how much Good he did with his Fortune, how many Trades he encouraged by his *Purple* and *fine Linen,* and faring sumptuously every Day, and how he conformed to the Ends and Advantages of Society by so spending his Estate." This is not an alternative, he says, to the New Testament command to plain living: "Having Food and Raiment, let us be therewith content." [9]

The fundamental reason for Christ's simplification of life is the subtle rivalry which riches set up with God. In the case of Dives "no Injustice, no Villainies or Extortions" are "laid to his Charge." His evil was simply "the bare pleasurable Enjoyment, the living in the usual Delights of great Fortune," [10] instead of in the love of God and mankind.

The power of money to wean the affections away from God can be seen among the poor as well as among the rich. The worldly cares that arise in the quest cause trouble for all alike, and worldly cares are just as destructive of the soul as are worldly pleasures. They are just as "vain and shameful, as any sensual Gratifications when they . . . divide or possess the Heart." [11]

Pursuit of wealth destroys the love of mankind also. Law attributes the rise of the whole system of social caste to it, declaring, "The Gospel has made no Provision for Dignity of *Birth* or Difference in Fortune." [12] The desire "to abound in wealth, to have fine houses, and rich clothes, to be beautiful in our persons, to have titles of dignity, to be above our fellow-creatures, to command the bows and obeisance of other people. . . ." [13] all have led to the present state of society, whereas "if we could submit to its (the Scripture's) plain and repeated Doctrines, it would never be asked, what people of Birth and Fortune are to do with themselves, if they are not to live up to the Splendour and plenty of their Estates." [14]

Law's literal and logical interpretations of Christ's condemnation of the love of money and its attendant evils were exemplified for Wesley in the lives and practices of the early Christians. He saw in them a demonstration of the quality of life demanded by pure, disinterested love. He seems to have been particularly impressed by Cave's and Fleury's accounts of the manners of the early Church, and for fifty years he enforced the principles learned from Law by illustrations drawn from these two authorities.

Fleury pointed out that direct acquaintance with Christ among the Christians of Jerusalem had prompted the "Communication of Goods." "They had always before their Eyes the Commandment of Jesus Christ, of loving one another, so often repeated by him, and particularly the night before he suffered, making this the distinguishing Character by which all men were to know that they were his Disciples."[15] Therefore many, acting upon this principle, reduced themselves to voluntary poverty by their gifts to the poor. The Christians had ushered in a new age by depending upon "the Grace of Jesus" to change, first, the motives and then the conduct."[16]

Wesley's vision of "a Christian world," which from the beginning of his ministry he presented as the inevitable goal of fully operative love, was inspired by his acquaintance with this phenomenon of the first century. It should be noted, however, that neither Cave nor Fleury influenced him to adopt a theory of communism. Cave says that, while at first all was held in common, this state did not long continue.[17] The Church "did not consider it unlawful to hold property and industriously mind the *necessary* conveniences of this life, so far as was *consistent* with their care of a better."[18] Fleury also stresses the fact that they lived as separate families, going from house to house to break bread. Poverty was banished through the operation of brotherly love rather than through superimposed regulation.[19]

Both authorities emphasize the Christian's freedom from

worldly care. Cave remarks that "they were not concern'd for more than what would supply the necessities of nature, or the wants of others." [20] Fleury says that they were careful to choose such callings as were "most consistent with Retirement and Humility." [21] They simply lived upon their labour and their estates, dividing "among the Poor, without distraction of thought, without the hurry of Business." They not only refused "all sordid Methods of Gain" but also "the very desire of heaping up Treasures and enriching themselves." [22]

The thoroughness with which Wesley sought to incorporate these principles and practices of the early Christians in the Methodist way of life will be apparent as we discuss his teaching on various aspects of getting and spending. We shall first consider his ideas about the gaining of money.

Work is worship in the fullest sense for Wesley. It is to be chosen and pursued in the same spirit of devotion as characterizes one's prayers. In support of this view he quotes Law: "If a man pursues his business, that he may raise himself to a state of figure and riches in the world, he is no longer serving God in his employment, and has no more title to reward from God, than he who gives alms that he may be seen, or prays that he may be heard, of men. For vain and earthly designs are no more allowable in our employments, than in our alms and devotions . . . . our common employment cannot be reckoned a service to him when it is not performed with the same piety of heart." [23]

It is apparent that Wesley adopts the Reformation doctrine of work as a calling, but it is also true that he carefully guards the doctrine from abuse by repeated warnings against the tendency of work to become something other than worship. He says: "If you act in the spirit of Christ, you carry the end you at first proposed through all your work from first to last. You do everything in the spirit of sacrifice, giving up your will to the will of God; and continually aiming . . . at the glory of God." [24]

When work fills the mind with secular interests it becomes the enemy of Christianity. The very best of employments may do this. Yet, the remedy is not to "give up" business, but rather to "contract it" in order that one "may have more leisure for business of greater importance." [25] Wesley talked a great deal to his followers about "sitting loose" to all earthly interests and would surely have condemned the complete absorption in commerce that characterizes many modern Christians.

He was greatly concerned for the spiritual life of his successful business friends, among them the banker, Blackwell. His frequent letters to him contain such counsel as this: "I find the engaging, though but a little in these temporal affairs is apt to damp and deaden the soul; and there is no remedy but continual prayer. What, then, but the mighty power of God can keep your soul alive, who are engaged all the day long in such a multiplicity of them? It is well that His grace is sufficient for you. But do you not find need to pray always? And if you can't always say,

> "My hands are but employed below,
> My heart is still with Thee."

is there not the more occasion for some season of solemn retirement (if it were possible, every day), wherein you may withdraw your mind from earth, and even the accounts between God and your own soul?" [26]

A decisive factor in converting all of work into worship is one's choice of employment. Wesley frequently said to Methodists: "Dare any of you, in choosing your calling or situation, eye the things on earth, rather than the things above?" [27] In his later ministry he became particularly outspoken against "the vile earthly-mindedness" that governed the choices made by many parents for the vocations of their sons, for he foresaw in this the secularization of second generation Methodists.

Any work pursued for the love of money kills the soul, but some sorts of work are inherently linked with evil. Such work

Methodists were advised to leave upon conversion, no matter what might be the arguments for continuing or the consequences of leaving.

Work which harms either body or soul should be refused. Wesley treats such work under two general heads: first, that which hurts the worker; and, secondly, that which hurts the worker's neighbor. No promise of gain should ever induce us to enter employment that deprives us of proper seasons for food and sleep or impairs the constitution through unhealthful surroundings. Since the life is "more valuable than meat," and the body "than raiment," we must not put gain ahead of health.[28]

We are reminded here once more of the comprehensiveness of the Methodist scheme. We shall find various instructions like these that seem to involve no immediate moral issue; yet they have importance because they bear directly upon the subject of effective Christian living. It is as Bebb says, ". . . if a man regards himself and his possessions as a solemn trust from God, his whole conduct must be thereby modified."[29]

The Methodist regulations have often been misinterpreted because they have not been understood as means toward the complete articulation of life in a plan for world Christianization. That was Wesley's reason for calling the Wesleyan way "the more excellent way." He said repeatedly that, while he did not unchristianize those who had not fully adopted it, he had little hope for world redemption without a general acceptance of it.

In his discussion of work which injures the mind of the worker Wesley gives particular attention to the preservation of healthful mental states. Too much stress cannot be placed upon early Methodist teaching concerning a healthful mind; this was a most important aspect of the theory of Christian Perfection. For example, the paying of customs was advised,[30] not only because it was required by law, but also because law-breaking created guilt and confusion in the soul. Then as now certain types of business, though innocent in themselves, had become so corrupted that a competent maintenance could not be secured from them without lying, cheating or conforming to some evil custom. No amount of gain could compensate for the accusing conscience created by such practices; starving was to be preferred.[31]

Wesley also made room for individual differentiation in choice of work. He cited as an example his own avoidance of those studies which inclined him toward atheism, although he recognized that another might not be similarly influenced. Each Christian must decide what work is most conducive to the health of his own body and soul.[32]

Of equal concern to the Methodist should be the effect of his chosen work upon his neighbor. In keeping with the Golden Rule he will treat the possessions, the body and the soul of his fellow as he would his own. "We cannot," Wesley says, "if we love every one as ourselves, hurt any one *in his substance*. We cannot devour the increase of his lands, and perhaps the lands and houses themselves," by an admittedly evil practice such as gambling, nor by a less condemned method, such as foreclosing for "overgrown bills," no matter whether it be medical or legal debts or any other sort.[33]

The General Rule on unlawful interest, "giving or taking things on usury," makes explicit the Christian's relation to his neighbor's substance. In Wesley's time the highest rate permitted was five per cent. Wesley saw clearly the fundamental conflict between the principle of Christian love and the economic principle of self-interest, and declared: "We cannot, consistent with brotherly love, sell our goods below the market-price; we cannot study to ruin our neighbor's trade, in order to advance our own; much less can we entice away, or receive, any of his servants or workmen whom he has need of."[34]

The only interpretation that can be given this passage is that he did not believe that free economic competition automatically fixes a fair price on goods. He held the ancient Christian theory of the " 'Just Price,' imposed upon commerce by ethical considerations."[35] He held, Lawson says, the belief preserved by

High Church Toryism from mediaeval times that "Church and State were to go hand in hand in regulating 'just prices' and conditions of work, and in preventing 'usury' and the making of profit by holding goods to await a rise in the market." [36]

This Christian economic tradition was soon to disappear completely with the triumph of modern industrialism, and what theory Wesley would have substituted for it is, of course, impossible to say; but this much is certain: Wesley would not have accepted any economic system which is inconsistent with brotherly love nor agreed with the contention of the modern industrialist that a man's position and wealth are to be attributed to his own ability and enterprise. He would have condemned this as "an excess of human pride." [37] The results of industry must be attributed to God and must be distributed under his direction.

He would have insisted that self-interest with its eye upon possessions, place or power cannot motivate the Christian business man, for it is the sworn and irreconcilable enemy of love of others. He would also have insisted that an economic society created by self-interest cannot be transmuted by any sort of specious argument into a Christian society. He would certainly have said to the modern business man, tempted to use commonly approved methods that ruin a competitor's trade, just as he said to his followers, facing equally severe temptations: "None can gain by swallowing up his neighbor's substance, without gaining the damnation of hell!" [38]

Wesley believed literally that "love will dictate the manner" by which to proceed in settling every problem. Was this a hopelessly impractical approach to the problems of the eighteenth century? So it seemed at the beginning of the Methodist movement, yet it proved amazingly workable in some cases where it was tried out. A good example of the successful application of the theory is to be found in Wesley's treatment of trades that harm the bodies of men.

The trade most deserving of this description in his time was the manufacture and sale of spirituous liquors. There is no question but that this constituted an evil of proportions never equaled before or since in England. All the social historians give facts to support this view. And when Wesley prohibited in the *General Rules* the "buying or selling spirituous liquors, or drinking them, unless in cases of extreme necessity," he was challenging the accepted practice of both the individual and the state. Besant says that drink "threatened, literally, to destroy the whole of the working classes of London,"[39] and Mrs. George finds, after a lengthy analysis of social and moral conditions, that "it would be impossible to exaggerate the horrors of the gin-drinking period at its worst between 1720 and 1750."[40]

The blame for this reign of horrors, during which the sale of liquor reached 11,000,000 gallons,[41] must be laid first of all at the door of an unchristian economic system. To compete with French importation of brandy and to dispose of an over-production of corn the English government encouraged distillers by a reduction of duties to greatly increase their output. The product was cheap, fiery and extremely intoxicating, brutalizing the drinker; but the profits were huge, and the greed which corrodes men's sense of social responsibility led many into its manufacture and sale. Besant reports that one in every four houses in London sold spirits either secretly or openly;[42] Bready says that of the 2000 houses in St. Giles 506 were gin shops.[43]

Taverns became the centers for social life, for business transactions, and even for certain types of religious groups. Apprentices spent all their evenings there, wages were paid there, with the consequence that little remained when the worker finally left; and the rector met his vestrymen there for church business.

With such a hold upon the national life and with vested interests so strongly entrenched, it is no wonder that the liquor traffic seemed to thoughtful men beyond reform—a force that could be used to debauch the whole nation,[44] and it is true that reform could have come only through a transformation in the ideals and appetites of the people. All moral perspective had been lost. The three acts passed by the government between 1736 and 1753 restricting the freedom of the distiller made little impression upon the trade[45] because they had no popular support.

Not until the Methodist Revival had changed the personal appetites of the worker and led him to regard the social and moral welfare of himself and all about him as his sacred responsibility did any extensive change take place. Methodist teaching struck at the root of the liquor traffic and awoke the national conscience.

It said to the worker, enslaved to drink:

> You strip yourself of your understanding. You do all you can to make yourself a mere beast; not a fool, not a madman only, but a swine, a poor filthy swine. . . . You stir up all the devilish tempers that are in you, and gain others, which perhaps were not in you; at least you heighten and increase them. . . . So you are now just fit for every work of the devil, having cast off all that is good and virtuous, and filled your heart with everything that is bad, that is earthly, sensual, devilish. You have forced the Spirit of God to depart from you. . . .[46]

It said of the manufacturer and seller:

> . . . all who sell . . . are poisoners general. They murder His Majesty's subjects by wholesale. . . . And what is their gain? Is it not the blood of these men? Who then would envy their large estates and sumptuous palaces? A curse is in the midst of them: the curse of God cleaves to the stones, the timber, the furniture of them! The curse of God is in their gardens, their walks, their groves; a fire that burns to the nethermost hell! Blood, blood, is there: the foundation, the floor, the walls, the roof are stained with blood![47]

It said to the English citizen:

> It is amazing that the preparing or selling this poison should be permitted (I will not say in any Christian country, but) in any civilized state. 'O, it brings in a considerable sum of money to the Government.' True; but is it wise to barter men's lives for money? Surely, that gold is bought too dear, if it is the price of blood. Does not the strength of every country consist in the

number of its inhabitants? If so, the lessening their number is a loss which no money can compensate.⁴⁸

Wesley was very patient with the habitual drinker, inciting him never to cast away hope, never to despair of conquering.⁴⁹ But he was neither patient nor tolerant with those who contrived or believed specious arguments for the continuance of the trade. He recognized how easy it was for vested interests "to procure ingenious men to plead for them," and how few men are "neither blinded by interests nor carried away by popular clamour," who "will attend to the voice of reason, and be persuaded to save their money and preserve" the health of their families.⁵⁰ Yet eventually there were enough of such men, transformed by the Revival into this character, to accomplish effective legislation. The nineteenth century saw the spread of a temperance movement of international proportions. This outcome for gin-drinking is an impressive instance of the power of the gospel of love when its full meaning is accepted and put into operation.

Not only the sale of liquor, but all trades which minister directly or indirectly to intemperance or unchastity were forbidden the Methodist.⁵¹ We have already seen that he included under this head "taverns, victualling-houses, opera-houses, playhouses." His criterion is exacting: "If these profit the souls of men, you are clear; your employment is good, and your gain innocent; but if they are either sinful in themselves, or natural inlets to sin of various kinds, then . . . you have a sad account to make."⁵² He who contributes to another's sin will share in the punishment.

These counsels on occupational choices first given by Wesley in 1744 in his sermon upon "The Use of Money," were repeated at least twenty-two times in the repreaching of the sermon and were circulated in print as well. So far as the records reveal, Methodists as a rule acted upon them and by and large refrained from entrance into questionable types of employment.

This cannot be said so certainly of Methodist acceptance of

Wesley's instruction on methods of business. For example, the rule which forbids "the *using many words* in buying and selling"[53] was not as fully observed among early Methodists as among Friends. Methodists were not known as were the Quakers for their refusal to haggle over prices. It is now recognized that "the Quakers introduced the one-price system into Europe in obedience to the suggestion of Jesus that 'your communication be Yea, yea; Nay, nay.' " Jones says that this "abandonment of the bargaining system which was prevalent in Europe, as it is now prevalent in Asia, has saved civilization millions of years in time and untold temper."[54]

The entire simplification of speech which produced such a remarkable result as this was nevertheless one of Wesley's ideals. It is true that he felt that the peculiar language of the Friends had become a mere formalism with them[55]; but he saw that the adoption of this elementary principle outlined in the *Rules* would inevitably preclude the other unchristian practices which he enumerates: *"Fighting, quarrelling, brawling;* brother *going to law* with brother; returning *evil for evil* or *railing for railing. . . ."* He was very severe with Methodists who took legal action against one another, considering it—as it was—a scandal to a Christian community.[56]

The Methodist convert, evolving often from a state close to sheer paganism, needed much education in the practical meanings of honesty. The rule against "Borrowing without a probability of paying, or taking up goods without probability of paying for them,"[57] was necessary. He was made aware also of the prevalent evils of bribery in voting and was told that he must not eat or drink at the expense of candidates for election. He was to regard his vote as seriously as though the election results depended wholly upon himself.

The practice which offered Methodists the greatest temptation was smuggling, which we might aptly compare to tax evasion in the twentieth century. The historian looks upon it as "part of the general situation of low business ethics."[58] Like gambling, it expressed the bent of the time toward speculation and the deterioration of the national sense of honesty. In high circles were the government lotteries, of which the South Sea Bubble was the most notorious,[59] and among the lower classes was an almost universal trade in stolen goods. Besant says that in mid-century London as many as three thousand people "bought without question whatever was brought to them for sale," the value of property stolen often amounting to 700,000 pounds. This along with other signs of the times is taken by Besant to indicate the total destruction of the moral principle "among a vast body of the lower ranks."[60] Really this condemnation should not be reserved for the common people alone, for some of the most scrupulous merchants dealt in uncustomed goods, as well as evading the excessive tax levies; and members of Parliament under Walpole frankly accepted bribery as "the normal process of government."[61]

It is no wonder, then, that Wesley struck hard at this particular symptom of national dishonesty found among Methodists and included in the list of prohibitions, "The buying or selling uncustomed goods." Church says that "even members of Society looked upon the practice as a minor offence"[62] and often local preachers defended it.[63] In the coastal areas the problem was especially acute. "At Dover and Sunderland, in East Anglia and Cornwall," he says, "it was a hard struggle to convince the ordinary people that it was more than a misdemeanour."[64]

Only continued education in the elementary principles of honesty and stern disciplinary measures in enforcing them could bring the offenders into line. Many were the letters written and the instructions given from the pulpit. In Wesley's pamphlet, "A Word to a Smuggler," he made the whole trade in uncustomed goods identical with robbery—robbery of the King's duties, robbery of the nation's taxes—and the smuggler "a thief-general, who picks the pockets both of the King and all his fellow-subjects."[65] When education failed to take effect, the offender was expelled from the Society; and this eventuality was all too frequent.

The discipline was effective however; in the nineteenth century one of the distinguishing marks of a Methodist was a scrupulous honesty which sometimes made him the butt of ridicule.

---

1. William Wordsworth, *Complete Poetical Works* (Boston: Houghton Mifflin Co.), p. 349.
2. E. D. Bebb, *A Man With a Concern* (London: Epworth Press, 1950), p. 93.
3. Baker, op. cit., p. 98.
4. Taylor, op. cit., p. 134.
5. Baker, op. cit., p. 98.
6. Law, *Works*, III, 60.
7. Loc. cit.
8. Loc. cit.
9. Ibid., p. 63.
10. Ibid., p. 50.
11. Ibid., p. 39.
12. Ibid., p. 64.
13. Law, *Works*, IV, 251.
14. Law, *Works*, III, 64.
15. Fleury, op. cit., p. 28.
16. Ibid., p. 28.
17. William Cave, *Primitive Christianity, or The Religion of the Ancient Christians in the first Ages of the Gospel* (London: Pr. by J. M. for Richard Chiswell, 1673), Part III, p. 284.
18. Cave, op. cit., Part II, p. 28.
19. Fleury, op. cit., p. 27. This was evidently Wesley's ideal—not an absolute communism. Each household would exist by itself preserving family life and carrying on its own vocation, but wealth would be so shared that there would never be poor among them.
20. Cave, op. cit., p. 26; also Fleury, op. cit., p. 132 et seq.
21. Fleury, op. cit., p. 55.
22. Ibid., p. 73.
23. *Sermons*, I, 474.
24. *Works*, VII, 32.
25. *Letters*, V, 257.
26. *Letters*, II, 131.
27. *Works*, VII, 304.
28. *Sermons*, II, 315.
29. E. D. Bebb, *Non-Conformity and Social and Economic Life—1660-1800* (London: Epworth Press, 1935), p. 89.
30. See Appendix. In *Sermons*, II, 315, he comments, " . . . We must preserve, at all events, the spirit of an healthful mind. Therefore, we may not engage . . . in any sinful trade . . . Such are all that necessarily imply our robbing or defrauding the king of his lawful customs."
31. *Sermons*, II, 316.
32. Loc. cit.
33. Ibid., p. 316.
34. Ibid., p. 317.
35. Lawson, op. cit., p. 269.
36. Ibid., p. 264.
37. Ibid., p. 265.
38. *Sermons*, II, 317.
39. Walter Besant, *London in the Eighteenth Century* (London: Chatto & Windus, 1892), p. 216.
40. M. D. George, *England in Transition*, p. 93; also George, *London Life in the Eighteenth Century*, p. 27.
41. Bready, op. cit., p. 146.
42. Besant, Loc. cit.
43. Bready, Loc. cit.

44. Walter Wilson, *Memoirs of the Life and Times of Daniel DeFoe* (London: Hurst, Chance & Co., 1830), III, 23-4.
45. Maldwyn Edwards, *After Wesley* (London: Epworth Press, 1935), p. 133.
46. *Works*, XI, 169.
47. *Sermons*, II, 318.
48. *Works*, XI, 510.
49. *Letters*, VI, 154.
50. *Letters*, VIII, 166.
51. *Sermons*, II, 319.
52. *Loc. cit.*
53. See Appendix.
54. Jones, *op. cit.*, p. 289.
55. *Works*, X, 187. In this Letter he points out "Once your zeal was against ungodliness and unrighteousness. . . . Now it is against forms of prayer, against singing psalms or hymns, against appointing times of prayer or preaching; against saying *you* to a single person, uncovering your head, or having too many buttons upon your coat."
56. See Dr. Church's account of the prosecution of Sally Brown, Church, *op. cit.*, p. 193. Wesley told the prosecutors, "They were not at liberty to go to law with each other, but are under an obligation to stand to the decision of me or the Assistant . . ."
57. See Appendix.
58. Botsford, *op. cit.*, p. 178.
59. See Bready, Besant, Botsford and George.
60. Besant, *op. cit.*, p. 218.
61. Botsford, *op. cit.*, p. 181.
62. Church, *op. cit.*, p. 194.
63. *Ibid.*, p. 195.
64. *Loc. cit.*
65. *Works*, XI, 175.

XII

Mammon and the Way

Wesley has often been called the St. Francis of Protestantism. Certainly in his efforts to found within the Church of England a sort of religious order which practiced a Christian theory of wealth he resembled his great predecessor. As we have already noted, the use of money was for Wesley the most important criterion of practical Christianity. No General Rule received quite so frequent treatment from him as the one that forbade "Laying up treasures upon earth."[1] He believed, in fact, that the continuance of the Wesleyan way depended upon the full understanding and practice of this rule. His directions about the spending of money are, therefore, as specific as those which deal with "getting."

The basic purpose in the expenditure of money, as Wesley saw it, is the satisfaction of natural need.[2] As soon as this goal is passed a desire and quest for riches begins. Riches he defined as "whatever is above the plain necessaries or at the most conveniences of life."[3] Whoever has sufficient food to eat and raiment to put on, with a place where to lay his head,[4] should be content; to desire more is to desire to "lay up treasures on earth." "They that will be rich" are all those that "calmly, deliberately and of set purpose, endeavour after more" than this,[5] yielding thereby to the "love of Money." They are clearly condemned by Christ, said Wesley, and "have practically denied the faith."[6]

The limits of expenditure set for the Methodist were: first, "to provide for giving all men their due"—to owe nothing; secondly, "to provide sufficient plain, wholesome food, plain raiment" and all "the household necessaries of life"—to be economically self-sufficient; thirdly, to leave his children upon his death "in a capacity of providing" for themselves within the standards he had set for himself"; fourthly, "to lay up from time to time, that needed for carrying on worldly business in such measure and degree as is sufficient to answer the foregoing purposes."[8] To spend or lay by more than this was to succumb to the love of money.

What are the consequences of exceeding these limits? First of all, desires are created for unnecessaries in food, clothing and furnishings. Luxuries begin to make an appeal. Sense demands of all sorts are stimulated and unchristian dispositions thereupon develop. When Miss Johnson, an early Methodist, came into a large fortune, Wesley wrote to her: "Hitherto you have been greatly superior to every delicacy in food; but even this may assault you now, and perhaps raise in you other desires which you are now a stranger to. At present you are above the follies of dress; but will you be so a twelvemonth hence? May you not easily slide into the pride of life, in this as well as other instances? especially considering how your vanity will be gratified thereby. For who will not admire and applaud your admirable taste?"[9]

The desire for wealth looses a series of ugly impulses. Vanity leads to costly dress. Pride leads to thinking one's self better than one's "poor, dirty neighbours,"[10] an attitude which constituted a denial of perfect love. In the wake of pride might come resentment and even the spirit of revenge, for few men with the means at hand can resist resentment at affronts and the temptation to revenge them. As these evil tempers are indulged, others follow until "every temper that is earthly, sensual or devilish" may take possession.[11]

The increase of material things beyond the rigid limits set removes the necessity for complete dependence upon God for all needs. Faith is thereby weakened, for faith is "the evidence of things unseen," and does not grow upon the abundance of "the things that are seen." The "exceeding deceitfulness" of riches consists in this subtle power to weaken faith in the eternal, to gradually make one a materialist or a "practical atheist," to use Wesley's term.

Another corrosive influence upon faith comes from the "acquaintance and conversation with worldly men" to which an accumulation of riches exposes one. This contact with Secularism undermines Christian ethical standards and makes one unresponsive or even hostile to the Christian messenger, when he attempts to recall one to eternal values. Superior circumstances and an unteachable spirit will finally render such a man unapproachable and Wesley says to him: "Who dares tell you the plain truth... And if any venture to deal plainly with you, how hard is it for you to bear it! Are not you far less reprovable, far less advisable, than when you were poor?"[12]

Increase in wealth is to be feared, also, for its dissipation of the spirit of meekness and patience. The sturdy fortitude, which is so much a part of true Christianity, is likely to be displaced by softness, a love of delicacy and luxury, and an abandonment of self-denial. The General Rule forbidding "Softness and needless self-indulgence" was aimed directly at this effect of wealth as much as at intemperate habits.

Wesley tells of his experience in the home of a man made effeminate and petty by his life of ease. "A servant came in and threw some coal on the fire. A puff of smoke came out. The baronet threw himself back in his chair and cried out, 'Mr. Wesley, these are the crosses I meet with daily!' Would he not," asks Wesley, "have been less impatient, if he had had fifty, instead of five thousand, pounds a year?"[13] Early Methodism, although not ascetic, valued the hardihood essential to active Christian service and obtained only by disciplining sense demands.

When the wrong use of money develops such unchristian tempers as these that have been enumerated the inevitable outcome is the loss of perfect love. This is first evidenced by an estrangement from God and a loss of the Christian scale of values and then by a growing indifference to the appeal of human need. The "exceeding deceitfulness" of riches thus breaks man's harmonious relationship with man as well as with God.

In view of these consequences, which Wesley believed always follow upon the use of money for non-essentials, it is no wonder that he dealt very firmly with all departures from simple living. He opposed, first of all, any outlay upon things that might be harmful to mind or body. Spirituous liquors, of course, belonged in this category, and we have already seen what he thought of those who bought them or sold them or tolerated a continuance of traffic in them.[14]

Included also among things that were detrimental to health and disciplined living were snuff, tobacco and even tea when drunk in excess. Irish Methodists, enslaved by dirty and harmful habits, were advised to "use no tobacco unless prescribed by a physician." He declared it "an uncleanly and unwholesome self-indulgence," saying, "the more customary it is the more resolutely should you break off from every degree of that evil custom."[15]

Of snuff he said, "I suppose no other nation in Europe is in such vile bondage to this silly, nasty, dirty custom as the Irish are. But let Christians be in this bondage no longer." Christians are men who refuse the rule of evil habit and know the power of Christ to make new men. He commands: "Assert your liberty, and that all at once: nothing will be done by degrees. But just now you may break loose through Christ's strengthening you."[16]

All such habits were included under the General Rule which forbids "Softness, and needless self-indulgence." Wesley believed that the Christian should have no need for stimulants; his faith in God should bring bodily and mental fitness. The use of narcotics interfered with this dependence upon inner resources and destroyed Christian fortitude. Control of all desires, therefore, natural and unnatural, was required for complete Christian living.

This included intemperance in food. When desire for sense gratification governs the expenditure of money, even the love of food can become a rival to love of God and others. Declaring that money must not be wasted on the pleasures of sense, especially the sense of taste, Wesley explained: "I do not mean, avoid gluttony and drunkenness only: an honest Heathen would condemn these. But there is a regular, reputable kind of sensuality, an elegant epicurism, which does not immediately disorder the stomach, nor (sensibly at least) impair the understanding; and yet . . . it cannot be maintained without considerable expense. Cut off all this expense!" he sternly commanded.[17]

The chief count against Dives is that "he fared sumptuously every day. Reconcile this," said Wesley, "with religion who can. I know the prophets of smooth things can talk in favour of hospitality; of making our friends welcome; of keeping a handsome table, to do honour to religion; or promoting trade, and the like." But to Wesley this was only a method of rationalizing sense-indulgence and God "will not be put off with such pretences."[18]

Another desire which must be held in check is the wish to gratify the sense of property. Wesley condemns as much the love of expensive houses and furniture as the love of dress. He asks that nothing be spent "in curiously adorning . . . houses; in superfluous or expensive furniture; in costly pictures, painting, gilding, books; in elegant rather than useful gardens."[19] This seems at first thought a disparagement of cultural environment, but it should be interpreted by reference to the context and what we know of Wesley's own taste and practice.

He followed this appeal with the explanation, "Let your neighbours, who know nothing better, do this," and then pointed out the motive that usually governs the neighbor in his accumulation of superfluities: "Men are expensive in diet, or apparel, or furniture, not barely to please their appetite, or to gratify their eye, or their imagination, but their vanity, too . . .

So long as thou art 'clothed in purple and fine linen, and farest sumptuously every day,' no doubt many will applaud thy elegance of taste, thy generosity, and hospitality." [20]

The Christian must not gather *things* about him merely for the joy he can get from them, nor to gain "the admiration or praise of men." The more these expensive tastes are indulged the more one becomes attached to *things* of sense and pride, and the less one loves God. Everything conspires to increase pride in the man who loves God's gifts more than God. "His noble house, his elegant furniture, his well-chosen pictures, his fine horses, his equipage, his very dress," all tend to elicit praise and to make him feel a better man than "those who do not have these advantages." [21] The only worth in *things* is the contribution they can make to fuller Christian living.

Now we know that Wesley loved books and gardens. Whether he cared as much for pictures is not so clear. But he certainly was not proposing here to deprive Methodists of the positive benefits to be gained from books or pictures or gardens or refined home surroundings. The books and publications issued by him and his brother for Methodists as listed by Green run to over four hundred.[22] In his later life he visited every famous garden within the compass of his extensive trips through England. He was a man of the widest culture, but he disapproved of the lavish and meaningless expenditure that has always gone into modish furnishings, unread libraries, unappreciated pictures and all that is involved in "keeping up with the neighbors."

Furthermore, if we base our final interpretation of his theory upon his life example, we shall have to say that none of these things are to make any real claim upon the Christian's affections. They are incidental to his chief interest and are to be relinquished without a tear. Wesley at his death possessed nothing but his furniture at the City Road house, six pounds for his pall bearers and a few shillings in change. As we have said before, Wesley "sat loose" to things, and so, he believed, did everyone in "the more excellent way." Like the early Christians they refused everything that catered to sense desires or aroused pride in possessions.[23]

One of the recognizable signs of freedom from the love of things and all the evils that spring therefrom is simplicity in dress. This was an accepted belief during the first century of the Christian church, and accordingly a few directions were given in the New Testament for women's apparel. These were accepted in all their literalness by the Church fathers. Cave says that the fathers condemned all finery and costliness and set up a pattern which would distinguish the Christian woman from "Heathen Ladies who cultivated arts of fineness and gallantry, all pomp and elegancy, richness and gaudiness, who spent fortunes on" ornamentation.[24] *The Apostolical Constitution,* so highly regarded by Wesley during his formative period, forbids all superfluities in dress.

Many other references might be drawn from Wesley's reading to account for his feeling that explicit teaching upon Christian dress is necessary to any religious movement. Contemporary writers of the more serious sort, both Anglican and non-conformist, gave him support in this view, and among the Friends he saw a living exemplification of the "primitive simplicity" which he believed should characterize the entire life pattern of the Christian. When expenditure is limited to the satisfaction of basic natural needs, plain dress becomes a necessity.

In his "Advice to the People Called Methodist" written after the Revival was well under way, he said: "Many years ago I observed several parts of Christian practice among the people called Quakers. Two things I particularly remarked among them—plainness of speech, and plainness of dress. I willingly adopted both, with some restrictions, particularly plainness of dress . . ."[25] Cheapness of material and simplicity in style were the features of Quaker dress which early Methodists were to imitate,[26] but they were not to adopt "little particularities . . . which can answer no possible end but to distinguish them from all other people." This seemed to Wesley being singular "merely for singularities sake," and "not the part of a Christian." In things "absolutely indifferent" he advised conformity to the customs of the country.[27]

Observing the trend among the Friends to stress what he deemed mere singularity he concluded that in their attention to one aspect of dress they had lost sight of another of greater importance, namely, costliness. They demonstrated what can happen to the most earnest believer when the outward symbol becomes more important than the inward motives, when the *pattern* of the Christian life is stressed more than the *principles* which created the pattern. A pattern given such pre-eminence obscures underlying principles.

He addressed the Friends directly in his *Farther Appeal to Men of Reason and Religion,* charging them with allowing great costliness of dress among their members. In their satisfaction with a singular, grave and sober garb they had forgotten a more important matter. Consequently, when they had begun to increase in wealth they had indulged their worldly-mindedness in purchases of high-priced linens and silks; in fact, they had become known for their manufacture of the exquisite and costly Quaker linens.[28] Thus, outwardly conformed to one requirement for Christian dress, they had ceased to conform to the higher law, the law of love, which bids us share our all with others.

Wesley wrote to them, saying, "You were at first a poor, despised, afflicted people. Then what some of you had to spare was little enough to relieve the needy members of your own society. In a few years you increased in goods, and were able to relieve more than your own poor, but you did not bestow all that you had to spare from, on the poor belonging to other societies. It remained either to lay it up, or expend it in superfluities. Some chose one way, and some the other."[29] But both had missed "the more excellent way," Wesley thought, and he hoped to prevent this outcome for Methodism by great emphasis upon the money problems relating to dress.

So serious did he consider this drift observable among young Quakers that he believed that they should be expelled from the societies. He wrote to the older folk: "Why do ye not vehemently reprove them; and if they repent not, in spite of all worldly considerations, expel them out of your society? In conniving at their sin, you make it your own. . . ." [30]

This is another instance of the comprehensiveness with which Wesley developed the implications of Christian love. Most advocates of plain dress, even among the professed followers of Wesley, have been content to emphasize the peripheral aspects of the question and have not seen the relationship between Christian dress and good works; but the early Methodists were taught that one cannot be adorned with good works at the same time as with expensive clothes, and that "costliness of apparel" is "immediately, directly, inevitably destructive of good works." [31] He agreed with leaders of previous religious movements upon the pride, vanity, lust and greed that may be engendered by unchristian dress, but he stressed even more than they the misuse of money entailed.

Perhaps the lavish outlay upon all personal adornment in Wesley's time made him unusually sensitive to this aspect of Christian dress. The early eighteenth century is notorious for its irrational expenditure of both time and money upon costume and coiffure. When even slovenly Dr. Johnson could spend thirty pounds upon a new suit and wig for a visit to Paris, what must have been the expense account of a London fop? [32]

Wesley, viewing the tendency of the poor to ape the fashions of the rich, a fact vividly presented by Cowper in *The Task,* attempted to forestall the drift which he had observed among the Quakers by teaching his people that love of mankind, if given full expression, necessarily involves the choice of simple, inexpensive clothing, and that this, in turn, involves a renunciation of the irrational fashions which occupy so much of the thought and time of a vain woman.

The fullest statement of Wesley's views on this subject is contained in a sermon "On Dress." He here declares: ". . . the more you lay out on your own apparel, the less you have left to clothe the naked, to feed the hungry, to lodge the strangers, to relieve those that are sick and in prison, and to lessen the numberless afflictions to which we are exposed. . . ." [33]

To those who see only the border-line problem of pride and claim that they can be humble in gold cloth, Wesley replies that, even were it true (which he denies), they are still guilty of a greater sin: "Every shilling which you needlessly spend on your apparel is, in effect, stolen from God and poor! . . . As a steward you are 'tearing from the back of the naked' what you put on yourself." [34]

From the day when Wesley as a student decided to wear the least expensive clothes he could buy, after having seen the half-clad condition of a poor maid who came to clean his college rooms, he believed that all that exceeds the essentials for living is bought with the blood of the needy.[35] The way of life that should characterize those who profess to the experience of perfect love was fully followed by Wesley. He may have bequeathed to his followers some problems in the exposition of the theory of perfect love, but he left them in no doubt as to the practice of it. Self-denying devotion to the needs of mankind is at the root of his insistence upon plain dress, as it is at the root of most of the disciplines he enforced.

However, other problems which may arise are discussed in the sermon "On Dress." Pride may be engendered or increased, causing us "to think ourselves better because we are dressed in better clothes." It is "scarce possible for a man to wear costly apparel, without, in some measure, valuing himself upon it . . . thousands, not only lords and gentlemen . . . but honest tradesmen" infer "the superior value of their persons from the value of their clothes." [36] Social inequality is the consequence.

Another problem is the appeal to vanity. Vanity is the enemy of simplicity, " 'that grace which frees the soul from all unnecessary reflections upon itself.' " [37] To the fine dresser Wesley says: "You know . . . it is with a view to be admired that you adorn yourselves; and that you would not be at pains were none to see you but God and his holy angels. Now, the more you indulge this foolish desire, the more it grows upon you. You have vanity enough by nature; but by thus indulging it, you increase it a hundred-fold." [38]

The matter of immodest dress had received the major emphasis in the discussion of dress at certain times in the history of the church, and might well have been pushed to the fore by Wesley at a time when sexual irregularities among the upper classes were accompanied by a studied appeal to lust in the daring fashions of the day. Law had asked whether women could "think themselves innocent, who with naked breasts, patched faces, and every ornament of dress, invite the eye to offend?" [39]

Wesley's treatment of this matter is brief but to the point. Confessing that he dislikes to shock the innocent-minded but finds it necessary to do so, he charges those who deliberately offend with poisoning "the beholder with far more of this base appetite than otherwise he would feel." "Did you not know this would be the natural consequence of your elegant adorning?" he asks. "Did you not *desire,* did you not *design* it should? And yet, all the time, how did you

'Set to public view
A specious face of innocence and virtue!' " [40]

Wesley distinguished always between conformity to general standards of dress and enslavement to ruling fashions and costliness. Evidently there were those who argued that they could not carry on their trade if they did not wear gold and costly clothes. He said to them: "If you mean only conforming to those customs of your country that are neither gay nor costly, why should you not dress like other people? I really think you should. . . . But if you mean conformity to them in what God has forbidden, the answer is ready at hand: If you cannot carry on your trade without breaking God's command, you must not carry it on." He doubted, however, whether any trade "may not be carried on by one who uses plain and modest apparel," and attributed such fears to an inordinate love of fine clothes. "If you were not fond of them you would never dream of their necessity." [41]

It would seem that such clear and continued teaching on Christian dress should have so molded the Methodist mind that there would have been a uniform understanding and practice of the principle involved. This was largely true until the last years of Wesley's life. Dr. Church in his study of *The Early Methodist People* describes typical Methodists of both city and countryside as very simply dressed.

At the City Road Chapel in London the older well-to-do women resembled Quakeresses in their plainness," and even women of rank, Lady Maxwell, for example, dressed "without ornament, or anything which could serve only for show." This Christian gentlewoman's apprehension of the real end of Christian dress is evident in the statement by her biographer that by her saving on apparel she found "that she could relieve many a suffering creature, and give education to many an orphan child, with what numbers expend in useless decorations." [43]

Yet the last years of Wesley's ministry brought him great concern over a growing spirit of worldly-mindedness, indicated most obviously by an increasing love of property and fine dress. The same change was appearing among Methodists as he had observed among the Friends, and he became uncertain as to the wisdom of his earlier policy, wondering if he should have dealt with specific details of dress and told the candidate for Society membership: "this is our manner of dress, which we know is both scriptural and rational. If you join with us, you are to dress as we do.' " [44]

On one occasion he became this specific and commanded: "Wear no gold . . . no pearls, or precious stones; use no curling of the hair, or costly apparel, how grave soever . . . no velvets, no silks, no fine linen, no superfluities, no mere ornaments, though ever so much in fashion. Wear nothing, though you have it already, which is of a glaring colour, or which is in any kind gay, glistering, or showy; nothing made in the very height of the fashion, nothing to attract the eyes of the bystanders. I do not advise women to wear rings, ear-rings, necklaces, lace . . . or ruffles. . . . Neither do I advise men to wear coloured waistcoats, shining stockings, glittering or costly buckles or buttons . . . any more than gay, fashionable, or expensive perukes. It is true, these are little, very little things, which are not worth defending; therefore, give them up. . . ."[45]

At the root of Wesley's efforts to clarify the thinking of his people on this subject was his conviction that Mammon was the greatest foe of the Wesleyan way and that here in worldly dress was a sure symptom of the encroachment of the enemy. The appearance of fine clothes, especially among the youth, was a danger signal, and an indication of their failure to comprehend the Wesleyan way which their parents, when "poor and despised," had taken. Wesley feared the day when Methodists would no longer be "poor and despised," not because there is any virtue in either poverty or persecution, but because they seem to be consequences of the full acceptance of the Christian Way.

---

1. See Appendix.
2. With Law, care after worldly things must be bounded "by the just wants of Nature." *Works*, III, pp. 36, et seq.
3. *Works*, VII, 3.
4. *Loc. cit.*
5. *Ibid.*, p. 4.
6. *Sermons*, I, 478.
7. *Sermons*, II, 322. Wesley asks: "Why should you throw away money upon your children, any more than upon yourself, in delicate food, in gay and costly apparel, in superfluities of any kind? Why should you purchase for them more pride or lust, more vanity, or foolish and hurtful desires? . . . nature has made ample provision for them: why should you be at farther expense to increase their temptations and snares . . . "
8. *Sermons*, I, 478.
9. *Letters*, IV, 59.
10. *Works*, VI, 333.
11. *Works*, VII, 7. See his complete analysis of all the problems that arise with riches in his sermon "On Riches," *Works*, VII, 215-221.
12. *Works*, VII, 333.

13. *Works*, VII, 13.
14. *Works* VII, 360.
15. *Letters*, V, 133.
16. *Loc. cit.*
17. *Sermons*, II, 321.
18. *Works*, VII, 250.
19. *Sermons*, II, 322.
20. *Loc. cit.*
21. *Works*, VII, 218.
22. See Richard Green, *op. cit.*
23. See Cave, *op. cit.*, pp. 40, *et seq.*; Fleury, *op. cit.*, pp. 66, *et seq.*
24. Cave, *op. cit.*, p. 51.
25. *Works*, XI, 466.
26. *Ibid.*, p. 467.
27. *Loc. cit.*
28. *Works*, VIII, 186. In this section of *The Farther Appeal* he says: ". . . you cannot but observe, upon cool reflection, that you retain just so much of your ancient practice, as leaves your present without excuse; as makes the inconsistency, between the one and the other, glaring and undeniable; For instance: This woman is too strict a Quaker to lay out a shilling in a necklace. Very well; but she is not too strict to lay out fourscore guineas in a repeating watch. . . . Surely you cannot be ignorant, that the sinfulness of fine apparel lies chiefly in the expensiveness: in that it is robbing God and the poor. . . ."
29. *Works*, VIII, 187.
30. *Ibid.*, p. 186.
31. *Works*, XI, 468.
32. Bready, *op. cit.*, p. 260.
33. *Works*, VII, 20.
34. *Loc. cit.*
35. *Ibid.*, p. 21.
36. *Ibid.*, p. 18.
37. *Letters*, V, 193.
38. *Works*, VII, 18.
39. Law, *Works*, IV, 307.
40. *Works*, VII, 19.
41. *Works*, XI, 473.
42. Church, *op. cit.*, p. 202.
43. *Ibid.*, p. 197.
44. *Works*, VII, 288.
45. *Works*, XI, p. 468.

XIII

Stewardship and the Way

We have found that the Wesleyan way was a way of utter simplicity prompted by the claims of compassionate love. We have seen, also, that love is outgoing rather than ingrowing, and that disciplines proposed for restoring life to simplicity are always to be regarded as means rather than ends. Since Wesley had discovered these facts only after years spent in substituting ascetic self-denials for the free operation of perfect love, he was not likely to emphasize the negatives set forth in the first section of the *General Rules* to the neglect of the positives, which follow them.

The function of the negatives was to throw light upon the common misuses of time, money and other talents and to cure these by imposing disciplines. On the negative side, therefore, the distinguishing mark of Methodists was to be their avoidance of "evil of every kind, especially that which is most generally practised."[1] This would inevitably produce singularity and might call forth persecution. The *Rules,* in fact, admonished the Methodist to submit "to bear the reproach of Christ; to be as the filth and offscouring of the world," and to look "that men should say all manner of evil of them falsely, for the Lord's sake."[2]

Yet, at the same time, the Methodist was warned to use "all possible diligence and frugality, that the Gospel be not blamed."[3] As the representative of Christ he must never give occasion for any misunderstanding of the nature of the Kingdom. For example, in his singular position of avoiding popular sins he must never give the impression of valuing singularity for its own sake. This tendency in other religious movements Wesley hoped to prevent by constant attention to all the implications of perfect love. He believed that if the negatives continued to be understood as *means* by which time, wealth, and talents could be conserved and devoted to fulfilling the demands of love such an outcome could be avoided and the Wesleyan way would never become a stereotype.

On the positive side, therefore, the distinguishing mark of Methodists was to be their "doing good" and "being in every kind merciful after their power; as they have opportunity, doing good of every possible sort, and as far as possible to all men."[4] The positives dealt with specific ways in which compassionate love will manifest itself in the world of needy men. In its outreach it was to include *all men;* hence the need for missionary endeavor was early recognized. It comprehended, also, in its diversity of expression ministry to *all the needs* of men, and at this point the *Rules* were very specific, perhaps because so many of these needs had not been fully served by the church.

Care for men's bodies was to be shown "by giving food to the hungry, by clothing the naked, by visiting or helping them that are sick or in prison."[5] Love for men's souls was to be poured out in "instructing, reproving, or exhorting" all with whom Methodists had intercourse. Constant concern for the good of others required that they trample "under foot that enthusiastic doctrine of devils that we are not to do good, unless our heart be free to it."

This positive objective was made clear by means of continued teaching and was implemented by one of the most efficient organizations in the history of religious movements. Let us first examine Wesley's elaboration of the social meaning of love in his sermons and letters. The core of his thought is to be found in his discussions of Christian stewardship.

Activated by the love of God and others, the Christian uses all he has in Kingdom building. He views himself as nothing more than a trustee for all that comes into his hands. Nothing, Wesley declares, is "properly our own." "Eternal things only are our own; with all these temporal things we are barely entrusted by another, the Disposer and Lord of all." [6] Soul, body, talents and goods—all are included in the Christian trusteeship.

Powers and faculties, such as understanding, imagination, memory, will, and affections are to be directed toward accomplishing God's plan—the only plan that will yield man real happiness. The body, with all the possibilities involved in the use of its members, the exercise of the senses, the gift of speech, is given the Christian to be employed in the service of God, the proprietor. Advantages, such as health, leisure, pleasing personality, opportunities for education, which seem so unequally distributed among men, are not of man's choosing or earning; hence, he should look upon them as gifts, for the use of which he must finally account.

The same is true of the worldly goods which come to him; food, clothing and shelter are granted him that he may effectively carry on God's plan. Money, in particular, is a trust which requires the most scrupulous administration. After the steward has supplied the reasonable wants of his household he is to restore the remainder to the Master through the poor, who have been appointed by the Master to receive it.[7] Recognizing the existence of economic inequality, Wesley makes the poor the appointed creditors, not the debtors, of the rich, the implication being that, had the rich always paid their debts, there would be no poor.[8]

The steward, in carrying out this commission, is to look upon himself actually as one of that number of the poor whose wants are to be supplied out of the particular substance placed by God in his hands. The only difference between the rich steward and the poor man to whom he gives is that the rich man has been granted two special favors by the Master, namely: the right of supplying his own needs first, and the joy that will come from giving rather than receiving.[9]

This is an exceedingly literal interpretation of the stewardship theory and distinguishes Wesley from others who have elaborated a Christian plan for the use of wealth. He was following through to its logical conclusion, as he attempted to do in all matters of conduct, the application of the doctrine of perfect love to human problems.

Wesley was not unique among Christian thinkers in his adoption of a theory of stewardship. The theory has repeatedly been a logical concomitant of a return to the original principles of Christianity. Even Judaism at its best viewed man as God's trustee, and many features of "the Way" in the early Church were a direct consequence of the feeling that material things were of little concern and completely subject to God's proprietary will.[10]

But the theory is easily susceptible to perversion, sometimes being urged simply because of the material rewards to be gained by the practice of it, and often only as a means of gaining merit. These two false interpretations were common in Wesley's day because of the loss of Christian simplicity under the impact of ruling materialism and secularism. They were both repudiated by him.

He was not interested in perpetuating traditional theories; he wished only to bring about a movement in which money would be used as it was in the early Church. With his primary emphasis upon practice rather than upon doctrine he envisioned a kind of stewardship which, when accepted widely, would create an equalitarianism such as was known only during the period when first-hand acquaintance with Christ had revolutionized men's thinking on every problem.

No one has grasped Wesley's theory of stewardship until he has seen these implications. Stewardship was much more than generous giving; it was real sharing, accompanied by the humbling realization that, but for the unfathomable favor of God, the role might be reversed and the giver be the receiver. If carried through it would mean inevitably the demolition of an economic caste system, accomplished, not by the interposition of the State, but by the spontaneous expression of compassion by each Christian as he fulfilled his duties as a steward.

It must not be concluded, however, that the ultimate objective in stewardship is the sharing of goods. The end of Christianity is not the creation of a society in which there are no poor. Fine as that might be, the removal of poverty will be, after all, only a by-product in the process of building a Christian community. Only gross materialism, such as characterizes our age, would substitute an economic good for a spiritual good. The end of all stewardship is the doing good to the *souls* of men, as enjoined in one section of the *Rules* quoted above. The sharing of material goods will open the way to the joyful sharing of the Good News. Every rich man, Wesley said, would be asked in the end, ". . . didst thou labour to improve all outward works of mercy, as *means* of saving souls from death?" [11]

A spirit of joy should attend every act of stewardship. Even the expenditure of money upon life-necessities calls for a happy accounting, the steward saying, "Lord, thou seest I am going to expend this sum on that food, apparel, furniture, and thou knowest, I act therein with a single eye, as a steward of thy goods, expending this portion of them thus, in pursuance of the design thou hadst in entrusting me with them. . . . And give me a witness in myself, that for this labour of love I shall have a recompense when thou rewardest every man. . . ." [12]

Continued training in stewardship was given all Methodists, but, when Wesley faced an audience of the rich, his teaching on the subject was heavily underscored. As we have said, from the beginning he accepted literally Christ's statement concerning the improbability of salvation for the rich; and his observation of attitudes toward the Christian disciplines taken by prospering Methodists only served to strengthen this belief. For this reason he did all in his power to inform his followers of the dangers of increasing wealth. Those who had come into a fortune he advised, "First, ask God what He would have you to do, feeling that you are standing 'on the brink of a precipice.' Consider, 'Having more means, I will do more good . . . than I did before.' All the additional goods . . . I am resolved to lay out, with all diligence in additional works of mercy." [13]

To those who talked about reaching a station where they could "afford" a change in their standards of living, he said, "This is the quintessence of nonsense. Who gave you this addition to your fortune; or (to speak properly) lent it to you ... informing you at the same time for what purposes he entrusted you with it? And can you *afford* to waste your Lord's goods, for every part of which you are to give an account? ..." [14]

To those who argued that it would be impossible in any case to supply necessaries for all the poor of the Societies he replied that it had been possible in the first church at Jerusalem, and that the decline in this church had begun in a failure to practice stewardship. The love of money was "the first plague which infected the Christian Church." All except Smyrna and Philadelphia had "increased in goods" and these which had less "retained more of the simplicity and purity of the gospel." [15]

Wesley's reading in the history of religious movements as well as his observations of trends among the nonconformists led him to believe that back of every decline in spiritual force lies failure in stewardship. During the seventeenth century in England he had found "a wonderful outpouring of the Spirit ..." But he observed: "from the time that riches and honour poured in upon them that feared and loved God, their hearts began to be estranged from him, and to cleave to the present world. No sooner was persecution ceased, and the poor, despised, persecuted Christians invested with power, and placed in ease and affluence, but a change of circumstances brought a change of spirit. Riches and honour soon produced their usual effects." [16]

The same story he found repeated in America after the Puritan era.[17] The "mystery of iniquity" is here solved. Riches "in all ages" have brought an end to the rise of "pure and undefiled religion"; they have been "the principal cause of the decay of true religion in every Christian community." Each time the wheel goes full circle: the natural result of the failure in Christian stewardship is apostasy. This in turn brings suffering upon the world. Then God by reducing men "to their former poverty" again restores them to their former purity." [18]

Hoping against hope to forestall such an outcome for Methodism he formulated a simple scheme by which he believed his followers could fully recognize the implications of the theory of stewardship and thereby cope successfully with the problems which attended their advancing economic status. This was his three-part formula of "Gain all you can, Save all you can, Give all you can.

The scheme was so simple that no one could fail to comprehend it. Money according to Wesley is not to be condemned *per se*. In the present state of society, to be sure, it is "the mammon of unrighteousness," but the handling of it may be Christianized, for "where unequal distribution exists, it may become 'food for the hungry, drink for the thirsty, raiment for the naked. . . .' " [19] Were all men Christian, the use of money would, of course, be superseded: in the early Church distribution was made "to every one as he had need." But in the present state of the world money is a good because it can be employed in leading the world to Christ.

Accepting world evangelization as the single goal of money-making, the Methodist was to enter fully upon his calling. Avoiding all businesses which harm body, soul, or substance, using those methods which are Christian, he was to use "all possible diligence" and bring to his work the finest understanding he possessed. "Every business," Wesley said, "will afford some employment sufficient for every day and every hour" and will allow "no leisure for silly, unprofitable diversions." [20]

The close relationship which exists between the Christian use of time and the Christian use of wealth and talents is to be seen here. Few restrictions would have to be placed upon diversions if both leisure and money were completely devoted to the building of a Christian community. But, when later on in the movement this end was obscured, and the principles which underlie Christian discipline were lost, Wesley's encouragement to business aggressiveness could readily be interpreted as praise of the economic virtues for their own sake, and the restrictions could likewise easily become ends rather than means, thwarting those legitimate cultural pursuits that enlarge the spirit.

Even before Wesley's death many Methodists had made gaining and saving rather than giving the goal of their rigorous living, losing the vision of a changed society and refusing, also, those uses of leisure time that are Christian. Perry remarks that the joylessness ascribed to the Puritans was not due so much to repression of legitimate interests as to the obligation which they felt to be forever improving their economic position.[21] There developed in time in Methodism, also, a type of individual who, grasping only the negatives of the *General Rules,* and, developing only the virtues associated with business success, lost the basic meaning of perfect love and became a cheerless, narrow-minded, obscurantist devotee to ceaseless work. He is no more to be condemned, however, than a type of Methodist who followed this generation of negativists. He, because he made the mistake of identifying the doctrine of Christian Perfection with inhibition and anti-intellectualism, renounced the Wesleyan way, lost all sense of trusteeship, and exalted cultural values to the exclusion of Christian simplicity.

Wesley's admonitions to "Gain all you can" and "Save all you can," when divorced from the third point of his formula, "Give all you can," proved no preventive to the decay of Christianity. Yet it should have been very easy for the early Methodist to pass immediately from the category of saving to that of giving,[22] for he was told repeatedly that a man who laid up the overplus that remained after life-necessities had been provided might as well "bury it in the earth."[23] Wesley's condemnation of large bank accounts, had it been heeded by the bulk of Methodists, might conceivably have had a marked effect upon modern banking, for only so much money as was needed for carrying forward a business was to remain long in the vaults.

Stewardship, it should now be clear, is not the same as tithing. It is, in one sense, a giving of all. Wesley commands, "do not stint yourself, like a Jew rather than a Christian, to this or that proportion. Render unto God, not a tenth, not a third, not half, but all that is God's be it more or less; by employing all on yourself, your household, the household of faith, and all mankind, in such a manner, that you may give a good account of your stewardship. . . ." [24] Only so does one acknowledge that all is God's and render to Him what is His.

Early Methodists saw in Wesley's own practice an illustration of the operation of the theory. His life-long attitude toward money was expressed when he said to his sister, Patty Hall, ". . . money never stays with *me*: it would burn me if it did. I throw it out of my hands as soon as possible, lest it should find a way into my heart." [25]

The reduction of his living expenses at Oxford to twenty-eight pounds a year continued throughout his college residence and, when his stipend rose to sixty, then to ninety, and then to one hundred and twenty pounds, he still maintained the same standard of living, and thereby increased his contribution to human need. He avoided all waste, even in small things, and showed utter indifference to possessions. To an inquiry from the Officer of Excise concerning his failure to make an entry for silver plate, which it was assumed that a man of his prominence must possess, he replied: Sir—I have two silver teaspoons at London, and two at Bristol. This is all the plate which I have at present; and I shall not buy more while so many round me want bread." [26]

An opportunity to carry out the injunction, "Gain all you can," came, quite without his seeking, in the book business which he started for the sole purpose of giving religious education to his followers. Such was his ingenuity and enterprise that during his later years he made an annual profit of one thousand pounds a year, all of which he gave away. He always closed the year's accounts, as he had advised his followers to do, with no balance remaining, except that needed for continuing the business and properly caring for his dependents.

Wesley's theory of stewardship has been subjected to much criticism. It is true that in our day of organized charities and increasing proposals for the removal by the state of all the economic conditions that create a need for charity his suggestions seem naive, if not useless. But a proper analysis of them will reveal certain fundamental features of great significance.

In the first place, it is not fair to judge Wesley's economic thought apart from the context of the eighteenth century. The social and moral needs of the day were extreme, and no one was meeting them. Neither economists, nor social workers existed, nor was the church doing a fraction of what it should. Wesley, acting upon principles learned from historic Christianity, rather than from modern scientific analysis, devised a simple plan for a simple people, which promised, first, a solution of the economic problems of the once idle and improvident convert; secondly, a provision for all the poor within the Societies and for many without; thirdly, a means for establishing all, both rich and poor, in the practice of the Christian disciplines; and, lastly, the organization of a movement which should resemble early Christianity in its indifference to material possessions and its responsiveness to the needs of others. Had the economic goal proposed by Wesley, "equal distribution . . . to all," been achieved even among Methodists, the Utopia of a shared economy, of which many men dare to dream today, might not have had to look to secular sources for its realization. Either Wesley was seventeen centuries behind his times or two centuries in advance.

The fact that Wesley's plan was not given a fair trial should also be considered. The amount of social amelioration accomplished under the influence of Methodism in the nineteenth century is a marvel to historians; yet it is very plain that acceptance of the full responsibilities of stewardship was far from universal in the Societies. Had it been, the chances are that Methodism would have exerted an influence upon economic conditions equal to that which it exercised upon moral reforms.

A third aspect is the validity of the economic principles which underlie the three-fold rule. Lawson observes that the command to gain is based upon the principle that diligence and enterprise are "necessary if society is to enjoy an income sufficient for a civilized standard of life." Saving achieved through the reduction of luxury and waste would divert income "into socially useful channels," and generous giving would pave the road to continuing economic prosperity, "for the basic cause of economic depression, and the tragic paradox of scarcity in the presence of plenty, is the desire of the individual to *accumulate for himself*." [27] How can a Christian society be created out of acquisitive professors of Christianity?

Let us go a step farther, then, and give Wesley the credit of recognizing in his interpretation of the implications of stewardship the principle that the moral use of property forbids great economic inequalities.[28] In Christ's command, "Lay not up for yourselves treasure in earth," he saw both the condemnation of economic inequality and the remedy for it. It is true that his Tory prejudices blinded him to the evils of political inequality, but the completeness of his acceptance of Christ's revolutionary principles led him into radical economic theory and practice. For this reason we make a great mistake when we dismiss his ideas as naive and inconsequential. They were workable at the beginning of the Methodist movement and continued to be effective among those who understood and accepted the whole meaning of Christian Perfection.

We must look now at one more criticism leveled at Wesley's scheme for a changed society before we go on to consider the organizational plan which implemented his teaching. He is said to have depended too much upon individual initiative. While, no doubt, he could have learned much from modern welfare institutions, it is surely of some significance that he had a warrant for his procedure in the social ethic of the primitive church. Christianity introduced into the world the belief in the infinite value of personality and the essential equality of all men. This belief is "a profound act of faith" that finds no support outside of traditional Christianity.[29] Out of a revival of this faith Western democracy was born, and Methodism, following immediately upon the Puritan revival, inherited and, also, added something to this concept of the individual's worth.

The erection by Methodism of Christian Perfection as an attainable goal for all believers is the supreme expression of faith in human potentialities. It is, likewise, the supreme expression of the democratic assumption that the responsible individual is the "ultimate moral unit" of society. "For unto whomsoever much is given, of him shall much be required." When faith in man's spiritual potentialities is so great as to envision Perfection as his predetermined end, then the responsibility of the individual for creating a Christian world becomes enormous.

The Methodist in his endeavor to spread Scriptural holiness through the world took upon himself greater responsibility for the redemption of society than had ever been assumed by any group of laymen. Herein lies the reason for the urgency with which Wesley viewed the evils of his day and his obligation to bring them to an end. Compromise can find no place in such an endeavor, either with sin in the individual life, or with evil in social and economic relationships. Wesley saw essentially what Barbara Ward sees when she says: "I doubt whether democracy will survive if it is to become at any time a society without saints." Furthermore, he was ready to take upon himself all the responsibilities entailed in sainthood, for he believed that "the quality of a free society depends essentially upon the quality of its citizens,"[30] that individual initiative is the final answer.

Now let us briefly survey the chief elements of the Methodist organizational scheme for putting stewardship principles into operation. The individual who loved his neighbor was to form the germ or cell of a Christian society. Accordingly, the first work of the church must be the "rooting and grounding" of individuals in love. Men must be saved from self-love to love of God and men. The "love of our neighbor," Wesley says, "springs from the love of God: otherwise itself is nothing worth." Purity of heart is the only remedy for self-interest.[31]

Wesley describes the original church as "a body of men compacted together, in order, first, to save each his own soul; then, to assist each other in working out their salvation; and afterwards, as far as in them lies, to save all men from present and future misery . . . and set up the kingdom of Christ."[32] The first object of the church is to save men; its second object is to help men attain their full moral stature. If these objects are achieved, the establishment of the kingdom is inevitable.

Wesley recognized from the beginning of his search for the Way that the Church was doing little toward the attainment of the second objective. The very organization of the Religious Societies had been an admission of that fact. Ritual and sermon, alone, were insufficient. The sermon, unaccompanied by opportunity for declared moral decision, and the ritualistic confession of daily sin, unaccompanied by actual change in conduct, seemed to him to produce only greater moral enervation. He believed that the church must provide incentives and occasions for confession, for decision, and for group intercourse concerning the problems of the Way.

It is interesting to watch the evolution of Methodist organizations to meet these needs. Utter flexibility characterized the process. They were purely "prudential arrangements," Wesley said, "not essential, nor of divine institution, constantly subject to change."[33] In one sense they were instruments for exploring all the meanings of Christianity for his age.

The original purpose of the parent group, the Methodist Society, was Christian nurture: "to pray together, to receive the word of exhortation, and to watch over one another in love, that they may help each other to work out their salvation."[34] But very soon the third purpose of the "original church" was added, that is, "to save all men from present and future misery ... and set up the Kingdom of Christ." [35] Each member was asked to contribute a penny a week for the care of the poor; collectors were appointed, and the welfare work of Methodism was begun.

These collectors on their rounds discovered persons and problems that needed closer attention than could be given in the large Society group, and so small classes were organized for the dual purpose of promoting Christian benevolence and providing Christian counsel. The leaders were laymen or women, whose duties were: (1) "To see each person in his class, once a week, at least, in order to inquire how their souls prosper; to advise, reprove, comfort, or exhort, as occasion may require, to receive what they are willing to give towards the relief of the poor," and (2) "To meet the Minister and Stewards of the Society, in order to inform the Minister of any that are sick, or of any that are disorderly, and will not be reproved; to pay the Stewards what they have received of their several classes in the week preceding." [36]

The class-meeting soon became the very heart of the Revival, providing it with its "life-blood." Workman believed it to be "the germ-cell of Methodism," remarking in 1912 that "in Methodism a church without a class-meeting is inconceivable." [37] Dale, who was a Congregationalist, thought that it was probably "the most striking and original of all the fruits of the Revival. It was not invented; it was the creation of the circumstances in which the Revival was carried on; it was the natural product of the soil." He warned the Methodist people to "take good heed how they treat so precious and wonderful a growth," saying, "It renders possible a far more effective fulfilment of the idea of the pastorate and a far more perfect realization of the communion of saints than are common in any other Protestant community." [38]

Dale wished that the Congregationalists could adopt it, for in it, he said, "we should secure a depth of religious earnestness, a fullness of religious joy, and a development of moral vigour and refinement which at present seems to be beyond our reach." [39]

As a matter of fact, such fellowships have been recurrent throughout the centuries in times of religious intensity. Harrison, after reviewing the various orders of mediaeval Christianity and such organizations among the Puritans as Baxter's weekly experience meeting, concludes that at all times "when the Christian religion has been alive it has discovered some form of intimate fellowship binding little companies of believers more closely together." [40]

The benefits of the Methodist class-meeting were many. It effectively nourished personal religion, throwing light upon wrong inward states, setting new goals each week, preventing the complacent formalism which Wesley so much dreaded. It exercised educational and cultural influences, also, upon the lowly, affording opportunities for self-expression and leadership, and thus increasing self-confidence and self-respect. It made of every Methodist "to some degree, a teacher, judge and preacher" and social worker. [41]

It was, above all, the major instrument in achieving the equalitarianism implicit in Wesleyan teaching. Through its intimate fellowship it became a common ground for rich and poor to practice democracy. The sharing of interests and problems of supreme consequence to all developed a mutual understanding and a bond of sympathy which forbade all social distinctions. It is true that the common task of rich and poor in building the Kingdom of God has always called for the adoption of democratic principles, but whenever the Church has provided no practical occasion for the operation of these principles, it has been the breeder instead of the extinguisher of caste. This has happened all too often. The Methodist class-meeting was the product of Wesley's genius for inventing effective implementation for his teaching. So long as it continued it achieved to a remarkable degree the purposes for which it was designed.

Wesley guarded jealously its democratic character. He wrote once to one of his preachers: ". . . you must immediately resume the form at least of a Methodist Society. I positively forbid you or any preacher to be a leader; rather put the most insignificant person in each class to be the leader of it." [42] It is true that it must often have been difficult to find in the societies leaders with the needed qualities of tact, spiritual insight and understanding of human nature; yet, when all who have studied early Methodist organizations have been convinced that in the class-meeting lies one of the chief causes for the success of the movement, we must conclude that these difficulties must usually have found a satisfactory solution.

The organization of bands was a further step in the process of providing care for soul and body. They originated in the popular request for smaller group meetings where complete freedom for confession and discussion of personal problems could be found. Men and women were segregated in this case, and the following rules were adopted: "1. Meet once a week. 2. Come punctually. 3. Begin with prayer or singing. 4. Speak out freely the true state of their souls, with faults committed in thought, word, or deed, and temptations since last meeting. 5. To ask some person of the group, after speaking his own state, to ask the rest 'as many and as searching questions as may be concerning their state, sins, and temptations.' " [43]

Another type of band, which seems not to have existed long, was composed of those who wished to consider more particularly the life of Christian Perfection. They were a "select company" to whom Wesley could speak without reserve, who needed no rules, and who bore the final responsibility for maintaining the high ideals of the movement. An interesting feature of this organization is their agreement to bring once a week all that they could spare toward a common stock.

Other organizational features which gave laymen opportunity for the practice of stewardship were the duties of the Society stewards, the very extensive activities of local preachers, and the full-time work of a lay ministry. Very early in the Revival Wesley brought before the Societies the needs of the sick and the poor and called for volunteers to assist stewards, class-leaders and preachers in their relief work. These visitors together covered the whole of London, seeing the sick three times a week, inquiring into their physical and spiritual needs, procuring the proper medical attention and spiritual counsel, and doing whatever was needed in the household.

This direct ministration to the needy was particularly expected of the rich. To those who asked that they be allowed to pay a doctor for such services Wesley replied that a doctor "cannot do them more good to their souls . . . . And if he could, this would not excuse *you*: his going would not fulfil *your* duty." [44]

The modern social worker will protest against such indiscriminate, unscientific procedure, but before we dismiss this advice, let us recognize that Wesley had his eye on the needs of the rich as well as the sufferings of the poor. He explained to the well-to-do parishioner, who shunned the homes of the poor, that positive good would come to him from seeing the living conditions of the needy: "One reason why the rich, in general, have so little sympathy with the poor, is, because they so seldom visit them. Hence it is, that, according to the common observation, one part of the world does not know what the other suffers. Many of them do not know, because they do not care to know; they keep out of the way of knowing; and then plead their voluntary ignorance as an excuse for their hardness of heart." [45]

He refers to "a person of large substance" who once declared, "I am a very compassionate man. But, to tell you the truth, I do not know anybody in the world who is in want." "How did this come to pass?" asks Wesley. "Why, he took good care to keep out of their way; and if he fell upon any of them unawares, 'he passed over on the other side.' " [46]

Wesley is again exposing the causes of social inequality and finding the remedy in the practice of Christian stewardship. The greatest danger in prosperity he once pointed out is that "it removes us from scenes of misery and indigence; we are apt to charge the great with want of feeling, but it is rather want of consideration. The wretched are taught to avoid them, and the poor fear to accost them; and in the circles of perpetual gaiety they forget that these exist." [47]

Is there any better method for counteracting the evils of wealth than the method discovered by Shakespeare's Lear: "Expose thyself to feel what wretches feel"? In Wesley's correspondence with Miss March, one of the well-to-do Methodists, he advises her not to confine her "conversation to genteel and elegant people." This, he says, he should like to do as well as she, but he "cannot discover a precedent for it in the life of our Lord or any of His Apostles." We must "walk as He walked." He then urges her to "converse more, abundantly more, with the poorest of the people." "Creep in among these," he says, "in spite of dirt and an hundred disgusting circumstances, and thus put off the gentlewoman." [48]

He grants that this "is not pleasing to flesh and blood. There are a thousand circumstances usually attending it which shock the delicacy of our true nature, or rather of our education." [49] Note the added phrase. It is eloquent in implying the kind of education Wesley wished to undo, an education which had made the upper class effeminate, afraid to face the ugliness in the world, while at the same time making the lower class coarser, more brutal, more to be feared. It had fostered class-consciousness, had kept the common people out of the church, and made the church a preserver of vested interests.

Wesley proposed to bring all classes together in the common cause of Kingdom-building. He found no provisions in the Kingdom plan for social or economic distinctions and he made none in his plan for the Societies. A class leader was as likely to be a blacksmith as a banker. A local preacher was chosen more for his natural gifts of spiritual insight than for his degree of education, and never for his bank account.

Wesley's wish to assign leadership only upon the basis of character and his deep antagonism to wealth as a criterion is shown in his comment on appointment of elders in Scotland: "In one parish, it seems, there are twelve Ruling Elders; in another there are fourteen. And what are these? men of great sense and deep experience? Neither one nor the other. But they are the *richest* men in the parish. And are the *richest* of course the best and wisest men? Does the Bible teach this? I fear not." [50]

The vigor with which Wesley enforced the necessity for the intermingling of rich and poor in direct ministration to the needy is to be seen in his conclusion to his sermon, "On Visiting the Sick," when he says, "All, who desire to escape everlasting fire and to inherit everlasting life, must practice this duty." [51]

Those "who are rich in this world," who have more than the conveniences of life, are here instructed, "As you are not under a necessity of working for your bread you have time at your own disposal. You may, therefore, allot some part of it every day for this labour of love. If it be practicable, it is far best to have a fixed hour . . . and not to employ that time in other business, without urgent necessity." [52]

Contrary to commonly held notions, the religion of early Methodists was not other-worldly. Every member, theoretically, at least, engaged in social work. No one was "too poor not to practise the rule," none too young. Parents instructed their children in this Christian duty. As a consequence social amelioration in the early years of the Revival held a place of equal emphasis with religious experience. Wesley could not have conceived of divorcing the two. Evangelism was not placed in one compartment and social work in another. This was impossible because Methodism saw personality as a whole and sought to minister to man's total well-being.

The joyous conviction that in "whole Christianity" is the panacea for all men's ills was never better expressed than in

Wesley's commission to George Shadford when he sent him out in 1773 on his mission to America. "I let you loose, George, on the continent of America. Publish your message in the open face of the sun, and do all the good you can." [58]

Methodism was a workshop in applied Christianity. It was not a doctrinaire movement, built upon an elaborate intellectualistic system and superimposed upon the masses; it was rather a natural, organic outgrowth from a principle which they had accepted. Wesley considered the origin of most of its organizational features comparable to the spontaneous appearance of similar practices among early Christians.

From his teaching on stewardship his followers caught a vision of a Christian society in which rich and poor shared not only their religious experiences, but also their wealth, their cultural advantages, and their talents for evangelism and social ministry, a society where the principles of Christianity worked as leaven to create a new order. They were not interested in building a new sect; the only reason for their founding of the Societies was that they had failed to find anywhere an organization which gave free operation to these principles.

The order which Wesley proposed and his failure to discover it in any existing religious endeavor was often stated in his early years in a poem entitled, "Primitive Christianity."

>Propriety was there unknown,
>None call'd what he possess'd his own;
>Where all the common blessings share,
>No selfish happiness was there.
>
>With grace abundantly endued,
>A pure, believing multitude!
>They all were of one heart and soul,
>And only love inspired the whole.
>. . . .
>Ye different sects, who all declare,
>"Lo, here is Christ!" or, "Christ is there!"

Your stronger proofs divinely give,
And show me where the Christians live.

Your claim, alas! ye cannot prove,
Ye want the genuine mark of love;
Thou only, Lord, thine own canst show;
For sure thou hast a Church below.⁵⁴

---

1. See *General Rules*, Appendix.
2. Loc. cit.
3. Loc. cit.
4. Loc. cit.
5. Loc. cit.
6. *Sermons*, II, 464.
7. *Sermons*, II, 477.
8. Loc. cit. Wesley probably accepted the theory of both Calvinism and the mediaeval church, which made room for a social hierachy; yet in practice he proposed to unsettle it.
9. Loc. cit.
10. See E. D. Bebb, *A Man With a Concern*, p. 44.
11. *Sermons*, II, 477.
12. *Ibid.*, p. 325
13. *Works*, VII, 308.
14. *Works*, VII, 360
15. *Works*, VI, 260.
16. *Works*, VI, 329.
17. *Works*, VII, 412.
18. *Works*, VI, 265.
19. *Sermons*, II, 314. It is interesting to know that the occasion for the first delivery of this sermon was a day proclaimed for a national fast, February 17, 1744, at the time when the young Pretender, Prince Charles, was preparing for attack upon England. Wesley here associates economic sins with national disaster. He is known to have preached this sermon at least twenty-two times.
20. *Ibid.*, p. 319.
21. Perry, *op. cit.*, p. 318.
22. *Letters*, V, 8.
23. *Sermons*, II, 323. Wesley said to his money-making members, "You who receive five hundred pounds a year and spend only two hundred pounds, do you give three hundred pounds back to God? If not, you certainly rob God of that three hundred pounds . . . O leave nothing behind you! *Works*, VII, 362.
24. *Sermons*, II, 326.
25. *Letters*, V, 108.
26. *Ibid.*, p. 230.
27. John Lawson, *Notes on Wesley's Forty-four sermons* (London: Epworth Press, 1946), p. 271.
28. W. J. Warner, *The Wesleyan Movement in the Industrial Revolution* (London: Longmans, Green & Co., 1930), p. 209.
29. Barbara Ward, "Christianity and Human Rights," The Atlantic Monthly, 1947, CLXXX, 40.
30. *Ibid.*, p. 41.
31. *Sermons*, I, 357.
32. Sermons, II, 482-3.
33. *Letters*, II, 298.
34. *General Rules*.
35. *Sermons*, II, 483.
36. *Works*, VIII, 253.
37. H. B. Workman, *Methodism* (Cambridge, University Press, 1912), p. 120.
38. R. W. Dale, *The Evangelical Revival and Other Sermons* (London: Hodder & Stoughton, 1880), p. 31.
39. Loc. cit.
40. Harrison, *op. cit.*, p. 26.

41. R. F. Wearmouth, *Methodism and the Common People of the Eighteenth Century* (London: Epworth Press, 1945), p. 221.
42. *Letters*, VII, 166.
43. *Works*, VIII, 258.
44. *Works*, VII, 119.
45. *Ibid.*, p. 120.
46. *Ibid.*, p. 122.
47. *Letters*, V, 181.
48. *Letters*, VI, 206.
49. *Loc. cit.*
50. *Journal*, IV, 317.
51. *Works*, VII, 123.
52. *Ibid.*, p. 124.
53. *Letters*, V, 22.
54. *Works*, VIII, 43.

XIV

Those Who Walked the Way

The audience which first received this teaching on stewardship was largely made up of lowly folk. Methodism in the eighteenth century was essentially a poor man's church. Its dominant characteristics were those which accompany the religion of the poor: an urgent sense of need, simplicity of faith, spontaneity in feeling, expressing itself vehemently at times, ready acceptance of rigorous disciplines, and emphasis upon the practice of religion rather than upon creed or ritual. In its main features it is seen to resemble, as Wesley had hoped it might, the early Church. Troeltsch speaks of it along with early Christianity as representative of the really "creative" movements that come from the lower classes, who unite "imagination and simplicity of feeling" with "an unconditional authoritative faith in a Divine Revelation."[1]

Hundreds of its converts came from the mass of idle, brawling, cursing, drunken semi-pagans who rarely entered the Church. Their response, once Wesley had broken through the wall that separated them from Christian influences, was astounding. The contrast between the results of his method and message and those achieved by the usual clergyman is illustrated by his own experience at Epworth soon after his conversion.

Having been refused the pulpit by the Epworth rector, Wesley preached from a tombstone in the adjoining churchyard to all who would hear him. In replying to the criticism called forth by his extraordinary method of approach and his equally objectionable message of "assurance," he said: ". . . many drunkards, many unjust and profane men, on whom both my father and I had for several years spent our strength in vain, from that time began to live, and continue so to do, a sober, righteous, and godly life. . . . If it be asked, But were there not 'the same hearers in the church—and the same God to influence in the church as on the tombstone'? I answer: (1) There were not all the same hearers in the church—not above one-third of them; (2) There was the same preacher in the church, but he did not then preach the same doctrine; and therefore, (3) though there was the same God, there was not the same influence or blessing from Him." [2] A new message was brought by a new method to a new people and a new and mighty religious movement began.

Wesley had discovered the essential gospel which Christ preached to the poor; he knew he had what they needed; and he was ready to sacrifice all conventionalities in order to become the instrument of God in reaching them. The same simple principle governed his unconventional use of ministers chosen from the people.

When it was said that Methodist ministers were "taken immediately from low trades—tailors, shoemakers, and the like" and were "a set of poor, stupid, illiterate men, that scarce know their right hand from their left," Wesley replied "I would sooner cut off my right hand than suffer one of them to speak a word in any of our chapels, if I had not reasonable proof that he had more knowledge in the Holy Scriptures, more knowledge of himself, more knowledge of God and of the things of God, than nine in ten of the Clergymen I have conversed with. . . ." [3] His need was for men, schooled or unschooled, who would not frustrate the grace of God in their own lives nor in its outreach to all men.

Every feature of church life was adapted to this same end. The early chapel and the behavior of its worshipers made a particular appeal to plain, common folk. Wesley describes the church as "not gay or splendid, but clean and plain, the people not gay or giddy, nor goodly, formal, outside Christians, but seekers of God. Not bowing or curtseying or staring at neighbors, but looking upward and inward." [4]

As for the service, "the person who reads prayers is above reproach, speaks from his heart, not in careless or hurrying manner. The addresses to God are not made by a drawling parish clerk, nor by screaming, bawling boys who do not understand what they say."[5] The music was spontaneous and completely congregational. "No unseasonable and unmeaning impertinence of a voluntary on the organ, no singing in the miserable, scandalous doggerel of Hopkins and Sternhold, but in psalms and hymns which are both sense and poetry. . . ." They were simply a medium for the direct approach of the soul to God and were "sung by the whole serious congregation all standing before God, and praising Him lustily and with a good courage."[6] The preaching was done "in plain, simple unaffected language."[7]

Here was a form of worship well within the comprehension of the lowly convert and in addition so conducive to his enjoyment and participation that Methodism drew, like a magnet, into its happy circle hundreds who had never known either a church home or Christian fellowship or any of the refining influences that such association brings. Their delight in these new-found joys sought spontaneous expression in ways that sometimes offended cultivated taste.

Gross exaggeration and even falsification undoubtedly accompanied the representation of early Methodist mass behavior,[8] but when proper allowance has been made for all this, there still remain those features of a poor man's church which will always arouse the antagonism of both the middle and upper classes. The protest of Hutton, a noble Christian, yet influenced by the aristocratic temper of the time, is illustrative of the difficulty that the refined man has to accept primitive Christianity.

Hutton spoke of the congregations as "composed of every description of persons, who, without the slightest attempt at order, assembled, crying 'Hurrah!' with one breath, and with the next bellowing and bursting into tears on account of their sins; some poking each other's ribs, and others shouting 'Hallelujah!'" He said it "was a jumble of extremes of good and evil; and so distracted alike were both the preachers and hearers, that it was enough to make one cry to God for His interference. Here thieves, prostitutes, fools, people of every class, several men of distinction, a few of the learned, merchants, and numbers of poor people who had never entered a place of worship, assembled in crowds and became godly." °

Those who know the spontaneity and directness with which the masses give expression to approval or disapproval of a popular appeal, especially an appeal for moral decision, can recognize in this description the earmarks of a revival of Christianity among the poor; yet these surface features always give offense to the sensibilities of the refined. No one ever liked decorum better than John Wesley, and it is a marvel that he did not retreat in dismay, as did Hutton, before these signs of religious enthusiasm. But his spiritual perceptions were far more powerful than his cultural prepossessions. The voice of God calling him to serve humanity was far louder than the cry of his injured sensibilities.

Another source of irritation to the upper class man inherent in a revival of Christianity is its threat to his latent sense of social caste. Southey's talk about Wesley's opinions being inconsistent with the existing order of society and his "rigid doctrine" on riches alienating the sympathy of the privileged classes is a pertinent illustration of this fact.[10] Movements which accept unequivocally the revolutionary principles implicit in Christianity *do* threaten the existing order of society. Southey was profoundly impressed by the consequences of the revival among the poor, but he refused to see that the major reason for these consequences was the revolutionary principle which he was criticizing.

Wesley had to be faithful to the teaching of Christ concerning both rich and poor. Furthermore, had he made any attempt to conciliate the "privileged classes," Methodism would at once have put on the garb of respectability, and its virility would have departed. This, in fact, we shall see, was what happened all too soon.

A further illustration of the class consciousness which refuses to give the poor man's religion its proper dues was the flippancy with which the equalitarianism of Methodism was commonly treated. It was considered a subject for satiric laughter, worthy only of such quips as that in Goldsmith's *She Stoops to Conquer*. The young Squire, referring to bedroom space at the local inn, reports "there are already in the bed two Methodist preachers and a chimney sweep." [11]

To the early Methodist the free association of high and low rich and poor, wise and foolish, clean and dirty, was not a subject for laughter; it was the urgent and attainable goal toward which all Christians move under the dictates of the law of love. And it must not be forgotten that while most of the Methodists were poor folk there were those of wealth and position who were not repelled by either Wesley's teaching or the character of the congregations. Numerous persons, like Ebenezer Blackwell and Lady Maxwell, accepted fully Christ's warnings on riches and became faithful stewards of the gifts placed in their hands, setting worthy examples that should have been followed by all poor Methodists when they rose in the economic scale.

Warner says that many of the well-to-do converts accepted the teaching on stewardship so completely that social relief became their avocation, consuming a large portion of their leisure time. Likewise, many converts whose moral uplift brought financial security retired from business and gave all their time to public charities.[12]

Working side by side in a fellowship that proposed to surmount all social and economic barriers, early Methodists discovered a great variety of ways for realizing their ideal. The plans for the care of the poor and sick mentioned in the preceding chapter were carried out with great ingenuity.[13] Money, clothes and medicine were provided. Employment was found for those capable of self-support.[14] A loan fund was made available for all strangers in need and the organization of this Strangers' Friend Society spread through all the English industrial centers.[15] So original was the work of Wesley and his followers that the Foundery, the first center of Methodism in London, became a pioneer social settlement where projects utterly new in the history of welfare work were tried out.[16]

The prison work initiated by Methodism led even by the end of the century to marked improvement in gaol conditions and furnished the incentive for extensive reforms in the succeeding years.[17] The education of the poor was undertaken through various agencies, such as evening classes for adults, boarding schools for poor boys, Sunday schools for city children.[18]

The acceptance of the obligations of stewardship by a representative Society such as that at the Foundery is attested to by the financial reports which have been preserved. Bebb in his study of them found that in twenty years London Methodists gave to the poor some 15,000 pounds, many of the givers being poor themselves. Moreover, an added sum which amounted to seventy-five per cent of this was given to the maintenance of preachers and their families, and a further fund was raised for new buildings.[19] Apparently, first generation Methodists were by and large practicers of the perfect love theory as it relates to the needy.

Yet ministration to physical want was not their final goal. Accompanying this great social experiment was a vast evangelistic enterprise. It has been said that "Wesley led more people to Christ than any man who has ever lived in England," and that his declaration in 1785 that "the number reached by the revival was greater than in any other age since the time of the Apostles can hardly be challenged by anyone who knows" the facts.[20] His desire to "take the whole world for his parish" was not an expression of egotism nor desire for power; it was simply a declaration of a concern for the good of all men so profound as to bridge distance, race and color.

He never forgot his unfulfilled mission to the American Indian, and when he was eighty-four years old he plead for someone to take responsibility for their conversion, lamenting, "How many millions of them (in South and North America) have already died in their sins! Will neither God nor man have compassion upon these outcasts of men?" [21] The last letter he ever wrote was an exhortation to William Wilberforce to "Go on, in the name of God and in the power of His might, till even American slavery (the vilest that ever saw the sun) shall vanish away before it." [22]

The result of Wesley's great yearning for the salvation of all men and his power to kindle this passion in others was the phenomenal growth of Methodist Societies in his lifetime and a continuing extension of Methodism after his death. In 1791 Methodists in Great Britain numbered 57,562 and in America 48,565. Eighteen years after his death these numbers had more than doubled, mounting to 171,590 in Great Britain, and in America to 159,500. [23]

So surely had he laid the foundations of evangelism and humanitarianism among his followers that they made the Christianizing of the English-speaking world their main business in life. Only a profound conviction of the truth of the principles which they had espoused and a contagious enthusiasm for the way of life which they had adopted can account for the amazing achievements of the Evangelical Movement in the nineteenth century. The followers of Wesley had set out to bring into being his vision of "a Christian world."

Wesley himself marveled at what he could explain only as "the work of God." "There is scarcely a considerable town in the kingdom," he said, "where some have not been made witness of it. It has spread to every age and sex, to most orders and degrees of men; and even to abundance of those, who, in time past, were accounted monsters of wickedness." In its swiftness he could find no parallel in religious movements since the time of Constantine. As for depth, multitudes have been "thoroughly convinced of sin; and shortly after, so filled with joy and love, that whether they were in the body, or out of the body, they could hardly tell; and, in the power of this love, they have trampled under foot whatever the world accounts either terrible or desirable, having evidenced, in the severest trials, an invariable and tender goodwill to mankind, and all the fruits of holiness." [24]

The repercussions of a movement so extensive in its outreach can never be analyzed fully or measured exactly. Many scholars have attempted to do so with varying results. But while they differ in their conclusions,[25] all agree that every phase of life among English speaking peoples had been touched by Methodism by the end of the eighteenth century—the moral, the social, the economic, the political, and even the literary.

By the time of Wesley's death the impact of the Revival upon the moral, social and economic life of the masses was being noted even by secular writers. The Annual Register of 1791 devoted an article to his passing, and after describing the one-time lawlessness of life around colliery towns, attributed to the "humane and active endeavors" of the Wesley brothers "the sense of decency, morals, and religion" that now characterized "the lowest classes of mankind." [26] "To you," declared Joseph Priestly in "An Address to the Methodists," "is the civilization, the industry and sobriety of great numbers of the laboring part of the community owing." [27]

The marked decrease in brawling, gambling and intoxication is attestation to the general acceptability of social standards radically different from those which we have earlier described. Lotteries were no longer approved, nor were masquerades. All the brutal forms of amusement had disappeared. As for the theater, although it lay outside the direct influence of Methodism because of the Methodist proscription of it, the change in the moral tone of late eighteenth century drama gives evidence of a salutary influence upon literary standards and audience taste.

The adherents of Methodism, those who never fully identified themselves with the Societies, have been estimated as numbering four times the active membership.[28] This larger circle responded to the peripheral influences of the Revival, and thus renewed moral insight came to a great number of religiously inclined people. Dormant Puritan influences were again released to produce reforms in amusement and various other social areas.

The report which Wesley gave for the neighborhood of Kingswood, a coal mining town just outside Bristol, could be repeated for every community where Methodism had established itself. Describing the people as originally "but one remove from beasts . . . without desire of instruction, as well as without the means of it," he told how in one year the scene had changed: "Kingswood does not now . . . resound with cursing and blasphemy. It is no more filled with drunkenness and uncleanness, and the idle diversions that naturally lead thereto . . . Peace and love are there."[29] City haunts of vice, also, like Moorfields, adjoining the Foundery, were converted into respectable residential and business sections.

But while all these social reforms are remarkable, the change which held the greatest promise for the future was the new spirit at work in the State Church. The outward signs of this leavening process were not yet very encouraging in 1791, the year of Wesley's death. The widening cleavage between the Societies and the mother Church was creating increasing official condemnation of the movement. This hostility was voiced in an act by Parliament passed in 1792 ordering an increase in church building for the express purpose of checking the rapid spread of Methodism and the menace it offered to the Establishment. Even yet the religious and moral needs of the poor had not entered into the thinking of official Anglicanism, the preservation of the *status quo* remaining its chief concern.

On the other hand, a study of the trends within the Anglican ministry at large has led to the conclusion that even by 1788 more than five hundred clergymen had been infected by the Revival.[20] Preaching was undergoing a change in its point of view and in its message. The emphasis was shifting from the purely speculative aspects of religion to the personal and evangelical.

What was happening to "the religion of reason" and "the way of humanism"? What had become of the claims of natural religion? The efforts of the speculative theologians to restore religious faith by an exclusive appeal to reason, the hope of the humanists to produce moral betterment by an appeal to natural goodness, had admittedly failed. Commendable as had been the efforts of Butler and other controversialists to prop "a falling church" by an attack upon the weaknesses of natural religion and deism, it could not save the day.

But Methodism, by its recovery of supernaturalism, by its discovery of love as the central principle of Christianity, by its fearless proclamation of a distinctive way of life growing out of acceptance of this principle—in other words, by its fresh recognition of the primal elements of Christianity—had led the way out of the dilemma which had threatened to reduce the boasted Age of Enlightenment to paganism.

Time had proved that Wesley had not been mistaken when he had said in his "Letter to Conyers Middleton": that the day would come when men of spiritual insight would no longer rest the whole case for Christianity upon a defense of the external and traditional evidences, but would be driven by deism to seek "a deeper and firmer support" in the experience and character of those who through the ages have taken the Christian way. The distinction was finally seen, as he had predicted, between the "real Deists," all those who have rejected the supernatural gift of faith and love, and the "real Christians," who, because they have accepted this gift, prove by their lives the transcendent truth of Christianity.[21]

Wesley did not live to see the triumph of the Evangelical movement once the ferment of Methodism had broken up the obstacles. Perhaps the old generation with their mistaken ideas of Christianity and the Way had to disappear before the new message could come to the fore. But its hold upon the incoming generation is remarkable, even the poets and philosophers seizing upon the love of God and mankind as a unique and exploitable theme.

One of the most impressive contrasts between the poetry at the beginning of the century and that at the end arises from a change in the conception of God. Whereas Addison and Pope had apostrophized God as the great *Maker* of a harmonious, intelligible universe in the intellectualized diction of that day, Blake, Wordsworth and Coleridge now extolled God as the supreme *Lover* of mankind and celebrated the humanitarian spirit among men in language kindled by the imagination.

Not since the metaphysical poets of the seventeenth century, had any literary leader voiced the emotion of personal religious experience as does Wordsworth in these lines from one of his "Inscriptions":

> But thou art true, incarnate Lord,
> Who did vouchsafe for man to die:
> Thy smile is sure, Thy plighted word
> No change can falsify!
> I bent before Thy gracious throne,
> And asked for peace on suppliant knee;
> And peace was given—nor peace alone,
> But Faith sublimed to ecstasy.[32]

The frequency with which the language of the Revival recurs in the poetry of these new leaders shows how deeply its influence had wrought upon the popular consciousness.[33]

By the dawn of the nineteenth century Methodism had done its great work of infiltration. It had been fortunate in the long life and astounding virility of its leader. He is estimated to have travelled on horseback more than 250,000 miles and to have preached 40,000 sermons.[34] Great success had attended the endeavors of a laymen's movement in which every man, woman and child was nominally, at least, both an evangelist and a social worker.

In another respect, too, it had been successful—perhaps more successful than any other movement on record. It had managed to cultivate religious tolerance at the same time that it maintained its own distinctive and exacting way of life. This was not the result of accident. It had been brought about, like many other features of Methodism, through the well-considered teaching and planning of its leader.

The Church of Wesley's youth was the preacher of religious toleration. After the dissensions of the seventeenth century it had been very ready to make great compromises in order to have peace. This end was mistakenly sought, however, as we have seen in our survey of the Ways that could not answer Wesley's need, in the formulation of a minimal creed which would be acceptable to all denominations through the exclusive appeal to reason. Accompanying this was a minimal ethical code which so eliminated the exacting requirements of the Christian way that it differed little from the codes of Stoicism and other pagan philosophies. The Latitudinarians bought toleration by surrendering to the secularists the doctrines which were fundamental to Protestantism and the ethics which are at the heart of Christianity. All this we have seen Wesley discovering in the course of his quest for the Christian way.

Yet at the same time that Wesley was recognizing the errors into which the Church had fallen in its attempts to destroy bigotry and establish a common basis for union, he was observing also the errors which had made the Puritan sects less effective than they should have been in bringing about a national reformation. He had the distinct advantage of coming at the end of a transitional era, when the weaknesses of both sectarianism and humanism had been fully exposed.[26]

Through his wide reading and his experience with the Moravians he had also the advantage of a historical viewpoint which threw into relief all those religious movements which had approximated the faith and the practice of the early Church. Recognizing in each sect certain excellences to which other sects had been blind, he was forced to admit that there might be various roads to evangelical truth. The sectarian had contended for his own particular road as the only one. He had not seen the particular elements of Christianity which he had recovered in their historic background nor in their relationship to other contemporary movements.

Wesley's perspective upon sectarianism and the various outcomes possible in the exercise of private judgment led him to say that no man can "be assured that all his own opinions, taken together, are true . . . to be ignorant of many things, and to mistake in some, is the necessary condition of humanity." [36] He goes so far as to say that opinion "does not depend on . . . choice: I can no more think, than I can see or hear, as I will." [37] And as for modes of worship, "this also is a thing which does not depend either on your choice or mine. We must both act as each is fully persuaded on in his own mind." [38] This being true, he concludes that "every wise man . . . will allow others the same liberty of thinking which he desires they should allow him; and will no more insist on their embracing his opinions, than he would have them to insist on his embracing theirs." [39]

The inevitable consequence of these observations was that when Wesley looked for a basis for toleration he should go beyond a common intellectual point of view, such as had been offered in natural religion or in sectarian opinion, and seek for a principle upon which to agree. That is, the union had to be spiritual rather than intellectual, inward rather than outward. Neither creeds nor ordinances nor prudentials could furnish the common basis.

This principle, we may be sure, would be love, and many are the declarations made by Wesley of the feasibility of this common meeting ground for all true followers of Christ, even to Roman Catholics. In his letter to this group he says: "I do not suppose all the bitterness is on your side. I know there is too much on our side, also; so much, that I fear many Protestants (so called) will be angry at me too, for writing to you in this manner." [40] After an effort to show that Protestantism and Romanism have much in common he pleads for love between them.

It is essential to an understanding of Wesley's plea for toleration to know precisely what he meant by love. It must not be confused with that pantheistic sentimentalism of the nineeenth century that made no distinction between God and man, nor even with that vaguely Christian sentiment derived from a purely theoretical belief in the Brotherhood of man and the Fatherhood of God.

The love which Wesley had in mind was God-given, and union was possible only between hearts that had been supernaturally transfused. In his letters to and about his nephew, Samuel, who had entered the Roman Catholic fold, he makes this the one essential for union. Unless a man has experienced an "inward change of the earthly, sensual mind for the mind which was in Christ Jesus" he will perish everlastingly. Opinions, "Protestant or Romish," even when they are "unscriptural, superstitious, and idolatrous" [41] will not keep a man out of heaven if he has the true religion of "happiness in God, faith working by love." [42] This is the basis for agreement between believers possible only to those whom God makes one through His gift. This, then, is what Wesley meant when he said so frequently that the only question he asked those who desired to unite with him was, "Is thy heart right, as my heart is with thy heart?"

This does not mean that a tolerant man is "indifferent to all opinions." Wesley had no patience with such a man.[43] The tolerant man "knows how to value . . . all the advantages he enjoys . . . in . . . doctrine, a form of worship, a congregation." But "retaining these blessings with the strictest care," at the same time he loves "all of whatever opinion or worship, or congregation, who believe in the Lord Jesus Christ; who love God and man; who, rejoicing to please, and fearing to offend God, are careful to abstain from evil, and zealous of good works." [44]

It is very evident that Wesley hoped through this new policy of toleration, not only to overcome the evils of humanistic latitudinarianism, but also to impregnate so effectively all the religious groups of the time with the ideal and experience of Christian love that a nation-wide reformation would take place. In 1786 he recalled how back in 1744 "at our first Conference, we considered ourselves (Methodist preachers), as extraordinary messengers whom God had rasied up to provoke to jealousy the ordinary messengers, the clergy; to preach the gospel to the poor, and to call all men of every denomination to worship Him in spirit and in truth." [45]

His followers were imbued with this ideal. In outlining his purposes in 1748 he wrote: "The thing which I was greatly afraid of all this time, and which I resolved to use every possible method of preventing, was, a narrowness of spirit, a party zeal . . . that miserable bigotry which makes many so unready to believe that there is not any work of God but among themselves." In consideration of this he decided frequently to read, he says, "the accounts I received from time to time of the work which God is carrying on in the earth, both in our own and other countries, not among us alone, but among those of various opinions and denominations." [46]

Probably one of the strongest reasons for Wesley's insistence upon remaining with the Church of England was his wish for the continuance of this opportunity of contact with the whole national life. In his sermon preached at the foundation of the City Road Chapel he mentioned this as one of the notable features of Methodism and said that the connection with the Church of England had made for greater results than had attended the seventeenth century sectarian movements. These after they had withdrawn from the State Church "did scarce any good, except to their own little body." [47] Anglicans thereupon formed a prejudice against them and since they were "immensely the greatest number, the hope of a general, national reformation was totally cut off." [48]

Wesley saw clearly that the Societies had brought into Anglicanism the doctrines and practices which were fundamentally Protestant. By his adoption of all the disciplines that had characterized both the early church and Protestant movements, he hoped to forestall bigotry and bitter zeal. In the City Road sermon he declared that Methodists are not "bigoted to any particular branch even of practical religion; they are not attached to one point more than another; they aim at uniform, universal obedience. They contend for nothing circumstantial, as if it were essential to religion; but for everything in its own order." [49]

Wesley, therefore, saw value in a connection with a State Church. However, it must not be concluded that he considered this a true Christian union, for true union can exist only between those who love one another out of a pure heart, and who endeavor in practice to abstain from evil and zealously promote good works. We have seen how very carefully he sought to nurture this kind of union within the Societies. This he was determined must not be destroyed by intimate association with the religious compromise and secularism of the mother Church. The very *raison d'etre* for the Societies was the need for a separate organization for those who, because of their ardent desire to "flee from the wrath to come," were ready to avoid "evil in every kind" and to do "good of every possible sort."

The channels for the widest overflow into national life were thus to be kept open, while the stream itself was to be kept pure. These two ends were to be accomplished, first, by a more or less nominal connection with the large body of the Establishment; secondly, by the closely-knit organization and the intimate fellowships of a "gathered church"; and, thirdly, by a union in spirit with all inside and outside the State Church whose hearts were right with God.

There can be no doubt as one reads the religious history of

the nineteenth century that Methodism accomplished this very union and through it achieved to an amazing degree its purpose of infiltration. One evidence is the rise of the Evangelical Movement in the Church of England, and the other is the unmistakable change in the spiritual temper of Nonconformity. Both of these outcomes have been so fully recorded by various scholars[50] that only brief reference to them need be made here.

Within the Church Puritanism for the first time came to its "full flowering."[51] From the clergymen whom we have noted as infected by the Methodist message in the last decade of the eighteenth century came the great religious and reform movements which include such names as John Newton, William Wilberforce, Thomas Scott, the two Milners, Charles Simeon, and, climaxing all, the men who made the Clapham Sect "a sect that moved the world."[52]

Strengthened by the very persecution which it had to meet, Evangelicalism took deeper root in the national Church at the same time as Wesleyanism was forced by elements inherent in its growth to withdraw. Although the separation which Wesley had fought took place, the seed planted in the Church flowered into a marvelous fruitage, and in the meantime the Methodist Societies were doubling their membership in the first two decades after his death.

With the appointment of the first Evangelical bishop in 1815 the accumulated forces were released to work a gradual transformation in the whole life of Church and State. The deep and fervid spirit of the Evangelicals revived an interest in both piety and Church tradition and in the middle of the century the Oxford movement came "as a logical development of Evangelicalism," rather than as a reaction against it.[53] By the end of the nineteenth century the Church of England was "a contrast in almost every way with the same Church of a hundred years before."[54]

Similar influences stemming from the Revival were at work among the Nonconformist groups before the end of the eighteenth century. We have seen the decadence in their spiritual fervor as they had settled down early in the century to a state of bigoted exclusiveness or dead rationalism and impotent respectability. We have seen also Wesley's criticism of their so-called "religion of opinions," their over-emphasis upon circumstantials and particularities, and their lack of disciplinary maintenance of their original principles.

The dimming of their spiritual perception is manifest in the violent hostility expressed by their leaders when, under the influence of the Revival, the very features which had characterized the early ardor of nonconformity began to reappear. Those features, in particular, which we have noted as typical of the poor man's religion proved most irritating. The report given by Walter Wilson in the appendix of his *History of the Dissenting Churches* in 1814 betrays this hostility as well as the welcome fact that a restoration of the old-time fervor was well under way.

He complains that " 'the great mass of modern Dissenters have thrown all the weight of their influence into the hands of *nondescript persons*, who are more remarkable for their religious zeal than for its judicious application.' " He admits that many Dissenters had been " ' sunk in apathy,' " but insists that there were still " 'a goodly number' " whose labours for the " 'extension of the Redeemer's kingdom' " were both abundant and successful, " 'though *without noise and parade.*' "[65] His real attitude toward evangelism he exposes when he says: " 'It is true they did not beat up a crusade in the religious world for the *wild purpose* of proselyting the savage Hottentot . . . but they conducted plans of instruction for the rising generation of their countrymen, which turned to infinitely better account.' "[66]

He is an advocate of religious education to the exclusion of evangelism at home and abroad, deploring the fact that the old Nonconformist ministers, who were notable for their literary attainments, are now " 'branded for their formality' " and have been superseded by " 'an irregular and enthusiastic class . . . a new race of Dissenters,' " who are " 'adopting much of the zeal that distinguishes the Methodists.' " Begrudgingly he grants that the " 'cause of Independency has *gained* ground considerably' " during the last twenty years, but yet, with the blindness typical of the opponent of revivalism, he insists that what Nonconformity has gained in numbers it has lost in quality."

Time, of course, proved the merits of those who led this forward movement among the masses; for the first time Nonconformity actually reached down to the lowest social levels. The work of Whitefield in England and Scotland, and of Howell Harris in Wales, the removal of many of the most vital Anglican clergymen and their followers to Dissent because of the opposition in their home churches, the creation by the Revival of a national climate more favorable to the practice of the Christian way of life, all combined to reinvigorate the Free churches.

Their numerical growth toward the end of the century is a reliable criterion of their new drawing power among the masses. A rough estimate indicative of the phenomenal change that was taking place, shows them to number one to eight in proportion to Anglicans at the end of the eighteenth century as against one to twenty-one at the century's opening.[58] Coomer says that the fervor infused into the old theology and organization that still remained in Dissent made of nineteenth century Nonconformity "an almost irresistible force." Probably by the mid-century their congregations equalled those of the Establishment, and at one time Nonconformity was so strong that it seemed that Disestablishment "was bound to come." [59]

Thus did the Wesleyan gospel of love work as leaven, first among the great unchurched masses, then in the State Church among the upper classes, creating a genuine evangelistic and humanitarian spirit, and simultaneously among the nonconformists, fanning their almost extinguished enthusiasm into a blazing fire which drew both the poor and the middle classes to its warmth. Seen from the perspective of the twentieth century the Methodists seem truly the "extraordinary messengers," that Wesley conceived them to be, arousing the Anglican clergy, preaching "the gospel to the poor," and calling "all men of every denomination" to a revival of true Christianity.

Wesley's belief in the possibility of a Christian union between those who love one another out of a pure heart was substantiated in a growing agreement upon Evangelical doctrine. "It may well be argued," says Harrison, "that the Evangelical Revival created more orthodox Christians than any popular movement of religion in the history of the Church."[60] In spite of wide differences in opinions about mode of worship and prudentials, the old wounds from sectarianism were healed and earnest Christians of all denominations united in many forms of religious, moral and social endeavor.

The consequence of such commonly shared faith and love was the common adoption of a distinctive way of life. The agreement upon the main features of the Christian way among the different sects of the nineteenth century is remarkable. There were, to be sure, differences about small particularities, and sometimes regrettable emphasis upon these, but the comprehension of the basic principles which characterized the Wesleyan way was so clear and the acceptance so unanimous as to seem almost phenomenal to us today. So also was the willingness among believers to adopt the rigorous disciplines essential to putting these principles into practice. The nineteenth century was animated by a buoyant hope of achieving in practice what was declared in the profession of faith, and out of that hope was born such heroic endeavor as makes the modern church look impotent and futile.

We may see areas where the principle of love was not put into practice; we may wonder why so little was done to christianize the whole social order; but we must admit that the great rank and file of Christians in the early nineteenth century courageously undertook to realize in their lives all that they understood about the meaning of love. This is certainly more than can be said today, when most discussions of the religious situation are prefaced with an admission that no one pretends to live up to his profession, when, in fact, the most earnest effort is made to accommodate Christian teaching to imperfect people in an imperfect world.

Wesley set out to organize a body of believers who would actually bring profession and practice together—that was, indeed, the only justification he offered for organizing another "gathered church"—and the consequence was that a great group among the whole body of believers followed suit. These formed a truly Christian union in the bonds of love and in the adoption of "the more excellent way."

From this union of like minds disciplined and dedicated to the espousal of great causes came the reforms of the nineteenth century. Sunday again became the Lord's Day; profanity was placed in the category of bad taste; successive Parliamentary acts brought the manufacture and use of spirituous liquors under control and a reformed popular sentiment gave support to a national temperance movement; amusement was Christianized and lost its brutality and profligacy; the spirit of gambling which had corrupted the national sense of honesty completely disappeared; literature (stigmatized sometimes today as Puritan and Victorian) mirrored belief in God, concern for moral and social reform, and faith for the realization of man's loftiest ideals. The great missionary enterprises were begun; Sunday schools spread throughout England; hospitals and children's homes were founded. Prison conditions were changed; factory laws improved working conditions; English trade in slaves came to an end.

These are some of the consequences of the adoption of the Wesleyan way. No one man or movement was responsible for this outcome, for the sources of moral and social change are too complex, too deeply hidden ever fully to be traced. But historians agree that towering above every figure that played a part in shaping these events is the man who took the world for his parish, and who, in his endeavor to reform the nation by a restoration of the national Church to the principles and practices of "The Way" came as near to realizing this dream as has any person who has ever lived.

---

1. Ernst Troeltsch, op. cit., I, 44.
2. Letters, II, 99.
3. Works, VII, 179.
4. Letters, III, 226.
5. Loc. cit.
6. Loc. cit.
7. Ibid., p. 227.
8. See Sydney G. Dimond, *The Psychology of the Methodist Revival* (Oxford: University Press, 1926)
9. Tyerman, op. cit., I, 236. Quoted from Hutton's *Memoirs*, p. 42.
10. Robert Southey, *The Life of Wesley; and the Rise and Progress of Methodism* (London: Longman & Co., 1820), II, 521.
11. Quoted by Bebb, op. cit., p. 139.
12. Warner, op. cit., p. 192.
13. Bready, op. cit., p. 269. Wesley's work in promoting household sanitation and general health makes him one of the "vital pioneers of the national health movement" according to Sir George Newman: *Health and Social Evolution*. His instruction given in *Primitive Physic* and his work with electrical treatments show his great resourcefulness.
14. See *Journal*, II, 453-4 for the plans for care of the poor, sick, hungry and unemployed. The first work provided was knitting for poor women.
15. *Letters*, VII, 308. This plan originated among Society members.
16. See Wearmouth's account: R. F. Wearmouth, *Methodism and the Common People of the Eighteenth Century* (London: Epworth Press, 1945), pp. 212-5.
17. Contrast conditions described by Bready, op. cit., pp. 126-134 with those described in pp. 365-72.
18. *Letters*, VIII, 34. Wesley says the Sunday Schools were "one of the noblest specimens of charity which have been set on foot in England since the time of William Conquerer." See Alfred H. Body, *John Wesley and Education* (London, Epworth Press, 1936)
19. E. D. Bebb, *Non-Conformity and Social and Economic Life—1660-1800* (London: Epworth Press, 1935), Appendix VIII, p. 143.
20. Bebb, op. cit., p. 10.
21. *Letters*, VIII, 24
22. Ibid., p. 265
23. Harrison, op. cit., p. 56. Cf. figures given by R. F. Wearmouth, op. cit., p. 178.
24. *Works*, VII, 425-6.
25. The opinion that the Methodist movement prevented the coming of revolution to England simultaneously with the French Revolution is an instance, scholars disagreeing widely.
26. *The Annual Register . . . for the Year* 1791 (London: Pr. by G. Auld)
27. Quoted from Joseph Priestly, *Original Letters by the Rev. John Wesley*, pp. xvii-xviii, by Warner, op. cit., p. 175.
28. Wearmouth, op. cit., p. 178.
29. *Journal*, II, 322-3.
30. Wearmouth, op. cit., p. 168.
31. *Works*, X, 77.
32. William Wordsworth, *Complete Poetical Works* (Boston: Houghton Mifflin Co., 1904), p. 566.
33. See Frederick C. Gill, *The Romantic Movement and Methodism* (London: Epworth Press, 1937), pp. 148, et seq.
34. Wearmouth, op. cit., p. 180.
35. See *Sermons*, II, 145, for hymn used in conclusion:
"I weary of all this wordy strife
   These notions, forms and modes, and names,
To Thee, the Way, the Truth, the Life,
   Whose love my simple heart inflames,
   Divinely taught, at last I fly,
   With Thee, and Thine to live, and die."
36. *Sermons*, II, 132.
37. Ibid., p. 139.
38. Loc. cit.

39. *Ibid.*, p. 133.
40. *Works*, X, 80.
41. *Letters*, VII, 230.
42. *Ibid.*, p. 216.
43. *Letters*, III, 35.
44. *Sermons*, II, 145.
45. *Letters*, VII, 332.
46. *Works*, VIII, 257.
47. *Works*, VII, 427. In 1790 he wrote, "I advise our brethren that have been brought up in the Church to continue there; and there I leave the matter. The Methodists are to spread life among all denominations; which they will do till they form a separate sect." *Letters*, VIII, 210.
48. *Letters*, VIII, 210.
49. *Works*, VII, 427.
50. Cf., Barclay, Bready, Coomer, Harrison and G. R. Balleine, *A History of the Evangelical Party in the Church of England* (New York: Longmans, 1908)
51. Maldwyn Edwards, *This Methodism* (London: Epworth Press, 1939), p. 52.
52. Cf., Bready, *op. cit.*, p. 289, and Balleine, *op. cit.*, pp. 278-316.
53. Harrison, *op. cit.*, p. 165.
54. *Ibid.*, p. 167.
55. Quoted by Barclay, *op. cit.*, p. 600.
56. *Loc. cit.*
57. *Loc. cit.*
58. Harrison, *op. cit.*, p. 129.
59. Coomer, *op. cit.*, p. 124. Cf. Barclay, *op. cit.*, p. 600, who says that they were not only increased in numbers but brought back to their first principles.
60. Harrison, *op. cit.*, p. 88.

XV

The Wesleyan Way in Perspective

"It was in a sense the tragedy of Methodism that, having accomplished so much, it was not able to accomplish more."[1] This is the judgment of Maldwyn Edwards, who knows Methodism as comprehensively as anyone now writing. Wherein did Methodism fail?

The full assessment of the results of the movement has been possible only within the last few years, when a proper perspective upon the decades which followed Wesley's death could be obtained. This perspective has revealed not only the glorious record which we have just surveyed but also areas of need which, in spite of the dominance of the humanitarian spirit, were ignored or, even worse, condoned by sophistical reasoning in the name of religion. These moral blind spots of Wesley's descendants have been subjected to merciless examination, particularly by modern sociologists and economists.

The most extreme of these criticisms have been answered by Methodist scholars, who have shown that Methodism, while outwardly conservative in its economic and political policies, possessed inwardly principles so radical that they worked creatively toward most of the social reforms which occurred during the nineteenth century. Above all, Methodism nurtured the social conscience which gave birth to these movements. Most historians would agree with Halevy that "in the vast work of social organisation, which is one of the dominant characteristics of nineteenth-century England, it would be difficult to over-estimate the part played by the Wesleyan revival."[2]

Yet the fact remains that the leaders of the Evangelical movement as the nineteenth century wore on were, as a group, actually less sensitive to the evils of the social and economic order than were non-Christians, and their failure to apply Wesleyan principles to all areas of life was greatly responsible for the complete secularization during the past century of many of the functions originally performed by the Methodist Societies.

The design of the Wesleyan way subordinated all of life to spiritual principles even more effectively and comprehensively than had the mediaeval church, in that it placed upon each individual the responsibility for the total welfare of the world. It relegated neither special religious experience nor special religious duties to the chosen few. It expected the utmost in both personal attainment and social responsibility of every man and woman.

For this reason the apathy of the Evangelical movement toward issues that deeply affected the moral and spiritual life of the last century does not seem to correspond with the alert sensitivity of early Methodists to human need nor to accord with Wesleyan teaching concerning the practice of perfect love. Did the principle of perfect love continue to hold its central place as the criterion for both personal and social religion? Did Methodists continue to respond flexibly to all the implications of this principle? Did the regulations by which Wesley had hoped to educate his followers in a "reasonable and religious" use of time and money continue to command their respect and obedience?

We must look for answers to these questions, first of all, to Wesley's own observations during his last years upon the state of affairs in the Societies. It is true that in sermons of this period we find a tone of marvel at the great "work of God." Nor has time proved that he was exaggerating when he said exultingly at the founding of City Road Chapel: "This revival of religion has spread to such a degree, as neither we nor our fathers have known."[3] Dr. Church's recent survey presents a host of early Methodists who joyously walked the Wesleyan Way.[4]

And yet, in spite of these very good reasons for unqualified satisfaction with the Revival, Wesley sounded a note of concern over and over again in later sermons on dress, worldly-mindedness and riches. A change was evidently taking place in Methodism in the last decades of the century.

His handling of the problem varies from sermon to sermon; sometimes he deals with the outward manifestations of change in costlier and gayer clothing, purchase of fine houses and furnishings, patronage of questionable amusements; sometimes with the indications of an inward change, such as absorption in business, indifference to private prayer, neglect of self-denial. But always his diagnosis of the causes of change is the same: the growing love of money is stifling the life within the soul and limiting the outward manifestation of perfect love. As Methodists grow richer they become less responsive to the teaching of Christian Perfection. Here, he declares, is the root of evils, which, if not ruthlessly destroyed, will obstruct the work of God in the future.

This is not the conclusion of an old man obsessed with nostalgia for "the good old days." It is an accurate observation from a man who, because he had had a closer contact with the classes which were rising through the Industrial Revolution than was enjoyed by any other person, and, because he had seen among the nonconformists a causal relationship between economic change and spiritual decline, had good reason for concern over the future of Methodism.

He realized that the spiritual decadence which he had observed among such nonconformist groups as the Quakers and the Baptists was bound to take place among Methodists if the full implications of the theories of perfect love and Christian stewardship were not continuously seen and put into operation. Only the persistence of uncompromising and courageous practice of the disciplines of the Wesleyan way would avert this disaster.

Long before our day of scientific analysis of economic processes Wesley recognized that the Puritan cultivation of the economic virtues tends to destroy Christianity. In a sermon on "The Causes of the Inefficacy of Christianity," seeking to explain past recessions in spiritual power, he came upon the discovery that the virtues which are developed by the adoption of a disciplined Christian life almost inevitably lead to the accumulation of riches, and that riches in their turn react upon this Christian way of life to destroy it.

He exclaims in this sermon: ". . . how astonishing a thing is this! How can we understand it? Does it not seem (and yet this cannot be) that Christianity, true Scriptural Christianity, has a tendency, in process of time, to undermine and destroy itself? For wherever true Christianity spreads, it must cause diligence and frugality, which, in the natural course of things, must beget riches! and riches naturally beget pride, love of the world, and every temper that is destructive of Christianity. Now, if there be no way to prevent this, Christianity is inconsistent with itself, and of consequence, cannot stand, cannot continue long among any people; since, wherever it generally prevails, it saps its own foundation." [5]

The same conclusion has been reached in the twentieth century by historians in their analyses of the course of all the Protestant movements which attempted to recover the Christian way. Perry in his discussion of the economic phases of American Puritanism finds that the "puritan cult of economic virtues represents an advancing worldliness in which Christianity arrived at a reversal of its original profession of faith . . ." [6] "Christian piety, having been transferred to the business of this world, suffered from its own success like a plant withering under the density of its own foliage." [7]

This strange coalition between ethical and economic virtues had greatly accelerated the rise of the middle classes in seventeenth century England and now when the lower classes had received through Methodism the first full impact of Puritanism the same threat to Christian piety reappeared. Wesley saw it as a serious ethical phenomenon and was disturbed; moderns see it mainly as an economic phenomenon and associate it with the rise of capitalism. But, if it is true that the complete Christianizing of life is the final answer to all problems, then Wesley's analysis is the more significant of the two.

Christianity, Wesley concluded, is not actually inconsistent with itself. It appears to be only when men who have once known perfect love and have received material rewards therefrom become unfaithful in their stewardship and deny the full operation of compassion toward others. So long as they remain responsive to the world's need Christianity continues to spread.

In his seventy-eighth year he attempted to waken rich Methodists to this fact, declaring, "You are so deeply hurt, that you have nigh lost your zeal for works of mercy, as well as of piety. You once pushed on, through cold or rain, or whatever cross lay in your way, to see the poor, the sick, the distressed. You went about doing good, and found out those who were not able to find you. You cheerfully crept down into cellars, and climbed up into garrets,

> To supply all their wants,
> And spend and be spent in assisting his saints.

You found out every scene of human misery, and assisted according to your power:

> Each form of woe your generous pity moved;
> Your Saviour's face you saw, and, seeing, loved.

Do you now tread in the same steps?"[8] he asked.

The heroic spirit of primitive Christianity which scorns delicate living and "exposes itself to feel what wretches feel," was disappearing and Wesley sought to arouse concern by probing questions: "Do you fear spoiling your silken coat? Or is there another lion in the way? Are you afraid of catching vermin? And are you afraid lest the roaring lion should catch you? Are you not afraid of Him that hath said, 'Inasmuch as ye have not done it unto the least of these, ye have not done it unto me'?"[9]

The radicalism implicit in the Wesleyan teaching about the real meaning of perfect love is apparent here. Early Methodism stood for something more than the bland sentimental humanitarianism of the nineteenth century, which stooped as it gave; and something far more than the impersonal and secularized administration of welfare work in the twentieth century. It demanded personal identification with the deepest needs of mankind. Men and women who deliberately place themselves in the way of pain, poverty and want cannot long remain indifferent to the injustices of an unchristian social order. The objection that such welfare work as Wesley sponsored was absurdly unscientific does not minimize in the least the significance of Wesley's teaching about the distinctive character of Christian philanthropy. The principle as well as the method must be evaluated.

In the last years of Wesley's ministry the supply for the needs of the poor was inadequate. This, said Wesley, could never have happened if benevolences had continued to keep pace with increasing riches. Growth in membership should automatically carry with it growth in resources for all needs. One of the most flagrant violations of the practice of stewardship which was creating this problem was the attitude of older members toward bequests for their children. Wesley protested frequently against this plain ignoring of the advice to "Give all." He speaks, for instance, of a Methodist who told him that he was leaving forty thousand pounds to his heirs, and says that half of that amount if given to God and the poor "would have set all the society far above want."[10]

In most cases these resources had come to Methodists as a direct consequence of their practice of the first two rules of Christian stewardship taught by their leader. The amazing phenomenon of their rapid rise to places of financial power and opulence was noted by Wesley himself and has since been described in detail by Methodist historians.[11] As early as 1763 Wesley reported that in "London, Bristol, and most other trading towns, those who are in business have increased in substance sevenfold, some of them twenty, yea, an hundredfold." [12] By the end of the century Methodists had become even factory owners, large scale merchants, and city officials.

It is no wonder that he spoke sternly to those who, having reaped the material rewards of the Wesleyan way, failed to share them by obeying the third rule of stewardship. The extent to which they were failing is indicated by Wesley's attempt to elicit a response by compromising the rigor of his original teaching. Satirically he proposed to "come to lower terms." "You might think this too high a price for heaven." "Are there not a few among you that could give a hundred pounds, perhaps some that could give a thousand, and yet leave your children as much as would help them to work out their own salvation? With two thousand pounds, and not much less, we could supply the present wants of all our poor, and put them in a way of supplying their own wants for the time to come." [13]

Even worse than insensibility to the physical wants of others was their indifference to spiritual needs, but there was a direct correlation between the two. Wesley reminded the well-to-do of the days when they reproved "directly or indirectly all those who sinned" in their sight and as a happy consequence saw many conversions among their associates. Now, he said, gold had so "steeled" their hearts that they could easily justify their failures in personal evangelism by saying that they had "something else to do." [14] The cares of this world had removed the love of God from its supreme place in their scale of values and soon would destroy the Wesleyan way of life.

Often from such people came active opposition to innovations in evangelistic method—field preaching, for example. They had lost their original sense of the urgency of human need and could turn a deaf ear to Wesley's appeal, ". . . our call is, to save that which is lost . . . we cannot expect them to seek *us*. Therefore we should go and see *them*." [15]

In some quarters the preaching of Christian Perfection was neglected or even in disrepute. This ideal, which at the beginning of the Revival had been considered the norm of Christian living, was regarded frequently in the same way as Catholicism had treated it, merely a "counsel of perfection," a spiritual experience to be enjoyed only by "elect" souls, such as might live in seclusion, but not the criterion for everyday ethical conduct. Even some of the preachers are said to have laughed behind his back about *Wesley's* doctrine of Perfection.

This produced either carelessness in the externals of religion or over-emphasis upon the externals to the neglect of the inner life. In 1771 Wesley complained: "The most prevailing fault among the Methodists is to be *too outward* in religion. We are continually forgetting that the kingdom of God is *within us,* and that our fundamental principle is, We are saved *by faith,* producing all *inward holiness*, not by works, by any externals whatever." [16]

The inter-relationship between the two was discussed in his "Thoughts upon Methodism," 1786. He here stated that "Methodism is only plain scriptural religion guarded by a few prudential regulations. The essence of it is holiness of heart and life; the circumstantials all point to this; and as long as they are joined together in the people called Methodist no weapon formed against us shall prosper." [17] "But," he warned, "if ever the circumstantial parts are despised, the essential will soon be lost; and if ever the essential parts should evaporate, what remains will be dung and dross." [18]

He is declaring a truth which seems difficult to hold steadily before any religious movement. If the outward signs of an inward work of grace, such as were described in the *General Rules,* came to be *despised,* then "holiness of heart and life" would inevitably be lost. Conversely, if holiness should gradually disappear from its central place in Methodism, slavish adherence to regulations would take its place and be simply the "dung and dross" reminders of a once powerful movement.

The correlation which he makes between this truth and another should also be known to every Christian. He continues, "I fear, wherever riches have increased, the essence of religion has decreased in the same proportion." [19] Riches were subtly undermining perfect love and in consequence were bringing into disrepute the disciplines of the Wesleyan way.

It was Wesley's belief toward the end that two-thirds of the rich in the Societies gave evidence of this fact, and he had little hope for the future unless his counsel to "Give all" was regarded by those who were advancing economically.[20] Profound pathos marked many of his parting messages. On one occasion he said: "After having served you between sixty and seventy years, with dim eyes, shaking hands, and tottering feet, I give you one more advice before I sink into the dust. Mark those words of St. Paul: 'Those that desire' or endeavor 'to be rich' that moment 'fall into temptation': Yea, a deep gulf of temptation, out of which nothing less than almighty power can deliver them . . . You, above all men, who now prosper in the world, never forget these awful words!" [21]

At another time he exclaimed in despair, "Lord, I have warned them! but if they will not be warned, what can I do more? I can only give them up unto their heart's lusts, and let them follow their own imaginations?" [22]

What was "the tragedy of Methodism"? "Having accomplished so much," what more should it have accomplished? Dr. Edwards says that Methodism "had an excellent opportunity of being the Church of the Industrial Revolution. The period of its rise was roughly coincident with the rise of industrialism. It affected the same areas and reached the same classes of people." [23] The mobility of its itinerant system, the simplicity of its chapels, the powerful appeal of its hymnody, its democratic use of laymen—these and other features were all well calculated to make it continuously the church of the common people and thereby to offer some solution for the moral, social and economic problems brought by the revolution to this class.

But gradually Methodism lost this unparalleled opportunity. Because it had failed in its purpose to Christianize all spheres of life, it finally ceased to attract the worker. Edwards reports that even by the end of the eighteenth century "the Methodist Church whilst still increasing greatly in numbers, and attracting artisans and workmen, had ceased to be the Church of the worker, and was controlled by respectable middle-class people. . . ." [24]

People of wealth, though in the minority, were given "importance out of all proportion to their numbers." [25] As Wesley had feared, granting leadership on the basis of economic success was a mistake. Just as he had predicted, when he drew a lesson from the experiences of the early church, the sequel of an improper use of money is always increasing "respect of persons." The equalitarianism of Methodism was doomed to go. The institution of pew rents was a long step in this direction and could result only in "the gradual alienation of the worker." [26]

Not until late in the nineteenth century did British Methodism awaken to the significance of this symbol of class distinction and remove its poor members from seats that looked "like so many pens in a cattle-market." [27] But by that time most of the poor had departed, some to strengthen the mission of the Salvation Army to the masses, for William Booth had been told one day when he came with a crowd of ragged people to the front door of the chapel to which he belonged that he must take them around to their proper entrance, the back door. [28]

Such an occurrence could never have taken place in a church that made perfect love the measure for all behavior. It could perhaps happen in a church that had identified Perfection with a mystical quest for personal religious experiences. But that is not Wesley's conception of Christianity; it is a "social religion." Hobson has pointed out that "the moral perfectibility which was the center of Wesley's creed was not limited merely, or perhaps mainly, to the end of personal salvation in another world. The perfection of the individual was a basis for a system of social ethics." For that reason Hobson insists that Methodism takes "higher ground as an economic doctrine than any of the earlier Protestant sects." [29]

It has been generally assumed that the failure of Methodism to make a positive contribution to the Industrial Revolution was due largely to its tacit acceptance of the same economic theory as thwarted Puritanism. It is true that Wesley's emphasis upon proper uses of time and money, serious application to industry, and accomplishment of the divine will in work pushed to the fore Calvin's teaching on "the calling." The consequences of this emphasis were the same as those attending the Puritan movement; honesty, sobriety, industry, frugality and various other traits which have both ethical and economic value were developed, and economic prosperity resulted.

It is also true that Wesley, like the Puritans, inherited an economic world that was rapidly becoming secularized. He did not believe in a withdrawal from this world; he stressed, in fact, the necessity for constant exposure to all the temptations to compromise offered by it. Neither he nor any of his age could have conceived of intervening in such matters as taxation, hours of work, or the wage scale; nor is it likely that such intervention would have had any effect upon the complicated economic problems of that time.

But he did question, as previously noted, evils which were developing under the emerging competitive system. He was sensitive to all problems created by self-interest and violation of the Golden Rule. He recognized the dangers inherent in the economic virtues. He saw that sobriety, industry, frugality, and all such means to material success are not in themselves good, but have ethical value only as they free the personality for enjoyment of God and provide resources to supply the wants of others. He knew that only by a radical form of stewardship could economic acts be kept Christian, that spiritualizing work is not enough: distribution of goods must also be spiritualized.

The chief reason for the failure of Methodism to make its

proper contribution to the Industrial Revolution was not, therefore, its evolution of the economic virtues. It was its refusal to adopt the Wesleyan way for the use of money, a refusal which amounted to a rejection of the doctrine of perfect love, the doctrine which had been central in the movement. To be sure, this renunciation did not take place at once. Doctrines are gradually modified before they are finally discarded, and in this case modification began at the point where economic considerations impinged.

The criticism leveled so frequently at Puritanism for affirming uncompromisingly "the vanity of worldly achievement" and then paradoxically investing "the acquisition of wealth with a glow of piety"[30] need never have applied to Methodism. Tawney is correct when he says that the new Puritanism enunciated by Law and Wesley was distinguished from the old Puritanism of the seventeenth century middle classes by the insistence that Christianity implies a distinctive way of life wholly different from the secularized religion of their day, a religion which was little more than "morality tempered by prudence," a religion which reproduced class distinction and economic inequality.[31]

The study given to early Christianity by Law and Wesley had made them so aware of this distinctive way of life that they could not be content with the inadequacies of Calvinistic Puritanism. In its prepossessions with the doctrine of Sovereignty it had undervalued the doctrine of Christian Perfection. As Perry has said, Puritanism, though apparently "a radical expression of Christianity," was radical only in its "Christian conception of God as the omnipotent ruler." This and not the Christian conception of compassionate love" was pushed by Puritanism to "its extreme logical conclusions."[32]

Wesley's logical development of the theory of Christian Perfection and his sensitive response to all the meanings of "compassionate love" made him question the whole economic process by which the Puritan way seemed to destroy Christianity. He had gone beyond the Reformers in his supreme faith in man's moral potentialities. He had inaugurated the first religious movement to bring the doctrine of Perfection and the disciplines for its attainment out of the monastic environment and present it as the norm of Christian living. He had furnished in the doctrine the needed criterion for measuring the actual worth of the economic virtues and bringing them under control.

Methodism had other advantages, as well, over Puritanism: in its sphere of activity, its type of organization, and its perspective upon both the weakness of Calvinism and the evils of Anglican aristocracy. Its beginnings among the lower classes gave it more precise knowledge of the problems created by a wrong social and economic system, its organizations for social work afforded opportunity for dealing directly with these problems, and its intimate fellowship in worship and welfare work would eventually have compelled abandonment of social distinctions.

Had the response to the dictates of love which led early Methodists to accept all the obligations of stewardship continued, there is no telling how radical an expression of Christianity might have ensued. If Methodism was strong enough, in spite of this failure, to impregnate Anglicanism and the old Puritanism with new Evangelical life and set in motion a national reformation, what might have happened if the equalitarianism inherent in Wesleyan teaching had been realized in the practice of three or four generations?

The oft-repeated statement of R. W. Dale will bear repeating once again in this connection: "There was one doctrine of John Wesley's—the doctrine of perfect sanctification—which ought to have led to a great and original ethical development; but the doctrine has not grown; it seems to remain just where John Wesley left it. There has been a want of the genius or the courage to attempt the solution of the immense practical questions raised—much less solved. To have raised them effectively, indeed, would have been to originate an ethical revolution which would have had a far deeper effect on the thought and life—first of England, and then of the rest of Christendom—than was produced by the Reformation of the sixteenth century." [33]

The strength of a religious movement depends upon the moral cohesiveness that has resulted from agreement upon goals and the urgency of their attainment. Most revivals only whip up a temporary concern, because the goals do not remain supremely real and therefore lose their urgency. Wesley, partly because of his genius, but essentially because of the intensity of his convictions concerning the distinctiveness of the Christian Way was able to convince others and to organize the convinced into a corporate body agreed upon the disciplines required. The moral cohesiveness which resulted and the approximation of the Methodist way to the early Christian way was truly remarkable.

Yet neither the reality nor the urgency of the highest goal of Methodism was fully accepted after Wesley's death. The ideal of Christian Perfection came less and less to be regarded as the norm of full Christian living; hence Wesleyan teaching on the uses of time and money were more and more treated as either counsels of perfection for the few or simply superimposed regulation that interfered with free expression of personality.

As a consequence Methodism on both sides of the Atlantic became content with the growing secularization of many areas of life and lost its hold upon the masses and its original character as a poor man's church. What Dr. Sweet says of the church in America is largely true in England as well: "Methodism, once a religious ferment, largely among the poor, has now become an upper-middle-class church. Once it was proud to be called the poor man's church; now it boasts of its colleges and universities, its great endowments and tremendous corporate power." [34]

Sweet's observations demonstrate the accuracy of Wesley's premonitions concerning the dangers of wealth: "As their churches tended to become increasingly costly and luxurious, the inevitable result was that the people no longer felt at ease in worshiping with their more fortunate brethren. Nor did the college- and seminary-trained minister stress the poor man's doctrines, such as 'holiness' and 'second blessing' . . . for the stressing of these doctrines caused the prosperous to feel uncomfortable." [85]

Perfect Love—the poor man's doctrine! Can any worse indictment be brought against the modern church?

---

1. Maldwyn Edwards, *After Wesley* (London: Epworth Press, 1935), p. 87.
2. Halevy, op. cit., p. 372.
3. *Works*, VII, 425.
4. See both his *The Early Methodist People* and *More About the Early Methodist People* (London: Epworth Press, 1949)
5. *Works*, VII, 290.
6. Perry, op. cit., p. 315. Cf. R. H. Tawney, *Religion and the Rise of Capitalism* (London: John Murray, 1937)
7. *Ibid.*, p. 317.
8. *Works*, VII, 14.
9. Loc. cit.
10. *Works*, VII, 286.
11. See Warner, op. cit., pp. 187-192, and Wearmouth, op. cit., pp. 236-8.
12. *Journal*, V, pp. 30-1.
13. *Works*, VII, 287.
14. *Ibid.*, p. 14.
15. *Works*, VI, 300.
16. *Letters*, V, 289.
17. *Works*, XIII, 227.
18. Loc. cit.
19. Loc. cit.
20. *Letters*, VI, 288.
21. *Works*, VII, 361-2.
22. *Works*, VI, 334.
23. Edwards, op. cit., p. 85.
24. *Ibid.*, p. 91.
25. *Ibid.*, p. 90.
26. *Ibid.*, p. 90.
27. Maldwyn Edwards, *Methodism and England* (London: Epworth Press, 1943), p. 209.
28. *Ibid.*, p. 208.
29. J. A. Hobson, *God and Mammon* (New York: Macmillan Co., 1931), p. 34.
30. Perry, op. cit., p. 297.
31. Tawney, op. cit., p. 191.
32. Perry, op. cit., p. 312.
33. R. W. Dale, *The Evangelical Revival and Other Sermons* (London: Hodder & Stoughton, 1880), p. 39.
34. Sweet, op. cit., p. 55.
35. *Ibid.*, p. 72.

Conclusion

What would Wesley say today to a world baffled by the problems which have followed in the wake of the failure among Evangelical Christians to accept in its totality Christian teaching on compassionate love? If he were to return, would he once again with the finality that characterized his utterances declare the same conception of the nature and design of Christianity?

What was the source of this conception, and what was the reason for this finality— a finality which is abhorrent if the way of life demanded is not really the Christian way?

Wesley's conclusions concerning the essential nature of Christianity had been the result of a moral awakening that had made him fully aware of sin—sin in his own life, and, as a sequel, sin in the national life. They were the conclusions of a man who had reached the end of his tether. Although he had begun his quest as a typical reasoner of the Age of Reason, he had come to the place where he no longer judged the Word of God. He himself was in question; the Word of God had judged him and had found him wanting. He stood morally naked in the presence of "the living God."

We have seen how desperately he fought to preserve a last remnant of faith in his own goodness. Only by a long and arduous process did he come to a recognition of the fallacies of humanism and a total abandonment of its assumptions. Every age has its own particular brand of humanism, for every man wants to believe the words of the serpent, "Ye shall be as gods," and the intellectual is particularly subject to the temptation to preempt the place of God.

Fundamentally, the humanism which Wesley had to abandon was no different from the humanism from which the modern man must escape before he can find "the living God." As C. S. Lewis has said, modern religion believes in a kind of God "who obviously would not do miracles, or indeed anything else," for the reason that it has ruled out "a God who has purposes and performs particular actions, who does one thing and not another, a concrete, choosing, commanding, prohibiting God with a determinate character."[1] Of this kind of God one does not become aware so long as one's approach to Christianity remains purely speculative. But let one shift to the ethical approach and begin to measure his life by the words and life of Jesus, and the same discovery will be made as was made by Wesley: that the teachers of humanism have substituted for the words of Jesus the words of man.

Measuring, likewise, the Christian church by the same criteria, one discovers, as did Wesley, that an appalling chasm separates Christian profession from Christian practice. This inconsistency in the eighteenth century church had been the concern of other thinkers as notable as Wesley for their logic: Swift, for example, commented satirically in "An Argument Against Abolishing Christianity" upon how little discernible effect the abolishment of Christianity would have upon professedly Christian practice. So, likewise, our own satirists dismiss organized Christianity with caustic contempt because of its secularism.

Measuring, also, by the Word of God the morality of nations which call themselves Christian one is forced to the same conclusion as that of Wesley: that a liberal Christianity is powerless to establish national righteousness. May it not even contribute to moral decadence? We have seen that the optimistic theory of human nature which it promulgated in the eighteenth century successively dulled the moral perception, encouraged toleration of evil, and defeated efforts at reform.

Paradoxically, the humanist's faith in man's reason and natural goodness seems always to produce far lower ethical achievements than does the pessimism bred by a belief in original sin. Orthodox Christianity, in spite of its apparent distrust of man, really develops more fully his potentialities. Humanism would seem to create a free morality in which all sorts of evil may flourish. Social injustice and moral corruption were glossed over by the apostles of the Enlightenment in the name of culture. In the same manner has not scientific humanism created some of the moral blind spots of our day?

A moral awakening such as made Wesley aware of these delinquencies in himself, in the church, and in the nation inevitably leads to the question, What really is Christianity? The answer can be found only in an examination of current religion in the light of the Bible and the history of the church. This examination calls for an honesty and a thoroughness such as few of us are willing to give. Wesley possessed these qualities to a rare degree, and he also had a capacity for appreciating supersensuous values such as has almost disappeared today under the pressure of materialism. What did Wesley's reexamination of Christianity yield?

He found that Christianity, when it is living and real, claims supreme direction of the believer's life. He found that a religion which does not do this, which makes room for counter claims in what are called unrelated areas, or which seeks to syncretize with foreign elements, is no longer living and real. Vital Christianity, he discovered, is far more than mystical experience, far more than devotion to a historic institution, far more than creedal correctness. It is a distinctive, all-inclusive way of life which has been shaped by dominant principles.

The road taken by Wesley was parallel with the roads taken by Paul and Luther. A sense of sin, a desire for righteousness, which had been deepened by disciplined living, revealed to each of them the inadequacy of current religion and brought them to an impasse where they could do no other than throw themselves upon the grace of God. The experiences which followed were so illuminating as to reveal the fallacies in popular conceptions of Christianity, so profound as to create faith for the attainment of goals unknown to the ordinary believer, and so convincing as to make the disciplines essential to this attainment entirely desirable.

Such an experience, inextricably interwoven as it was with ethical considerations, leads inevitably to an adoption of a well-defined way of life. As Taylor has said, ". . . though a richly living religion is always something much more than a rule of conduct, it is never, for those whose religion it is, less than this." [2]

No wonder then that Wesley spoke with finality of his conception of Christianity and the Way. He knew that he had confronted Reality, and because he had, he assumed that his message would reach not only the morally sensitive but the hardened and unbelieving as well. And it did. We have seen how the new conception steadily gained ground until by the mid-nineteenth century thousands of people on both sides of the Atlantic had accepted it and had adopted the main essentials of the Wesleyan way.

It has been said that the early Christians—those of "the Way"—outthought the world, outlived the world and outdid the world." [3] The same claim can surely be made for Methodism and the Evangelical movement in their first hundred years or more. So long as they remained faithful to the implications of the principle which they believed to be central to Christianity they were "the salt of the earth," rendering palatable all of life. Is it conceivable that any such changes in English society as we have surveyed could have been accomplished without the thorough-going adoption of the principles and the disciplines of the Wesleyan way?

Do we not have need once more for such a restatement of the nature and design of Christianity as will bring a profound conviction of its truth, a renewed sense of its primary principles, and an insight into its applicability to the needs of the twentieth century? Does the modern man hold a conception of Christianity that creates a profound sense of sin and at the same time inspires a faith for its remedy? Is our current form of Christianity a match for the quasi-Christian isms which command great followings from the masses? Is not its greatest fault its moral flabbiness? Does the modern church offer a way of life which claims supreme direction of the believer's life and develops thereby his highest moral potentialities? Can non-Christian movements, such as Communism, be offset by a form of Christianity which does less than this?

What is popular religion today but an impotent belief in the goodness of man and the sentimental benevolence of God? The miracle has departed, and the greatest reason why we have not sunk to the rawest paganism is that we still benefit by what remains of the Christian faith upon which America was founded and by means of which Great Britain advanced to the state of civilization which it enjoyed during the nineteenth century.

But how long can any nation subsist upon the cultural by-products of a decadent religion? When the church no longer stands for a way of life vital enough to produce Christian character, how long can the by-products continue? The supreme need in the world today, as in Wesley's day, is for Christian character. Christian character can be formed only by the adoption of the Christian disciplines. No one has enunciated more explicitly than Wesley the dominant principle of this way. He was not unique in his recognition of the principle of love; he was unique only in his attempt to explore all its meanings for the ordinary life of the ordinary Christian.

The modern church has ceased to explore the meanings of love for the world which it serves. For years it has viewed with complacency the divorce between profession and practice and has dismissed the historic ideal of perfect love as only a counsel of perfection. History has repeated itself and the greatest talent of the church has again been devoted to the speculative approach to Christianity. But no victory of apologetics, however laudable, can save the modern church from defeat if the formation of Christian character and conduct does not become its imperative and primary concern.

It is still just as true as when Wesley wrote his "Appeal to Men of Reason and Religion" that the final evidence for the truth of Christianity is its miraculous power to make genuinely Christian men and women. The dismal failure of eighteenth century humanists who sought union through adoption of a minimal creed should be sufficient warning to those of our times who, in their desire for a united Christian front, would reduce theology to terms that would be acceptable to a Socinian, and would equate Christian ethics with good citizenship. No mass movement, however well it might seem to serve some immediate need, is Christian unless it is composed of Christian individuals.

Before we can see any great change in the social order we must have genuine Christians in politics, in economics, in education, in social work, in every sphere of modern activity, who confidently and courageously bring to the solution of our pressing problems the principle of compassionate love and the personal integrity and moral insight developed by the disciplines of the Christian way. Those of "the Way" must be the cells for the new order, if it is to be a Christian order.

---

1. C. S. Lewis, *Miracles* (London: Geoffrey Bles, 1947), p. 101.
2. A. E. Taylor, *The Faith of a Moralist* (London: Macmillan & Co., 1930), p. 10.
3. Frank B. Clogg, *The Christian Character in the Early Church* (London: Epworth Press, 1944), Preface.

Appendix

Text of the Rules of the Society of the People Called Methodists

4. There is only one condition previously required in those who desire admission into these Societies, viz. *"a desire to flee from the wrath to come, to be saved from their sins."* But wherever this is really fixed in the soul it will be shown by its fruits. It is therefore expected of all who continue therein, that they should continue to evidence their desire of salvation,

Firstly, By doing no harm, by avoiding evil in every kind, especially that which is most generally practiced.
Such is

The taking the name of God in vain;

The profaning the day of the Lord, either by doing ordinary work thereon, or by buying or selling;

Drunkenness; *buying* or *selling spirituous liquors,* or *drinking them,* unless in cases of extreme necessity;

Fighting, quarrelling, brawling; brother *going to law* with brother; returning *evil for evil,* or railing for railing; the *using many words* in buying or selling;

The *buying* or *selling uncustomed goods;*

The *giving* or *taking things on usury;* i. e., unlawful interest;

Uncharitable or unprofitable conversation, particularly speaking evil of Magistrates or of Ministers.

Doing to others as we would not they should do unto us;

Doing what we know is not for the glory of God, as—

The *putting on of gold or costly apparel.*

The *taking such diversions* as cannot be used in the name of the Lord Jesus.

The *singing* those *songs,* or *reading* those *books* which do not tend to the knowledge or love of God;
Softness, and needless self-indulgence;
Laying up treasures upon earth;
Borrowing without a probability of paying, or taking up goods without a probability of paying for them.

5. It is expected that they should continue to *evidence their desire of salvation,*

SECONDLY, By doing good, by being in every kind merciful after their power; as they have opportunity, doing good of every possible sort, and as far as possible, to all men:—

To their bodies, of the ability that God giveth, by giving food to the hungry, by clothing the naked, by visiting or helping them that are sick or in prison;

To their souls, by instructing, *reproving,* or exhorting all they have intercourse with; trampling under foot that enthusiastic doctrine of devils, that 'we are not to do good, unless *our heart be free to it.*'

By doing good especially to them that are of the household of faith, or groaning so to be; employing them preferably to others, buying one of another, helping each other in business; and so much the more, because the world will love its own, and them *only.*

By all possible *diligence* and *frugality,* that the Gospel be not blamed.

By running with patience the race that is set before them, *denying themselves, and taking up their cross daily;* submitting to bear the reproach of Christ; to be as filth and offscouring of the world; and looking that men should *say all manner of evil of them falsely, for the Lord's sake.*

6. It is expected that they should continue to evidence their desire of salvation,

THIRDLY, by attending all the ordinances of God; such are,
The public worship of God;
The ministry of the word, either read or expounded;

The Supper of the Lord;
Family and private prayer;
Searching the Scriptures; and
Fasting or abstinence.

7. These are the General Rules of our Societies: all which we are taught of God to observe, even in His written word, the only rule, and the sufficient rule, both of our faith and practice. And all these we know His Spirit writes on every truly awakened heart. If there be any among us who observe them not, who habitually break any of them, let it be made known unto them who watch over that soul, as they that must give an account. We will admonish him of the error of his ways: we will bear with him for a season. But then if he repent not, he hath no more place among us. We have delivered our own souls.

May 1, 1743.   John Wesley
                                         Charles Wesley

About the Author

Convinced that "they really had something," Dr. Tenney has, for many years, been interested in early Methodists and in the Wesleyan Revival. She chose as her doctoral thesis subject, "Early Methodist Autobiography," and has continued throughout the years her study of the early Methodist movement.

Born in Nora Springs, Iowa, Mary Alice Tenney attended grade and high school in that state, later doing undergraduate work at Drake University and at Greenville College, where she received an A.B. degree. In 1939, during a leave of absence from Greenville College, where she has been chairman of the English department for the past twenty-five years, Miss Tenney received her Ph.D. from the University of Wisconsin.

In 1948-49, on a fund raised by Greenville College alumni, Dr. Tenney continued her study of early Methodism in England, investigating the sources on the early Methodist movement in the historic Methodist Book Room and in the British Museum.

Index

Addison, 74
Age of Reason, 36, 53, 279
Aldersgate, 94
Amusements, 159-83, 223, 247, 259, 265
Anglicanism, 42, 43, 45, 46, 47, 53, 65, 69, 71, 72, 75, 89, 90-3, 103, 106, 107, 131, 133, 139, 148, 149, 209, 247, 253, 254, 257, 275
Appeal to Men of Reason and Religion, 38, 53
Apostolical Constitution, 209
Arianism, 48
Arminianism, 54, 104
Asceticism, 70, 72, 83, 84, 86, 94, 139, 205, 217
Assurance, 55, 65, 70, 71, 91
Atonement, 104

Baker, Eric, 187, 247
Bands, 232
Baptists, 49, 50, 135, 265
Barclay, Robert, 50
Bebb, E. D., 187, 193, 244
Belden, A. D., 148
Besant, Walter, 200
Blackstone, 31
Blackwell, Ebenezer, 144, 192, 243
Boehler, Peter, 76, 91-94
Botsford, J. B., 165
Bready, J. W., 19, 164, 196
Butler, Bishop, 33, 57, 74, 93, 248

Calvin, 124, 273
Calvinism, 45, 54, 90, 104, 273, 274, 275
Card playing, 164-6, 170
Catholicism, Roman, 46, 60, 72, 90, 107, 108, 131, 188, 251, 252, 270
Cave, Wm., 131, 190, 209
Christian Library, 169
Christian Perfection, 69, 81, 88, 97, 108-17, 120, 121, 124, 128, 129, 131, 145, 224, 227, 228, 232, 265, 270, 274-6. *See also* Perfect love
Church, Leslie, 166, 200, 214
Church of England, *see* Anglicanism
Class-meeting, 135, 230-32
Clayton, John, 84
Coleridge, S. T., Foreword, 249
Collier, Jeremy, 176
Congreve, Wm., 178-9
Conversation, 140-46, 148
Conversion, 92, 93, 96, 97, 106, 114, 129
Coomer, D., 48, 104, 257
Cowper, Wm., 155, 211
Cranmer, 13, 16
Crouch, J., 175

Dale, W. R., 230, 275
Dancing, 126, 144, 155, 158, 162-64, 166, 246
Defoe, D., 150
Deism, 48, 55-58, 61, 67, 98, 103, 248
Dissent, 26, 27, 45, 48, 70, 91, 103, 148, 256, 257
Diversions, *see* Amusements
Dives, 204
Dodd, W., Dr., 110-11
Donne, John, 89
Dress, 207-15, 265

Early Christianity, *see* Primitive Christianity

[289]

Early Church, *see* Primitive Christianity
Economic virtues, 224, 266, 273
Edwards, Maldwyn, 255, 263, 271-72
"Enthusiasm," 14, 25-27, 29, 35, 36, 43, 44, 55, 56, 58, 75, 92, 106, 171, 242
Epworth, 66, 239
Equalitarianism, 227, 231, 233-34, 243, 272
Evangelical, 48, 96, 103, 105, 108, 133, 152, 171, 245, 248, 251, 255, 258, 263-64, 275, 279, 282
Evangelism, 223, 235, 236, 244-5

Faith, 71, 72
Fielding, Henry, 141
Fielding, John, 148
Fitchett, W. H., 21
Fleury, C., 131, 169, 173, 190-91
Flew, R. N., 111, 116
Foote, S., 179
Formalism, 41, 43, 45, 53
Formula, three-part, 223, 224, 227
Fox, G., 38, 126
Friends, *see* Quakers
Furniture, *see* Property

Gambling, 155, 164-7, 200, 246, 259
George, Dorothy, 31, 155, 180
Georgia, 85, 89, 95
Gibbon, 75
Gibson, E., Bishop, 29, 36, 59, 156, 163, 164
Godley, A. D., 19, 20

Halevy, E., 152, 263
Haller, Wm., 175
Harris, Howell, 257
Harrison, A. W., 86, 91, 231
Hawkins, John, 177
Herbert, George, 144
High Church, 45, 47, 65, 69, 75, 84, 91, 92
Hobson, J. A., 273

Hogarth, W., 163
Holy Club, 35, 83, 105
Hooker, R., 54
Horse-racing, 161, 165, 183
Humanism, 28, 29, 38, 53-59, 62, 97, 103, 248, 250, 279
Hume, D., 57, 62
Huntingdon, Lady, 15
Hutton, J., 241

Imitation of Christ, The, 67-8, 157
Independents, 47, 48, 50, 135
Industrial Revolution, 271, 273, 274

Johnson, S., Dr., 75, 144, 177, 178, 211
Jones, E. S., 60, 199
Justification by faith, 55, 89, 91, 94, 96, 103, 104, 106, 107, 131

Kempis, Thomas a, 67, 69, 76, 97, 105, 110, 120, 151
Kennicott, Dr., 14, 16, 18

Latitudinarianism, 250, 253
Law, Wm., 28, 32, 34, 66, 73-79, 82, 88, 97, 103, 105, 107, 108, 110, 120, 124, 125, 126, 140, 142, 157, 158, 162, 179, 182, 187, 213; *The Case of Reason,* 57; *Treatise on Christian Perfection,* 73, 75, 81, 168; *The Serious Call,* 75, 141; *Remarks upon "The Fable of the Bees,"* 74; on the theater, 173-4, 179; on riches, 188-91
Lawson, J., 227
Lewis, C. S., 30, 280
Lincoln College, 20, 73
Lindstrom, H., 107
Locke, Wm., 55, 72
Luther, 55, 94, 95, 124, 281
Lutheran, 90

Mandeville, B., 74
Masquerade, *see* dancing

INDEX

Maxwell, Lady, 214, 243
Methodist Societies, 126, 134, 135, 145, 187, 226, 229, 230, 232, 233, 236, 244, 245, 247, 254, 255
Middleton, Conyers, 98, 248
Milton, John, 175
Money, see Riches
Moravians, 86-88, 91, 93, 98, 107, 126, 250
Mysticism, 81, 82, 83, 90, 98, 119

Natural Religion, 29, 55-59, 66, 68, 72, 248, 251
Nonconformity, 47, 89, 98, 151, 209, 222, 255-57, 265
Nonjuror, 74

Original sin, 55, 66, 103, 104
Orthodoxy, 44, 48
Oxford Methodists, 35, 84, 85, 159
Oxford movement, 13, 255
Oxford University, 13-15, 19, 22, 35, 81, 83, 84, 95, 107, 187

Pascal, 158
Perfect Love, 109, 110, 119, 124, 126, 128, 132, 139, 145, 146, 205, 218, 220, 224, 244, 264, 265, 267, 268, 272, 274, 283
Perry, R. B., 123, 224, 266, 274
Plato, 55
Play-houses, see theater
Poor, The, 219, 222, 233, 235, 239-42, 244, 258, 277
Portus, G. V., 32
"Practical atheism," 25, 32, 33, 205
Presbyterians, 47, 48, 49, 50-53, 92, 135
"Primitive Christianity," 35, 84, 86, 101, 173, 220, 226, 227, 236, 241, 267
Prison, 83, 218
Profanity, 146-9, 259
Property, 207-9, 214, 226, 227, 265
Protestantism, 42, 46, 60, 91, 92, 106, 107, 117, 131, 132, 188, 203, 230, 252, 254, 266, 273
Puritanism, 46, 63, 65, 75, 101, 102, 117, 126, 127, 149, 171, 174-6, 222, 224, 228, 231, 247, 250, 255, 259, 265, 266, 273, 274, 275

Quaker, 27, 49, 50, 135, 199, 209, 211, 214, 265

Rattenbury, J. E., 92
Reformation, 71, 90, 95, 124, 191, 274, 276
Religious Society, 32, 83, 85, 149, 229; Society for the Reformation of Manners, 148, 164
Rich, The, see Riches
Riches, 187-91, 203-9, 215, 219, 221-3, 233, 234, 243, 265, 266, 268, 271, 274
Rousseau, 62
Rules and Exercises of Holy Living, 69-73
Rules of the Methodist Societies, 126-36, 139, 143, 146, 149, 162, 167, 170, 179, 196, 203, 205, 206, 217, 218, 224, 270

Sabbatarianism, 149-52, 259
Sacramentarianism, 42, 83, 84, 86, 98
St. Francis, 203
St. Mary the Virgin, 13, 19, 22
Salvation Army, 272
Sanctification, see Christian Perfection
Sangster, W. E., 113, 115
"Scriptural Christianity," 15-19, 38
Secker, Bishop, 35
Sectarianism, 45, 46, 47, 49, 50, 53, 250, 251, 253, 258
Secularism, 29, 58-63, 66, 101, 106, 147, 151, 205, 220, 254
Simon, J. S., 87, 101
Simplicity, 209, 212, 217, 220, 222, 224, 239

Smuggling, 134, 199-200
Snuff, 206
Social welfare work, 83, 235, 243-4, 268
Societies, see Methodist Societies
Socinianism, 48, 53, 103
South Sea Bubble, 165, 200
Spirituous liquors, 126, 196-8, 206, 246, 259
Stewardship, 218-27, 232, 243, 244, 265, 267-9, 273, 275
Stillingfleet, E., 149
Supernaturalism, 25, 248
Sweet, W. W., 102, 276
Swift, J., 148, 176
Sydney, W. C., 178
Sykes, N., 31

Tauler, 178
Taylor, J. 68-73, 76, 82, 97, 105, 110, 120, 139, 140, 142, 188
Theater, 126, 144, 155, 158, 161, 170-83, 198, 246
Tillotson, Archbishop, 31, 59
Tithing, 224
Tobacco, 206

Toleration, 250-53
Trapp, J., Dr., 34, 36
Troeltsch, E., 239

Unitarianism, 48-9
Usury, 194-5

VanBrugh, J., 178-79
Voltaire, 62

Ward, Barbara, 228
Warner, W. J., 243
Watson, E. W., 31
Watson, Wm., 48
Wealth, see Riches
Wearmouth, R. F., 231, 244
Wesley, Charles, 15, 83
Wesley's father, 35, 66
Wesley's mother, 65-67, 70, 71, 162
Whitaker, W. B., 149-52
Whitefield, George, 148, 171, 177, 257
Witness of the Spirit, 26
Wordsworth, Wm., 187, 249
Work, 191-94
Wycherley, Wm., 179
Wycliffe, J., 13, 102

www.ingramcontent.com/pod-product-compliance
Lightning Source LLC
Chambersburg PA
CBHW051749040426
42446CB00007B/279